M. SCOTT PECK (1936–2005), author of *The Road Less Travelled*, wrote of Suzanne Claire Olaski's *Remembrance of a Path Well Lit*:

> *"As a non-denominational Christian myself, I thought your theology was remarkably accurate and solid. Your Chapter 'Touching the Feet of Jesus' is a gem . . . it strikes an extraordinary balance between arrogance and humility and between consciousness and a healthy kind of 'unself-consciousness' . . . exquisitely balanced."*

M. SCOTT PECK was a world-renowned author of many books. *The Road Less Travelled: A New Psychology of Love, Traditional Values and Spiritual Growth* (1978) is one of the most influential books of modern times, remaining for 10 years on the New York Times Best Sellers List – longer than any other paperback book. Other works include *In Search of Stones, A World Waiting to be Born and People of the Lie*.

Please visit his official website, www.mscottpeck.com, for biography details and further publications.

Remembrance

OF A PATH WELL Lit

Remembrance

OF A PATH WELL *Lit*

Suzanne Claire Olaski

REMEMBRANCE OF A PATH WELL LIT
Copyright © 2009 Suzanne Claire Olaski

ISBN-10: 1-897373-71-6
ISBN-13: 978-1-897373-71-2

All Scripture quotations are taken from the King James Version of the Bible.

Published by Word Alive Press

WORD ALIVE PRESS
Just Write!
131 Cordite Road, Winnipeg, Manitoba, R3W 1S1
www.wordalivepress.ca

Printed in Canada.

But the Comforter, which is the Holy Ghost,
whom the Father will send in my name,
he shall teach you all things,
*and bring all things to your **remembrance**,*
whatsoever I have said unto you.

~John 14:26

*****

God has never hidden His Word or His Truth from us

*****

… as the story goes in the Garden of Eden …

… so it goes with you and I …

It is WE who are desperately hiding from Him

*****

Table of Contents &

Foreword	xv
Introduction	xix
In Service	1
Touching the Feet of Jesus	27
The Visit	59
In the Garden	69
In the World	83
The Walkabout	115
Wanting to See the Light	119
Demons of Darkness	133
Encounter with the Enemy	141
The Path	189
In Conclusion	257
Endnotes and Scriptures	267

Foreword ❧

If you have ever wondered if there is a God and if there was, what role He might play in your life, you owe it to yourself to share this true life journey and decide for yourself to what conclusions you might have come had these events happened to you.

From the author's miracle healing of breast and lymph cancer in 1975 to her political exploits, from childhood through maturity, you will find a strength of conviction, vulnerability and meekness, the combination of which proves itself both charming and irresistible.

Much controversy exists today and throughout history regarding the connection with the realm of God that awaits us AFTER death. Though Suzanne faced near-death experiences on more than one occasion, her testimony bears witness that an 'encounter' with the light is possible without the necessity of *having to die.*

The required 'death of self' is more spiritual than physical, though rebelliously we choose not to seek it; hence, the encounter is more widely spoken of during an actual physical near-death experience, where the choice has been taken from us.

What arises out of the gift presented here is the knowledge that an undeniable relationship with God is possible in the here and now …

while we live …

because He lives.

Neatly woven within the boundaries of the supernatural you will find a series of autobiographical encounters that challenge the reader to question the validity of their belief system and subsequent faith in it.

Suzanne Claire's *Remembrance* enables the reader to get in touch with the child in each of us. She takes us casually and believably into those regions that encourage us to consider incidents in our lives wherein the possibility exists that the Creator has been reaching out to us.

With continuous personal experiences to draw from, she calls us to return to an atmosphere of innocence which inevitably allows the reader to fall prey to the ability to believe in the impossible and delight in the incredible.

Often disarming, always thought provoking, this offering, which amounts to the very breath of her life, will bring tears of both pain and joy as she manages to touch those intimate parts of the heart we like to hide so carefully from public display.

intimate ... inspirational

*****

It is difficult to present my story in its entirety in this first book.

Through what I can only call a collection of personal experiences, I hope to encourage readers to search for evidence in their own lives of blessings that have reached down to them from above, not from an often unidentifiable 'higher power' but from '*The* Highest Power.'

Though your encounters may be more or less interesting than my own, your encounters belong to you; they are uniquely yours for you to cherish as your own classified connections with the heavenly realm.

Once you know what to look for in your own walk, you will find, as have I, confirmations that surface without number that Our Creator is continuously present, in even the least events of the day.

Having come into an understanding of how these glorious blessings have enriched my own life, it is now my privilege to share the way 'home' with those who can receive it.

*****

Introduction ❧

Many deny the possibility that God speaks to people.

Recently I heard a well-known preacher say that he is highly skeptical when he hears anyone say, "The Lord spoke to me and said..."

Funny, it occurs to me that if Jesus said that we would 'hear' His voice,[1] then surely 'hearing' is a part of the equation. Usually one hears when one is spoken to. To be sure, hearing includes a variety of wavelengths, but without getting into physics, let us simply understand that the Lord often talked of 'hearing' and He indeed said that we would 'know' ... Him ... His Voice ... The voice of the Shepherd.

Some preachers have decided to become a little more liberated, possibly because they themselves might be 'hearing things,' and have gone so far as to accept the saying "The Lord spoke to my heart."

I understand their concern, for to assume that every 'voice' you hear is the voice of God can be dangerous.

There is a definite caution to be exercised.

There are many voices that come to us. Sometimes we simply hear our own, convincing us to do that which we have already chosen; there are demons (or, if you like this concept better, counter-productive thoughts that tend to mislead you); and yes, I believe there is ... the Voice of God.

Does any proof exist today to confirm that God speaks to man?

A study of Scripture will categorically confirm that it is filled with examples of God's intended directives. In fact, the list below indicates plentifully how God speaks to men in eight different ways:[2]

1. Prophesy
2. Tongues and interpretation
3. A still small voice
4. An audible voice
5. Angels
6. Visions
7. Dreams
8. Impression upon man's spirit

This last item could be called intuition, impression, inner consciousness or inspiration. It can come in various forms and ways.

The difficulty, then, is not in determining IF God speaks to men but whether or not we can tell when it is actually God who is speaking.

There are many ways to discover whose voice or voices we are responding to. We might wish to explore these theories, for there is so much to cover on this one topic alone.

For the purposes of this book, however, and in order for me to help you feel more comfortable with the concept, it may be best for you to simply assume, for the time being, that the possibility does exist. In this assumption, you will be assisted while reading this text, for I will often refer to times when ...

... 'the Lord spoke to me' ...

After years of developing a keen awareness about information moving through my senses, I came to know very distinctly the 'Lord's voice' and subsequent 'conversations' and eventual 'revelations'. For me, His communication came in many ways.

And so it was that, after a multitude of opportunities to do His will, where I was sometimes obedient and oft' times not, I had become highly sensitive to what is known as an 'unction' from the Holy Spirit.

This is not some dream, a fantasy or just wishful thinking; it is very real, so real, in fact, that you cannot survive 'in the spirit' without it.

Below you will find a Scripture which confirms the benefits of working with the Holy Spirit. It is my hope that these benefits, through this book and others like it, you will one day learn to employ.

For ye have an unction from the Holy One,
and ye know all things.[3]

*****

Some have questioned my right to speak of the things of God as I do. Though their arguments provide a great deal of worldly sense, as I have had no formal biblical teaching, I have been unable to bring myself to cease following the leading of my heart, continuing to preach the gospel, I am told, with a certain measure of authority.

I had always a sense that eventually there would come a time of confirmation that what I knew as Truth was true.

It goes without saying that in the name of Christianity the darkest days of history are recorded, and even to this moment in time despicable acts are performed under its guise. Violence, judgment, cruelty, unforgiving and hate are not the acts of a

Christian, though the word be loosely tossed about in the midst of these.

There is a time when you might truly come to know what it is the Lord would have you do and how to behave, and on such a day, you are indeed provided the Holy Spirit to teach you 'all things.'

The Bible clearly dispels the rumour that human teachers are necessary for one to be granted permission to become apprised of the ways of God. The apostle John assuredly tells us:

> *But the anointing which ye have received of him abideth in you, and ye need not that any man teach you: but as the same anointing teacheth you of all things, and is truth, and is no lie, and even as it hath taught you, ye shall abide in him.*[4]

There had always been, it seems, an underlying mystery about my life. I had a sense of this from the days of my youngest memory. Did the possibility exist that such an anointing like the one described by Paul had been steadily increasing since the days of my childhood...an anointing that had unmistakably included inordinate peace?

I was about to find out.

*****

I began writing my first story, *Miracle Miles*, in November, 1992, while visiting friends in California. It was a recounting of how the Lord had miraculously provided for me during what might have been a trying car trip to Danville, California, the previous Thanksgiving.

On Christmas morning, I presented the finished product to the family involved. Sandra took the copy of some eight pages in length and began reading it aloud while several of us were lounging about the cheerily decorated living room. As she read on, each of us was moved in a very special way. There were a few tears, some laughter, moments of deep reflection . . . the words had touched us.

I was pleasantly surprised to note such a favourable response. I felt that it was clearly a sign for me to press on with the various compositions currently running around in my mind. I was already formulating a piece about a close friendship with a young woman struggling with terminal cancer. This and other documentation would eventually become part of a larger work on illness, its relationship to emotional and spiritual well-being, miracles and other stories. These would tie in with my own personal history of facing death through illness and living to tell about it.

I was happy for the encouragement, for I had long ago determined that a different perspective from Betty Rollins' account in '*First You Cry*'[5] needed to be presented. I hoped to make room for the experiences of others in order to bring into focus the very broad range of situations that occur when words like 'breast and lymph cancer' take over a person's life.

Having worked extensively with cancer patients in a variety of ways, having been part of the Canadian Cancer Society for a term, having been spared a death sentence more than twenty years before, I felt there was much to be said.

Returning to Canada at the end of the season gave me some free time where I drew outlines of *Touching the Feet of Jesus*, *The Visit* and *The Path*. I had no definite goals about where the writing would take me . . . it just seemed like I was supposed to!

While in Canada, my dad had a severe heart attack, which eventually cost him his life in February of 1993. After the matter of a small estate had been settled, I returned to

California to continue the work of assisting a whole medley of strangers who needed help: some without housing, some without food, others without family or friends, most without hope!

I continued to write.

Over time, the completed work began to swell. Much of the writing covered insights into faith, hope, compassion, forgiveness . . . insights that were offered up from the very streets wherein we laboured with love. I would write short stories, long stories and many in-between.

Because I was often asked to preach, mostly at missions, some of the writing covered topics that had surfaced during question and answer periods after the address. There were many selections to cover the tragedy and triumph of facing illness, terminal or not.

Usually, though, the writing captured incidents along the way, many of which I have gladly shared during my seminar called *Forgiveness is Freedom*, an 8-hour seminar where participants actively engage in their own deliverance.

There was no real rhyme or reason to the writing. This did not really concern me, however, since having formerly been a paralegal I was used to such a dilemma while preparing for a case. I would often have pages and pages of work strewn all over the office, some with whole paragraphs and others with nothing more than a sentence or a word. Time would be running out as the court date was fast approaching with the work still to be found in that scattered condition. Suddenly, and when you might least expect it, the pages would somehow fly together ... in a flash! Not a word would have been wasted, not even a thought! This process always amazed me somehow, but then I proceeded to accept its happening as if it were the norm, dismissing my amazement so as not to confuse the issue.

In similar fashion, the writing came as though I was preparing the work for some future need, although I was completely unaware of what that need might be.

Most days, there was little money to be had. But what we did have, we were more than willing to share. And what I had to share, I found, was proving to be more valuable than oodles and scads of money, for the privilege of knowing simple truths was priceless, truths that had been garnered from every corner of the 'walk' ... including inspiration which flows both to and from the hearts of the men and women and children of America.

*****

In Service ❧

Although the spectacular autumns that I was used to mattered not to Californians, Marin County, just 30 miles north of San Francisco, is considered Northern California and, quite surprisingly, experiences a fall of its own that is not at all unpleasant. A variety of trees take on yellow, red and orange flavours, though certainly not with the iridescent intensity that happens in Canada.

As I was taking in one of these pleasant fall afternoons, I realized that I was bent on completing two recent compositions, hoping to put them to some kind of use, although at this point in time it was not clear what that use might be.

I decided to stop in at the deli, pick up a sandwich and spend an hour or two at the park, where I would for about the sixth time begin again the seemingly endless job of editing.

The sandwich came to $3.95.

I reached into my purse, which was small and, as a result, provided great difficulty in extracting money.

I pulled out a $10 bill, which obviously would have taken care of the matter, when I heard the Lord say to me, **"Not the ten-dollar bill."**

He didn't say why, and I was slightly startled because it was an audible voice this time, not particularly loud, but definitely audible.

Obediently, I pulled out some miscellaneous selections of change and paid the bill.

The next stop was the gas station. As I got out to serve myself, I was adding up in my head the money that I had left to decide what amount I would put in the tank. "I still have that ten dollar bill," I mused.

Using what seemed to be relatively good logic, I considered that this was probably why I had kept the ten.

But there it was again. *"Keep the ten-dollar bill."*

"All right," I thought slowly, "what other change do I have?"

(Our obedience, by the way, must become that instant!)

"A five, a one and another one from the change at the deli. I'll use that."

I thought no more about the incident and headed over to the park. After spending an hour or two there, I decided to make my way home, where I would hopefully finalize the edit.

*****

It was usual for me to work late into the evening.

Tonight was no different, other than I was able to complete a major re-write, which happened only every month or so. I printed one copy and gathered my notes together.

As I headed out to Kinko's, an all-night copy center, the still night air bid a strange expectancy.

It was just before midnight.

The parking lot at Kinko's was overflowing, indicative of the creative nature of Marin. The side lot, used little because of its location, had several vacant spots. There was no difficulty manoeuvring into a relatively wide spot, and as I scurried to secure my material, I could sense a man approaching the car just as I was about to disembark.

He seemed embarrassed and somewhat shy.

As I stepped out of the car, he spoke to me.

"Excuse me, ma'am, I hate to disturb you, but may I trouble you for some change? I wouldn't ask, except neither my wife nor myself have eaten today."

His use of the English language told me that he'd been properly schooled.

"Of course," I replied. "Where is your wife now?" I asked, looking to see if she was with him.

"She's at the Safeway, asking for handouts too."

"Oh, I'm sorry," I said, hoping he could tell that I sincerely meant it. "Believe it or not, I understand your plight."

This was indeed the truth, since there had been many occasions when I had not a penny to my name and had wound up sleeping in my '82 Dodge. In fact, it had happened so often one fall that when anyone asked me where I lived, I would say 82 Caravelle.

I was leaning into my vehicle now, determined to find something to give.

"Do you have a place to stay?" I called over my shoulder.

"We've been sleeping in our car, trying to save enough for a rental deposit." He sounded hopeful.

I continued to rummage through catchall spots, including the ashtray for some change, unable thus far to locate my purse. Since I already had a credit at the copy store, I had not intended to take it in with me.

"Here it is," I called out to the man reassuringly. I had found the elusive purse.

Surfacing from the car, I began to walk toward him.

He was standing slightly out of the way.

Just then I noticed how very dark it was in that part of the lot. There was no one outside and I could barely see the man's face. It seemed that he was comfortable with this, for he was definitely not easy with his current occupation.

I was digging into the purse, obviously for change, when I heard the Lord's voice for the third time that day.

"Give him the ten-dollar bill."

"Oh, of course," I said, seemingly to myself, smiling contentedly, "that's who the ten was for."

I was only slightly surprised, but happily so, knowing that I had been obedient for an intended result.

In the shadows, it would be difficult to tell what denomination the money was, what with American money being all the same in colour, no matter what the amount. The man was somewhat overwhelmed to receive paper money at all, having again repeated, "Just some change, ma'am, any change that you can spare will do."

Realizing he had received not one dollar but ten times that much, tears quickly filled his eyes.

"Oh my God . . . thank you . . . thank you. I . . . I just don't know what to say."

He kept looking at the money in disbelief.

"I wish it could have been a hundred," I said apologetically. And I meant it.

"You need to know, however, that in spite of the amount, God IS watching out for you."

It is my guess that he could not have been privy to how very well I knew this to be true.

"If I had a home of my own," I added heartily, "I would take you there now, but I'm merely a visitor here, having little myself. I'm involved with missionary work, presently staying with friends. Please give my regards to your wife and let her know that everything is going to be all right."

I smiled encouragingly and began to walk away.

He called anxiously after me, "God bless you for this. God will surely bless you."

The words echoed in the still night air.

I smiled thankfully, knowing that what he said was entirely true.

*****

I proceeded to make the copies of my edit when the Lord caught my attention yet again.

"You could give him a copy of Miracle Miles."

Immediately, I thought, "Yes! What a great idea!"

I set the copier to printing and quickly scurried to determine if the man was still outside. I found him not far from the entrance to the door.

"Excuse me," I called out, while making my way towards him, "I thought you might like to read a story I wrote about one of the many miracles I've experienced during my walk with the Lord."

He came to meet me, accepting the story greedily, happily. I was touched that he had not rejected my approach nor had he appeared to simply appease me due to his thankfulness for the money received.

I returned indoors. Some fifteen minutes or so passed before I was finished what I had come to do. Gathering my papers together, I made my exit.

To my surprise and delight, the man had moved under a street lamp and was eagerly devouring the words. He held the papers above his head for better light. I could tell that he had already read several pages.

He was entirely engrossed in the story, and as I passed by, saying, "I'm glad there's enough light there for you to see," he barely acknowledged me, despising to take his eyes from the copy.

"Oh … (he was speaking in my direction now) … thank you … thank you once again. This is great. My wife is going to love it!"

His eyes did not leave the paper.

"Good night," I called softly to him.

*****

As I left the property, the car leading me deftly into the night, I was joyfully grateful.

The day's events scrolled before me.

I was taken aback in the realization that the Lord had quietly and patiently guided me throughout the day in order to bring a blessing to this man, a man for whom He obviously cared a great deal, in the same way He cares for each of us.

Without warning, hot, full tears began to pour over my face. My heart was leaping, and not able to contain my joy any longer, I blurted out my appreciation to the Lord for having called upon me in this very special way. "What a wonderful use of the stories, Lord! Thank you! Thank you so much."

*****

Should this be the reason for writing …

… to touch a fallen heart from time to time
… at the Lord's direction
… I couldn't imagine anything more sublime!

And on that note, I flew home with the angels …

*****

Is it so hard to imagine that every one of us may be privileged to participate in encounters such as these? If you really think about it, you may recall from your past those moments when you knew beyond a shadow of a doubt that something mysterious was happening, as if ordained from another time and place. There were probably occasions when you did something you had not planned to do and you wondered afterward how it was that you'd ever thought of doing such a thing.

What about synchronicity or serendipity, times that seem to meld together as if the very moments themselves belonged to one another? Days when destiny calls, when the pieces of the puzzle fit so perfectly together that you just know that everything is exactly as it should be and that you are right where you were meant to be. Is it possible to be connected to this 'sensitivity' more often, perhaps even for all eternity?

Whether we want to admit it or not, there are many times when we behave in certain ways in which we surprise even ourselves.

How is this so?

Like the detective following a hot lead, I was continuously encouraged within my spirit to move toward the unravelling of these life mysteries. In days gone by, my baby steps of obedience touched not only the lives of the lonely and afflicted; there had been Bay Street lawyers and Provincial Premiers too. Sometimes those baby steps felt more like giant leaps.

*****

One afternoon in the late eighties, high above all there is in Metropolitan Toronto, before I came to the war torn ghettos of Oakland and San Francisco, there was the voice…

...the voice that began taking me away from the things of this world to those things *not* of this world...

...a voice that leads me onward to this very day...

...to more service...and yet again...more.

*****

The team members who put together the multi-million-dollar transfer of funds from one large trust company to one of its subsidiaries were mostly unknown to one another. In such a way, it appeared that no one person knew absolutely everything about the deal. This, of course, was not completely true.

During this transfer an inspired 'thought' came to me something like this.

"You know there is no money here. You're just moving paper around."

Well, naturally, one really does know this to some extent, but just not quite as innately as I did at that moment.

"It's like cheque kiting, you see," came my 'thoughts.'

"And although cheque kiting is quite against the law," (the thoughts were becoming a voice outside my head now) ***"if the corporate world is doing it, then they will somehow manage to slough it off as being in the best interests of the country or something equally moral. The rules are different at every level."***

The dialogue was just beginning. The 'voice' then asked me, more directly, with precision and direction:

"Why don't you stop using your communication skills to help the rich get richer but instead speak for those who have no voice?"

The thought was compelling. Why not, indeed?

I knew immediately that I could. I had spent many hours volunteering in pediatrics as well as helping drug afflicted teens while yet a teen myself. After my bout with cancer, I had been mysteriously launched into serving as a death and dying counsellor. It seemed a perfect 'next step.'

The following day brought my priorities to the fore.

I had been assisting the Senior Partner in Securities.

Attorneys were flying all over the office.

There had been a securities leak on Bay Street!

The situation was serious!

Lists were being made of all individuals who'd had access to any of the files involved and, one by one, those individuals were being brought in for questioning.

In the very midst of this furious activity, a call came in on my personal line, the caller hopelessly in tears. After listening for several moments to indistinguishable words smothered in uncontrolled sobbing, I was eventually able to determine who was calling. I was dumbfounded, as this was a gal who was usually quite well put together.

She continued to sob . . . more than ten minutes passed this way.

All she could manage to eke out were the words, "I'm sorry . . . I'm so sorry."

I continued to reassure her that whatever was wrong, it would be okay, to take her time to compose herself, that I was not going anywhere and that she could take as long as she needed in order to tell me what was going on and how I could help.

As these comforting promises ensued, heads began to pop into my office to let me know that I was wanted at an emergency meeting. I shrugged my shoulders as if to alert them to the fact that I was unable to get away just now, pointing quizzically at the phone in my hand.

As the frenzy continued outside my door, my friend on the line was matching the intensity … becoming almost hysterical as she braced herself to get to the bottom line. I continued to speak softly to her, yet with more deliberation so as to assure her that she was not disturbing me in the least.

I knew in my heart that if for any reason we became disconnected, there was no telling what next steps she would resort to taking.

As the clock ticked feverishly away, thirty minutes turned into an hour. She was still unable to couple sentences together without intermittent outbursts, but we were at least getting to the beginning of what her anguish was all about.

More than one senior partner was now growling at me to explain myself, which made it all the more obvious how afraid everyone was becoming. No one had ever before shown me anything but complete respect. Putting my hand over the mouthpiece, I whispered quite loudly, "You're going to have to take someone else just now. I have an emergency here!"

More annoyed than concerned, they did nothing more than turn their backs, pouting their way out the door. It was obvious they were not the least bit interested in any emergency other than their own.

"What emergency," they must have thought, "could be any worse than a securities scandal, and in particular, one that involves our firm?"

The call with my friend lasted more than two hours!

The partners had eventually taken me at my word, having found someone to fill in for me and then to finally cover for me. This should not really have been too much of a problem, for we had at least a half dozen 'floaters' on staff, extremely competent gals who did whatever overload required immediate attention.

The outcome of the day was one of relief, for me at least. My friend, who, that very morning, just prior to her call to me, had decided to commit suicide, had now found a way through our conversation to put that thought aside, at least for the time being.

Throughout the four floors of the firm, there were certain grumblings that included my name.

I never knew the outcome of the 'leak.'

I presume it was somehow resolved.

I was all but ignored the following day.

Cold shoulders were turning up everywhere.

This behaviour on their part might be considered understandable, due to the non-personal relationship of our acquaintance. I had been for many years a free-lancer, meaning I usually worked for someone different every day and I had not been with this particular company for very long. I was mostly known as a 'trouble-shooter,' able to perform with superiority in highly stressful predicaments as well as being known as the 'presenter' of difficult truths to staff that were not getting along. Although I certainly had my position, in a firm of several hundred attorneys this had not made for a lot of bonding.

Nevertheless, is there ever a time when a crisis, no matter for whom, can be taken lightly? Had I been a 'personal' secretary, perhaps there may have been more of a commitment to supporting my situation…classic discrimination!

It seemed more than obvious that, to them, no matter what the circumstance, since it had not involved their own private little world, it was, quite simply, irrelevant.

One week later, I resigned.

Their moves were not what I would classify blatant constructive dismissal, although my having been transferred to work for the most difficult partner in the firm had to be construed as an obvious demotion. I could have fought for, and probably won, a nice little separation package. I declined the suggestion.

What came up clearly for me was simply the realization that if, as was the case with many of my contemporaries, my job had been too important to me, I might have been intimidated into disengaging my friend in order to keep my bosses happy and my position intact. Had that been the case, who knows what might have happened to my friend that day?

I was grateful that I had never been insecure about employment. This, in itself, gave me the freedom to make the right choice that day. A further lesson learned from this experience was that in the future, any employment would have to guarantee my right to react in exactly the same way.

Steps taken from that day to this have continued to remove me from the fast lane. I participate only in positions where my employer knows that if the Lord should call, my response can be quick and secure . . . "I'm 'outta' here." This only works with those who understand that there IS such a thing as God's work and that indeed His work comes first, and further, that I must be trusted to discern the difference.

Even so, from time to time I can be found enjoying lunch at a specialty cafe or visiting exclusive shops with members of the wealthy or 'intelligentsia.' I do not refuse such associations for many reasons, but mainly because Philippians 4:12 shows us how to live when Paul says:

I know both how to be abased, and I know how to abound: everywhere and in all things I am instructed both to be full

*and to be hungry, both to abound and to suffer need. I can
do all things through Christ which strengtheneth me.*

Self-imposed poverty or lack does not serve well, mainly
because of the word *self*. If we have chosen it, then we have
taken over God's rightful position in determining His desire
for our walk. To 'deny oneself'[6] is imperative. This means to
put others first and to give up that which we have for someone
else.

Self-determined wealth, followed by the choice of
overabundance, does not usually equal the word 'deny.' Of
course, it is never ours to judge. It is for those who find
themselves in such positions to search with diligence the
meaning of their circumstances.

The high road looks like this: the more received, the more
available to give away . . . "freely ye have received, freely give"[7]
. . . like a thoroughfare from heaven to those around us.

When one enjoys immense financial blessing, it is an
enormous responsibility. For example, how would we want the
report to the big boss to look after handling his portfolio of
investments? In a similar fashion, how will we answer for our
stewardship of those things in our care?

I do not fault those unaware of their positions for what
they really are. I remember once shopping with a friend who
was not in the same financial category as myself. It did not
occur to me at the time that my totally unnecessary purchase
of three jackets might have hurt her deeply (it was likely she
could not afford even one). For my part, it was selfish and
narcissistic, and I sincerely regret having done so.

Gratefully, my viewpoint is much different today.

We intentionally avoid such guilt trips by shopping only
with those in similar income brackets, and quite assuredly, this
is the way it usually works. Assume for a moment that you

enjoy a respectable income. I challenge you, under such circumstances, to walk aisle by aisle through a supermarket with a welfare mother of four; she would make her choices and you would make yours.

How easily could you purchase all that you would normally, suited exactly to your liking, with nary a second thought for the 'lack' of the woman beside you? Would you consider it nothing more than "I've got it and, sadly, she doesn't" or "just lucky, I guess?" More likely, it would not occur to us at all. We may distance ourselves from situations like these, but that does not eliminate them.

During our days of plenty, we would do well to seek ways in which to employ our assets to care for those without. I personally have passed through many days of abundance without realizing how much more I could have done with what I had.

Our day of reckoning will come ... best to get on with it now.

I know these things are often difficult to hear.

It takes courage to rigorously continue pouring over the things of God, for it is not comfortable to discuss the truth truthfully.

At the end of the movie version of *Schindler's List*,[8] in spite of the fact that he had performed beyond the capabilities of most, Schindler discovers that had he not kept his car, he could have saved others their grief and their pain.

His brokenness at the thought of it broke us too.

It occurs to me that we are each of us like Schindler : we, too, are at war, and everything that we hold onto of monetary value for no other reason than our comfort or pleasure or pride, could be used to transform someone else's life, sparing others their grief and their pain.

14

And when our war is over, will we not, like Schindler, be overtaken with grief that we did not keep less for 'us,' giving more to 'them'?

This concept was not entirely new to me. For quite some time I had been aware of things in my life that I could easily give up in order to serve another. I had been letting them go, one after the other, for some time.

Thanks to my own children, this really came home for me. One spring, I drove to Saskatoon to visit the boys. They were each in hot pursuit of hockey careers, seemingly managing without too many problems. On my arrival, I found their fridge empty and there was no shampoo, no laundry detergent, no deodorant, no toothpaste – items that the 'civilized' consider staples. I was mortified.

Considering that I was already well into the 'path' taking me 'out of the world,' I myself was in no monetary position to help them.

I did, however, still wear a half-carat diamond on my left hand, the original engagement ring given to me by their dad. Since the diamond was a VVS (very very slight imperfection) it was of a higher quality than most. It was the only asset I had worth salvaging.

I thought about giving up this ring and whether or not the amount I might garner from its sale would be 'worth the sacrifice.' I called around. Most places said that even though the equivalent was selling for $7,000 retail, I'd be lucky to get $300. This certainly wasn't much and I wondered about the wisdom of such a move. The diamond itself was such a beauty that hardly a day passed without someone commenting about it. It would be strange, almost lonely, without it.

My last call was to a friend, a jeweller in town. I did not really want to impose my friendship upon a deal, but I wanted a comparison. He told me that he would give me a thousand dollars AND put a cubic zirconium in the setting. That way, few would know that the ring was gone. (This component itself proved fascinating, with a follow-up story of its own.)

"Further," he told me, "mostly these days people aren't looking so much for diamonds of VVS standing because a lesser quality buys them a larger stone, thereby supplying seemingly more for the money." Accordingly, he suggested, "I'll tuck it away and hold onto it for some time, in case you want to one day buy it back with a nominal penalty."

I began to think more seriously about the concept now. What did me in was the thought that I could hardly, in all good conscience be walking around with a beautiful diamond on my hand when my children didn't have food in their fridge.

Suddenly, the most amazing thing occurred to me.

"How, in good conscience," I asked myself, "could I walk around with a beautiful diamond on my hand when there are ANY children without food in their fridge?"

This concept should never leave my mind.

*****

These days, most of my excursions with those enamoured with the world tend to be brief. I quickly find myself, through no profundity of my own, longing rather to comfort just one lonely soul than ogle over the latest evening gowns deemed elegant enough for the opera or ballet. Fortunately, I have experienced what it is like to be there and therefore have no sense of lack without them.

Long gone is my treasured condo with immaculate and charming interior, my closet brimming with Simon Chang suits. My favourite little Honda, which is not that big a ticket item even at best, has been exchanged for a brutal 1980 Dodge

Window Van, which holds the barest of necessities, including a bed and some clothing. For a while, I pulled a little trailer behind the van, which managed to house a homeless man or woman from time to time.

Often, for lack of proper sleeping arrangements, my bones ached. My physical condition was often deteriorated due to frequent poor nutrition and difficult living conditions.

Make no mistake about it, though, what I am describing to you here compares in no way to the countless missionaries around the world who live in despairing circumstances month in and month out, with nary a whimper or glint of sorrow about it.

In spite of any adversity, and I am sure I speak for all who serve in this way, to witness but one hopeless heart come to the knowledge that you actually care about them for no other reason than they are who they are ...

... Oh Sweet Charity!
There is nothing to compare!

*****

It has long ago become obvious to me that my friend's phone call during the securities scandal came just hours after I had responded in my heart to the words of the Lord:

"Come with me to serve the less fortunate."

The call was strategically placed in my path in order for me to take the necessary steps to respond.

There are no accidents.

*****

*****

Not unlike the majority of middle Americans, I have been often known to be seriously going about the business of my life and, given my particular gifts, exercising those strengths to the very best of my ability.

My letters of reference clearly confirm this.

Throughout the years there have been tremendous challenges with, I suppose, an appropriate number of wins and losses, a typical combination of excitement and melancholy, the varying 'passages' that one normally associates with the 'ups and downs' of life.

At the time that I would eventually come to know to be 'the days that radically changed who I was and where I was going,' I found myself, and not for the first time, to be moving rapidly in an *up*wardly mobile fashion.

Even in the midst of such exhilarating times, never far from my memory was the understanding that not only was Jesus a simple carpenter who taught us simple truths, He had declared Himself to be the Son of God.

It had never really occurred to me then, and it would take many more segments to bring it 'home,' that the *down*wardly mobile position *He* took while making this claim was in direct contradiction to how I had come to understand what *my* life was expected to be.

In his book *Descending into Greatness*,[9] Bill Hybels showcases real people who experienced tremendous success but eventually realized that becoming 'first' is to inevitably position ourselves 'last.'

"But how does one do that?" you ask.

And more importantly, "Why would anyone *want* to?"

It is, like all things in life, a process.

First comes an understanding of that process, followed by the implementation of the smallest of baby steps. Eventually, with some surefootedness, you might begin to act as if you 'knew' what you were doing. Over time, you have opportunities to believe in those elements which were carved out of your own life's enterprise.

Finally, should these three stages be irrefutably forged into every fibre of your being, culminating in what can clearly be considered 'faith'…faith in the very process itself…you would find yourself beginning to lead others to this same place: the truth about who we are.

Having become 'utterly ourselves' it becomes our task routinely to free others to do the same.[10]

This seems to be a laborious journey, and to be sure, it is. Nevertheless, in spite of its difficulty, we must determine to make fast work of this process. If we do not, we will fail to know who it is we are as individuals, resulting consequently and more importantly in the inability to bring about the necessary changes to allow our fellow countrymen and women to experience the freedom they were intended to enjoy.

There is everything to lose if but one of us delays.

*****

There came a time, I know not when, I began to centre my thoughts on questions being raised within the silent recesses of my heart. They had been intermittent at first, brought on usually by either a traumatic or exceedingly favourable experience. More often than not, the 'moment' had been distinctively overshadowed by something supernatural, inexplicable.

As my soul strained to touch that force that holds all of eternity's records in hand, I was moved beyond measure to understandings that I had never before heard spoken;

...the words appeared to be written somewhere deep
within me...

...words that continued to surface over the years with
greater and greater frequency...

...words that began something like this...

Was not Christ's lowly position precisely why His claims to
being the King of Kings were rejected?

Was this not also why those who killed Him, mocked Him
and spat upon Him? They had wanted Him to use His gifts to
take what was rightfully His, to display His power in order to
convince those who doubted, to present Himself in a kingly
fashion. This, they believed, was the only way to prove
Himself to be the One whom He said He was.

And yet, I mused, in spite of the fact that He knew at all
times who He was, having the ability without question to fully
demonstrate His power and authority, He never did so simply
to please Himself, and especially, not to 'save Himself.'[11]

This was an awesome concept and it began to weigh
heavily upon me.

Since Jesus had called us to be like Him, how on earth
could we possibly do so when we were obviously heading in a
totally opposite direction from the road taken by Him?

There seemed to be so much distortion, yes, and even
perversion of such a simple truth. It appeared that all of us had
gathered Christ's teachings sparingly, choosing for ourselves
only that which was comfortable – a sort of makeshift
Christianity.

When the Word of God seemed too harsh or too
restrictive, we convinced ourselves that there had been so
many translations, who could really count on it anyway?

Another favourite route for dismissal of a particular issue
was that Christ was speaking only to *that* particular person for

that particular time, thereby bringing no relevance to our own personal lives today. Putting it another way, "Times have changed." However, if God 'changes not,'[12] then the teachings remain the same.

There have been too many arguments, often putting to shame the Pharisees of old, speculating on the variety of meanings of a specific word or phrase.

Added to all of this was the consideration that each person had the right to create their own destiny, applying to their lives only those scriptures chosen specifically to fulfill their personal needs.

There did not appear to be two Christians who agreed on absolutely everything! For the most part, they could agree on practically nothing at all.

Such confusion!

Something must have gone terribly, terribly wrong!

So, what were the right answers?

Better still, what were the right questions?

For starters, it was clear to me that forgiveness was not something we came by easily, if at all, that boundary setting was the order of the day if we wanted to sufficiently protect ourselves from abuse and co-dependent relationships. Allowing oneself to be taken advantage of was becoming sociologically more of a sin than most civil misdemeanours. To serve in such a way as to be 'wasted' (be that your time or your very life itself) for the sake of another would be considered dysfunctional, requiring possibly years of therapy in order to determine what lack of self-esteem had manifested itself to drive you to such unseemly behaviour.

In essence, such conduct today is simply not tolerated.

Such conduct might also be termed 'service.'

True, there are times when we admire lives of sacrifice, but cautiously, after a fashion. The one making the sacrifice, who might otherwise be known as a 'good servant,' will have to put in so much time serving that the world cannot possibly deny that he or she is not going to stop, that they were not really just doing it to get something for themselves – our attention, perhaps – that yes, they are surely, truly serving and it appears they are really for real, thereby deserving some recognition of the deed.

Little is understood, unfortunately, about a true servant's heart. It is one that has become so full, through the very act of serving, that such human accolades actually get in the way of the purity of the service.

Often, when others lead by serving, it makes the rest of us look so bad that we are literally forced to make it our business to encourage those enduring with so much longsuffering to simply 'get over it' and 'get a life.'

We cannot ask ourselves often enough: Whatever did the Lord mean by the following words?

> *Whosoever will save his life shall lose it; but whosoever shall lose his life . . . the same shall save it. For what shall it profit a man, if he shall gain the whole world, and lose his own soul? What shall a man give in exchange for his soul?*[13]

When we finally have to admit that yes, so and so is doing quite a bit of good after all, we begin to heap some kind of praise upon that person, as if by our so doing, we ourselves become elevated, vicariously perhaps, due to our self-righteous speaking about the individual.

I continued to question.

How was it we had become so sidetracked, especially on this continent of plenty, that millions upon millions were walking as far from Him as was humanly possible, all the while convinced that we were somehow doing it right?

The doubts that surface as a result of the need for us to understand our own lives are enormous, but happily, the answers are available to each and every one of us who are willing to expose our own dark corridors while 'judging not'[14] the mistakes of others.

There need be no confusion about this, no confusion at all. "So, where *are* these answers?" you ask.

It is a promise of God that we have been given our own teacher, not needing man's wisdom and attention to our every waking thought and deed.

> *. . . ye need not that any man teach you . . .*[15]

The difficulty, then, must lie in discovering how to access that teacher, and then, having made contact, developing a relationship that is supportive, exhortative, edifying and instructive.

This is the issue at hand.

*****

I have found that the most important things I have learned came, not surprisingly, through service to others.

I had few formal instructors, experienced no college education, attended only a handful of seminars and, in particular, knew no one willing or able to speak privately at any length of the things of God, as if I'd even wanted to. I had abandoned my parents' home church at the age of thirteen, so one could not consider me 'churched.'

What I noticed filtering through me were certain immovable understandings. I eventually came to know that this had been made possible by my own personal acquaintance with the Holy Spirit.

When I met up with a man who had succumbed to the practices of a number of cults, I was instinctively aware that he was in some kind of trouble. I had no idea what that trouble was. It seemed impossible not to meet with him, and with each meeting, because of the cry of my heart to help him, came a knowledge from somewhere deep within me. I was not channelling; I did not lose consciousness, nor did I experience voice change. My willingness to simply hang in there coupled with my acknowledgement that I didn't know what to do, prompted the Lord to provide me with specific instructions and the power to break down strongholds, eventually enabling this man to be loosed from his bonds.

Throughout our relationship, I faced dozens of demons, skilled beyond measure at their craft. With the help of God, I was able to 'stand' in spite of their threats. After many years of gruelling work, this man came to know the Lord and is a missionary today.

Astonishingly, the immutable fact was that the information that had passed through me, once deciphered and then challenged by what is commonly known as the Word of God, stood those fiery trials with shining colours.

The Bible speaks of a time when "men will not endure sound doctrine; but after their own lusts shall they heap to themselves teachers, having itching ears; and they shall turn away their ears from the truth, and shall be turned unto fables."[16]

Although times like those described have crept in and out of history, our currently voracious appetite for mindless chatter and authorities who 'know not God' is evidenced in the continuous talk shows that titillate the imagination through fear and lust.

Surely, this is a time like none other.

Now that a 'remembrance' has been awakened within me of who I was before I came to know the Truth and, as a result, who I am to become, it is amazing for me to discover the hundreds of incidents that happened throughout all of my life, each and every day, when I could have knowingly participated openly and daringly in an intimate relationship with God.

He was always there, waiting with the greatest of patience, for me to 'see the light.'

What I will attempt to encourage you to seek is your own personal opportunity to determine how you may have been missing a life of continuous blessings in the face of either adversity or abundance.

And in this discovery, may you become compelled to waste not one minute more of your precious life on those things that can in no way compare to the marvellous Kingdom of Heaven.

*****

Who, for a better physical body, would not attend a gym, walk a mile a day or swim 20 laps?

Who, for a better job, does not frequent seminars or take additional college courses?

Who, then, for a better spiritual life, would not engage in the process required to produce the qualities necessary for peak performance?

This having been said, let us begin!

*****

Touching the Feet of Jesus ✑

Be ye followers of God, as dear children.

~Ephesians 5:1

I was 5 years old when my parents enrolled me at Loretto Academy, a Catholic girls' school overlooking Niagara Falls on the Canadian side.

My mother, although a staunch Protestant, had been auspiciously schooled by nuns in Hamilton, some fifty miles away. Having become a teacher herself and now privy to both sides of the learning curve, she was thoroughly convinced that the nuns were the most devoted to their students and hence best able to provide her eldest daughter an education.

Rules at the convent were strictly enforced. Navy uniforms with white blouses reduced competitive dressing and I recall actually enjoying how I looked and felt in my neatly pleated jumper. Less than pleasant were the hard plastic removable cuffs and collars, used to enable such easily dirtied areas to remain snowy white. They could be scrubbed with Ajax and bleach, which we applied once a week.

At the end of each day, within moments of the sounding of the dismissal bell, one could hear from floor to floor the snap, snap, snap of collars and cuffs as they were ripped away from each body. Accompanying this freedom came the right to head for the playground for a variety of activities such as baseball, swimming or the building of snowmen, depending on the season. Within the hour, school buses filled the circular drive patiently waiting to return us to our respective homes.

Once on board, it was my particular delight to position myself directly in the center of the bench that stretched across the breadth of the back of the bus. From this vantage point, I could witness everything that was happening in every seat and at the same time defy the forces of gravity while standing for most of the ride. Such precarious balancing was, I suspect, a type of entry level position for the administrative work to which I would be drawn throughout most of my life.

It was a regular circus, the ride to and from school.

Such harrowing road experiences were long before the days of seat belts, however rarely such belts might be used. Had our parents been even slightly aware of the true nature of any one of these junkets, they'd have surely been aghast at the mere thought of it. Children tore up and down the aisles and from seat to seat, delightfully screaming and carrying on at great length.

There can be no doubt that angels travelled close by, keeping us continually out of harm's way.

On mellow rides, we would sing. This relatively peaceful behaviour, which the driver welcomed with great relief, would occur, however, only on Thursdays, our last class that day having been choir.

Loretto's curriculum included valuable life principles, which were meticulously woven throughout every subject matter. This rated high on my parents' list of reasons to make the Academy my alma mater, which, when one considered my fairly outrageous personality, is not at all surprising.

It was not their intention for me to become a Catholic, quite the contrary. They were ardently both anti-French *and* anti-Catholic, prejudices that were to remain with them throughout their lives. They would continue to have difficulty separating the sinner from the sin, making it not only often impossible for them to forgive, but frequently forcing closed the door to relationships built on unconditional love.

Though we would come to debate quite fiercely this issue, it was never possible for me to convince them that individuals must be encouraged and loved, despite their incorrect choices, whether real or perceived.

After concluding that obtaining the most disciplined schooling was worth the risk of receiving unsolicited religious indoctrination, I was taken to meet the Mother Superior, whom I immediately noticed cared for me not at all.

The school selection having been made, nevertheless, one can easily understand the extent of the continuous dilemma in which my parents found themselves. The desire for my highest education seemed to be laden with cost.

To compensate, Mom and Dad went overboard in their statements against Catholicism, so much so that by the time I was 17, I was so well trained that I actually stopped dating a very nice young man simply because, as if to impress me, he pointed to St. Patrick's Cathedral as we drove by, declaring proudly, "There's my church!"

I never told him why I refused to see him again. I hardly knew myself.

Years later, we met at a mutual friend's 25th wedding anniversary party. We had not seen each other since high school. In fact, I had all but forgotten him, except for the vague recollection of having once decided against dating a boy because he was 'R.C.' (Roman Catholic). He, on the other hand, confessed that he had been plagued by the incident as he had no idea what he had done to cause me to spurn him.

As it turned out, he had married the daughter of a lady who had worked for my father. She had occasion to tell me confidentially that she was certainly glad that I had dropped him as he was not only her husband and father to her children but was indeed her very best friend.

I was relieved that it had all turned out so well.

There is no doubt that my parents had my best interests at heart, knowing full well that a marriage with dissimilar backgrounds makes for additional adjustments, the number of which should be kept to the barest minimum.

Unfortunately, they never explained, perhaps because they themselves did not know, why 'Christians' vary so greatly from one denomination to another. Their sole motive was one of historical account. They never gave me the details; that was just the way it was.

Protestants attending Loretto were supposed to be part of a separate class during the study of religion. However, we were but a handful of students, and so it was not a surprise that my closest friends attended what was called 'catechism.' Naturally, I did too. The nuns didn't seem to mind, never mentioning the matter. Perhaps they saw a budding young novitiate in their midst. I do not know.

As a result of the experiences I relate to you here, which occurred entirely without the influence of any personal instruction, I was given the opportunity to know that we are often directed solely from 'above.' This has further allowed me to understand how Jesus meets us wherever it is that we are, provided our hearts are open to His love with a willingness to believe in who He is.

So, whether a Moslem or Jew, tucked away in jail or a concentration camp, living in luxury or poverty, following a religion or a cult, healthy or sick, living in sin or piety, I rest in the confidence that if you "draw nigh to God, He will draw nigh to you."[17] This belief brings about the ability to comprehend the countless numbers who follow Him, despite their diverse life histories.

Though I had little or no interest in discussions at catechism (I was there mainly for the 'fellowship'), and although I kept a relatively safe distance from becoming 'one of them', no one could have guessed the spectacular results that would unfold in this seemingly mismatched atmosphere. No matter what the daily lesson, whether it be saints, Mary or Joseph, transubstantiation, communion or prayers, throughout my brief attendance there, I only had eyes for Jesus.

He was, for me, the Name Above All Names!

Quite mysteriously, He had become my 'first love.'[18]

*****

The ceilings throughout the building were enormously high and I would venture to say that some of them were no less than forty feet. It was a formidable sight for a child my age, to say the least. The floors were cold, European marble I think, with no carpets. When you walked through the corridors, some twenty feet or more in width, the echo of your thundering oxfords could be heard throughout the mezzanine.

Known to be an especially precocious child, which was probably just a polite way of saying that I was basically a brat, I appeared to have little or no fear of authority. Nevertheless, with thoughts that your every move was monitored from somewhere hidden from your view, as well as the notion that behind every pillar lurked something strangely sinister, even I was frequently intimidated.

Trouble found me everywhere. A regular chatterbox, something that has not really changed over time, I was the recipient of frequent disciplinary actions. At this tender age, I became accustomed to printing across the blackboard countless lines stating "I will not talk in class."

Unfortunately, such measures failed to noticeably deter me.

*****

There were two chapels to serve the Academy. One was in a separate building between Loretto and Mt. Carmel College, the boys' counterpart situated on the adjacent property. The other was actually in-house, on the second floor.

The in-house chapel was basically off-limits, except for morning prayer or special religious occasions held once or twice a month. At such times, the entire school would be in attendance.

Being precocious, it was often my style to do the opposite of everything I was told. It was therefore not unusual that I would decide to secretly visit the chapel.

The Stations of the Cross, a sequence of the fourteen most notable occurrences during the proceedings leading up to and during the crucifixion of our Lord, were hollowed deep into the walls and very faintly lit. Known as the Passion of Jesus, I remember them being extremely sobering as I would creep along in stocking feet so that no footsteps could be traced. I would peer into these silent caverns to witness the unfair suffering that the Son of God had endured on my behalf.

I can't recall thinking about anything in particular during those times, only that I was, for the most part, numb at the thought of His suffering. There became for me an understanding so intimate that the very feelings, thoughts and motives of my Saviour seemed readily comprehensible.

Growing out of this experience was my exquisite fascination with the Lord.

Upon the entrance wall of the chapel, one could not possibly miss a life-size clay model of our Lord as He hung on the cross at Calvary. It was a towering figure, placed just above the wainscoting. Keeping a respectful distance, I would pass solemnly by, with my eyes in wonderment lifted high to look upon His precious face. I imagined running my finger across His cheek as if to comfort Him.

Following one of my secret visits, my courage began to increase. I bravely moved up close to the entrance wall. With all the nerve that I could muster, and standing on my very tallest tippy toes, I reached up as high as I could. Since the structure was hung quite low, I was curious to discover if I could touch it.

To my amazement, not only had it become accessible (I surmised that I must have grown some), but my little fingers slipped into the frightful hole dug out by that awesome spike that had pierced the feet of my Jesus.

The very instant this took place, I knew beyond words the measure of His love.

From this 'knowing,' there became an unspeakable assurance that for all time we belonged to one another.

It was as if I would never be the same.

There would be nothing that anyone could ever say or do to take this love away, as I understood for all eternity exactly who He was!

*****

From a child's point of view, it was beautifully simple. It was perfectly understandable and completely real. I would not come to realize until many years later that the gift I had so simply received that day was more precious than gold. This gift of 'life' is desperately sought after by millions today. Oddly enough, only the very youngest at heart are apt to gain it.

It is not wisdom that obtains it, nor age, nor knowledge; in fact, the older and more worldly-wise one becomes, the less likely the success, for "unless we become as little children, we cannot enter…"[19]

Oh, how I pray for the world to set aside their cleverness of doctrine, their need to be right and, worse yet, righteous. For to experience such a meeting, one must seek Him out in the humility and dependency of an innocent child.

Without understanding the enormity of the moment, my heart scarcely skipped a beat. I sensed His presence, however, from that time to this, which has never failed to comfort me.

With nary a second thought, I moved on into the following days of my life, which, on the outside, and for the most part, appeared only slightly different from the days before. My 'conversion' was to be surely by degrees, for the remembrance of this specific appointment eluded me for most of my life, the process having been underway nonetheless.

In the meantime, my overwhelming fascination with spiritual mementos prompted me to continue to steal rosaries of every description: black pearl rosaries, pink crystal rosaries, wood bead rosaries. You name it, I had it! Over time, my drawer at home became quite full.

One day, our cleaning lady discovered the cache and, to my dismay, disclosed the find to my mother, who was absolutely horrified!

Concerned that I was somehow becoming ensnared by the icons of Catholicism, I was pulled, at the age of six, from the embrace of the sisters and plummeted into public school.

*****

My parents, seriously considering a multitude of consequences, decided, somewhat despairingly, that one hour a week at the Academy would cause me no greater harm than had already been done. Consequently, it was decided that my piano instruction, which was progressing rather nicely at the time, would be continued. This avenue brought forth the privilege to encounter a teacher who was the highest spirited and most joyful nun I have ever met.

Sister Magellan displayed a sweeping gait that made you long to wear her flowing robes. Her gestures were grand, her smile infectious. She moved with amazing speed and yet propelled as if upon a rail, so smooth was her passage from one room to another. Her slim and graceful figure, with head held high as if seeking someone above an invisible crowd, told you that each of her movements was a dance to the Lord. You could tell she was pleased to serve Him.

This weekly companion over the next eight years, through love and dedication, managed to enhance greatly the musical gifts that had befallen me strictly through heritage on my mother's side. This unique sister had a particular way about her that seemed to create the desire in her students to perform *with excellence*.

She never raised her voice nor brought us to shame, despite our occasional lack of diligence. These divine characteristics were in marked contrast to other encounters at the Academy.

One such unpleasant remembrance was an occasion when the Mother Superior was to visit our class. We had all been thoroughly instructed that while 'Mother' was present, anyone talking, or for that matter, even making so much as a move, would bring upon themselves grave repercussions.

Everyone knew what that meant!

'Mother' was no sooner in the room, with all apparently going quite well, when suddenly the girl in front of me came down with a gushing nose bleed. She turned to look at me and I was stunned to see that she was already soaked to the waist.

Obviously not old enough to have undergone CPR training, never having witnessed anyone with a nose bleed, and my experiences having been somewhat limited due to my age and all, I did what any responsible five-year old in my situation would do. I took my friend's hand in mine and placed it on the bridge of her nose.

"Pinch here tightly," I said with authority.

"And put your head back...here, I'll help you."

Now the little girl was bending nicely back, head tilted as far back as possible with her little fingers pinching her nose. (How could I have known to do this?)

This had all occurred within less than a minute, at which time I looked proudly toward the front of the room, now that everything seemed to be nicely settled.

The fury on the Sister's face raced towards me and I nearly shook from its intensity.

The Sister flew to my side, grabbed me viciously by the arm and dragged me to the back of the room, where she proceeded to instruct me that I would be strapped a dozen times for my disobedience.

And Mother Superior was about to do the honours!

I did not cry, nor try to explain; somehow I sensed that this would only make things worse. All the while this was happening, I continued to think upon the action that had brought me to this moment. Upon reflection, I was well pleased and content that I had done what was right.

A twelve-inch ruler was brought forth and the Mother Superior proceeded to hit me hard...six smacks on each little hand.

You may find this difficult to believe, but I recall the instant with brilliant clarity. I found myself wondering, as the ruler continued to strike me, how anyone in this class would ever get the message, as a result of this punishment being mercilessly inflicted upon me, that it was worth helping another person when they were in trouble.

Further, I knew then, as I always have, that those in positions of authority often either willingly abuse their power or more accurately, "know not what they do."[20]

It is my guess that these thoughts, which were completely removed from the situation at hand, made the punishment barely noticeable. I must also add that there was the faintest notion that in some way it was I who was actually the one in power. There was no explanation for this feeling but I knew that it was true. I sensed no ill feelings toward the two nuns, merely a sense of puzzlement and inevitable pity.

In those days, to arrive home with broken blood vessels in your hand was something you hid, if at all possible, from public view, for if your parents uncovered the secret, one might endure further reprimands, most notably their disapproval and disdain. In this particular case, I was not found out, thereby ducking further difficulty.

*****

Sister Magellan's most specific achievement was the confidence and authority she instilled in us in our approach to any opportunity to perform in competition. The rituals of such events were followed to the letter, the children managing to behave with enormous precision and obedience. Without her encouragement, the successes many of us enjoyed would have been entirely impossible.

Prior to the formalities, each candidate would be given a number, taking a seat in corresponding numerical order. The adjudicator would then take his seat in the center of the theatre. After a respectful pause, he would tinkle a small bell to indicate that he was ready for the competition to begin.

The first aspirant would then climb a small flight of stairs to the stage, become situated comfortably at the piano, place often shaky fingers above the keys, take a deep breath and begin.

At the conclusion of each performance, you would stand before the audience, making a small curtsy or bow. When you returned to your seat, a deafening silence would fall upon the auditorium while the adjudicator made his comments upon the certificate which would eventually be yours.

It was always difficult to know whether the amount of time he took was because he loved or hated what you had trained so tirelessly to perform.

In the meantime, the next candidate waited anxiously for the anticipated sounding of the bell to acknowledge that it was their turn to mount the stage.

One competition of measured difficulty found Boris Berlin to be our adjudicator. He was brilliant as both a composer and a musician. Most of the contestants were quite in awe of him.

At the conclusion of the twenty-or-so performances, he gathered together the certificates that would either make or break us and proceeded to take his place before us.

As he made his comments to each of the candidates for gold, he would move along the row of seats so that he might face directly the pianist in question. He was often long winded, covering in detail crescendos and staccatos that had gone awry throughout the piece. He might even spend several minutes discussing the particular performance and how it might be improved upon. This characteristic constantly caused serious delays in the scheduled programming.

As he approached me, he removed his glasses, meeting me with a deep and penetrating gaze. I was aware that I had performed well, and yet I could not have been more surprised at his response.

"How can I speak to this excellent accomplishment?" he asked, as if expecting an answer.

"I have written only one sentence on your certificate, young lady." He paused dramatically as if to enlarge upon what he was about to say.

"You...have...talent!'

Every eye and ear came to full attention as the enormity of what had just been said rang throughout the hall. I smiled meekly back at him.

"I have given you the highest mark of the day to earn you the honour of first place," he continued.

"Congratulations!"

With this last comment, he nodded ever so slightly, as if we were long lost friends, placed his glasses upon his nose and proceeded to the boy on my right.

Such accolades that continued to come my way over the next several years were clearly due specifically to the disciplined tutoring of Sister Magellan, and though I was too young to understand the extent of her contribution, I gladly speak of it now.

In spite of all that our partnership included during my happily attended weekend lessons, in addition to many successful public appearances, the most delicious moments came when I would occasionally have an opportunity to slip unnoticed past the central office, down to the chapel, for a much-loved rendezvous with the Lord.

*****

Throughout adulthood, a certain revelation began to unfold. Over time, it became clear to myself and others that there must have been some extraordinary influence upon my life that had provided me with some kind of built-in mechanism designed specifically to handle life's numerous and varied challenges.

During the many crises that came my way, I found that I rarely had difficulty dealing with them. All problems had for me a simplicity and truth that was virtually impossible for those involved to comprehend.

When, in 1979, the interest rate in Canada rose to an enormous 20 and 21 percent, we lost virtually everything that we had due to the fact that we had several executive homes under construction. As we juggled payments and fell behind in mortgage on our home by some six months with foreclosure papers looming ever larger, I was in no way daunted by the dilemma.

It never occurred to me to find the situation anything more than just 'life.' I clung to my usual good nature since there was absolutely nothing anyone could do.

You take your lumps and move on. Right?

Another noticeable irregularity had always been that whenever I had done something wrong, my guilt was only momentary. My mother declared in exasperation that it was impossible to punish me as my ability to surmount the apparent inconvenience frustrated all attempted penalties.

The story goes that once she had grounded me for three days from using my toboggan on the hill next to our yard. This was one of my favourite things to do and so it stood to reason that this should have caused me sufficient grief to sustain at least a moderately contrite spirit.

Making no comment whatsoever, I proceeded outside.

Little time had passed when Mother was both astonished and amused to view from her kitchen window a happy little girl sliding down the hill on a cardboard box!

It had obviously never occurred to me to become even remotely defeated by the intended restriction.

This very odd behaviour, which allowed for little or no remorse, gained me much resentment and accusation from my superiors. I was often labelled a sociopath, a horrible condition known by psychologists to mean 'without conscience.'

As I grew older, I began to wonder myself, from time to time, if that might not be true. There was no doubt about it, I had a very different way of viewing things from, seemingly, the rest of the world.

After much soul searching, I had concurred, however, that the concept that I was operating from a lack of conscience was impossible, for one of my most notorious habits was to bring home the lost and hurting. This was in addition to my constant examining my motives for any given thing as to what I might have done differently or better. My mother was continuously aghast at the sight of my unusual acquaintances and reminded me that to associate with people from the 'wrong side of the tracks' would bring nothing but trouble and heartache into my life. To her credit, she eventually came to fully understand and appreciate my 'calling.'

Not until I was in my mid-forties, when it was insisted by a friend that I read Andrew Murray's book, *The Power of the Blood of Jesus*,[21] did it begin to seem possible that I had been somehow led on a journey of precision and promise. Murray delicately explains what it means to be 'cleansed of an evil conscience.' I read the book several times before I was hit, as if thunderstruck, by the remarkable conclusion that I may have somehow become thus 'cleansed.'

More difficult to comprehend was the receipt of accusations so often hurled at me from those who seemed to be guilty of the very things of which they were accusing. Such treatment was often startling; nonetheless, the Lord provided me with the grace to avoid defending myself or retaliating in any way. Although I was not yet aware of the particular stages of preparation that He was providing for me, there was always present a quiet assurance that everything that was taking place was not without reason.

Finally, the most spectacular element was some kind of innate wisdom, which often catapulted me well beyond my years and experience, in addition to the provision of obvious instincts that one might classify as paranormal.

Puzzling remarks from friends and associates finally prompted me to eventually investigate and, at long last discover, what it was that seemed to separate me in a most peculiar way.

Questions continued to plague me, like "How do you manage to be so calm when everything seems to be falling apart?" or "However did you acquire such a forgiving heart?"

Once, during a serious political interview, I was asked, "What aspect of your upbringing would you say contributed the most to your incredible outlook on life?"

In an attempt to respond, I realized that I couldn't think of any particular things that might have contributed to my ability to so easily accept whatever life brought my way. As the question ran around in my head, memories of my youth began to surface, including practising the piano and a voracious appetite for reading ... lots of mysteries ... like the entire Enid Blyton series with titles such as *The Sea of Adventure*[22] and *The Castle of Adventure*[23] ... and ... everything that was ever written about or by Mahatma Ghandi, who eventually became my favourite subject matter, year after year, for public speaking.

I loved baseball, largely because everyone in the neighbourhood congregated daily in a large field across from our home in the country where a baseball diamond had been diligently carved. We played for hours each evening from early spring to late fall.

Having no siblings until the age of ten, I had found myself alone a great deal.

Mother's teaching duties had kept her very occupied, and although we spent musical time together, she was otherwise mostly inaccessible. In retrospect, I have to say that the times we shared added enormously to my walk with the Lord as she herself had known Him for a very long time.

Unfortunately, we rarely spoke of this in any meaningful fashion until her dying years, for which memories I was extremely grateful. As a child, I missed telling her about my experiences and, for the most part, I was unaware of any intimate details regarding her own relationship with the Lord. I think it was more a case of knowing that she knew Him that influenced me most.

As for my earthly father, he regularly found disagreement with almost everything about me and so we had infrequent conversations of any warmth. This situation sadly remained throughout most of our lives, though I came to understand his way and was therefore able to 'let it go.'

There could be no doubt that he loved me, for he protected me from any path that I might have eagerly yet misguidedly pursued. In fact, he cared about me so much, I believe, that he feared for me regularly, making it impossible for us to be comfortable together.

His love, which he most often demonstrated with inappropriate anxiety, was always difficult to receive due to the accompanying odd behaviour.

Here follows one example: my dad's friend was at the wheel of a four-door sedan that was travelling down the highway at top speed. There were probably six, and maybe even seven, of us packed into the car. I was sitting in the back, quite squashed into the corner next to the door, and directly behind my dad, who was sitting in the front passenger seat.

I was barely three.

Intending to open the window, I inadvertently unlatched the door. Suddenly, I was falling out the door, rolling dozens of times along the roadway's not-so-soft shoulder.

It was several moments before anyone realized what had happened! By the time the car was stopped, pulled to the side of the road and reversed again at top speed, I had covered several hundred feet of gravel and dirt. Miraculously, there were no broken bones and I was fully conscious. However, I suffered many abrasions and tiny stones were imbedded into almost every part of my body.

I looked a terrible fright, to be sure. My frilly pink dress and curly blond hair were covered in dirt and blood. As everyone from the car came running to fetch me, my dad approached me, yelling at the top of his voice at my stupidity for having done such a thing.

Although at the time I had little understanding for such an emotion, my own similar instinct brought about by my own motherhood provides me with little doubt that this was the only way in which he could deal with the horrifying thought that such a thing could happen to his little girl.

He was very angry that I had somehow hurt him.

I spent several months so covered from head to toe in bandages that I resembled a mummy. My time was spent in a comfortable chair that was placed in the centre of the picture window where I watched longingly as my friends played ball throughout the summer.

It does seem unfortunate that in spite of his obvious desire for that which was best for me, Dad and I never really became friends, having been sadly unable to penetrate the barrier that one often finds between parent and child.

I count it a blessing, nonetheless, for perhaps the distance between us encouraged me to embrace the Lord more earnestly.

*****

From what I could gather, after searching the files of my youth, the most character-building aspects of adolescence, it seemed, were my years of competition in piano and voice at the Kiwanis Festival. To be sure, the opportunity to perform had made it possible for me to learn that I could win or lose with equanimity. I had to admit, however, that such understanding was uncharacteristic for one so young.

Clearly, there had to be something more.

Over the years I had begun to see that hardly anybody lived like me. At least, hardly anybody I knew then. In fact, what I had come to discover was that such optimism and joy was, without a doubt, unique.

As I became more vocal about the Lord, though I attended no church and associated with no known Christians whatsoever, my ability to talk about Him with confidence grew steadily.

There became a suggestion that my childhood encounter and ensuing association with Jesus must have had a major impact on my life. I was more and more frequently asked to share my 'testimony.' It occurred to me that perhaps I didn't have one, but as this could not really be possible, I knew there was a missing link, one that I had either forgotten or somehow missed.

Unlike other Christians who were increasingly coming into my life, I couldn't point to a particular moment when I accepted the Lord and then became somehow transformed. I had no recollection of when I had become 'saved', although I knew without a doubt that I was.

But more than this, it was clear that I was no angel, and hence, it never really occurred to me that I may have something special to do for the Lord. Oh, I knew that I loved Him and all, and without a doubt, I could feel His love for me, but I was not unaware of my unworthy deeds.

Though I accepted His forgiveness without question, I could never have anticipated the Lord's calling on me to go 'fishing' for Him.

It had not yet become known to me that, as Charles Spurgeon so perfectly points out:

> ... a man may be saved and yet know none of the details of his conversion.
>
> No doubt, there are many strong believers who could not point to any special event or means by which faith was born within them. In general, faith came by the hearing of the Word of God and the operation of the Holy Spirit; but those believers do not remember, as some do, a remarkable text or thrilling sermon or striking providence through which they were turned from darkness to light.
>
> Thousands in the fold of Jesus came back to the good Shepherd by degrees. Many who now walk in the light

received daylight, not by the leaping of the sun above the horizon in a moment but as our days usually begin: a little light tinged the eastern sky, and then came a rosy hue, followed by a dim dawn; and afterward the actual rising of the sun out of its chambers of the east, and the sun runs his course till he has created perfect day. Many are gradually brought to Christ, and yet they are truly brought to Christ.[24]

As the Holy Spirit is the Author of spiritual life, so is He the Author of all true instruction. You may profess to be a believer but you know nothing at all unless the Holy Spirit has taught you. To be taught of the minister is nothing, but to be taught of the Lord is everything. It is only the Spirit of God who can engrave the truth upon the fleshy tablets of the heart.

The knowledge of the letter only puffs up those who rest in it, and eventually the letter kills; but the inward whisper, the secret admonition, the silent operation of the Spirit of God that falls as the dew from heaven upon the heart – this is quite another thing. Without it we are blind and ignorant, though we may be esteemed a theologian. We are still in the dark unless the Spirit of God has shone in upon our soul.[25]

Knowing full well that the light had been presented to me gradually over the years, I determined to discover, if it was possible, the approximate time when my salvation had been secured. Seeking clues took me as far back as my earliest school days.

And then, unmistakably, I felt drawn to pay a visit to Loretto, as a keen suspicion began to grow that an answer must surely wait for me there.

*****

We set out for the Academy on a cold and sunny day. As we drove through the iron gates, winding our way toward the front of the building, I felt a flurry of excitement.

There were no cars and the grounds seemed deserted.

We climbed the stairs to the main entry and pushed the buzzer. After waiting a very long time, it occurred to us that perhaps the building was actually closed. Just as we were about to turn away, the old wooden door creaked slightly open.

The tiniest nun I had ever seen peeked out at us warmly and with obvious curiosity. She asked if she could help us.

I began to tell her that I had attended the school many years ago, and that I was hoping I could take a look around for old times' sake. She said that she would be happy to take us on a tour.

She opened the door wide.

My glance was drawn high above me to those fabulous ceilings. Before us rose a magnificent oil painting of Archangel Michael with his foot on the head of a serpent. The masterpiece was so large that it literally filled the foyer. I remembered the picture having been there, but recalled that, although it was incredible in size and spectacular in content, it had had little impression upon me as a child.

I have since learned that the sisters of this order give a certain prominence to this magnificent Archangel, for it is said that the Bar Convent of the walled city of York, in England, during a raid upon it by 16th century rebel forces, had been divinely protected by a supernatural event.

The story goes that as the rebels approached the door, prepared to seize all, a figure of Michael's stature and strength appeared in a suit of medieval armour riding a magnificent white horse. In his right hand he had strategically positioned a huge spear. The appearance was so threatening that the rebels, fearing for their lives, turned and hastily departed.

To this day, there graces each building of the international order – from Dublin, Ireland to Sydney, Australia – an acknowledgement of Michael's support for their mission.

This acknowledgement comes in many forms.

Sometimes, a modest figure of Michael hangs on the wall by the entrance door. Now and then a larger tribute is found. I presume that the one before us would rank among the most splendid in the world.

Our petite escort appeared to be happy for the company and told us that the Academy was no longer used for a school but instead was a center for retreats and conferences. The huge play rooms were now dormitories lined with single cots, which provided no familiarity whatsoever.

We let her show us as she pleased until finally I asked if the chapel was in the same place at the north end of the building. She said that it was and that it might be easier for me to remember as that part of the building had never been changed.

"The chapel," she went on, "was part of the very first construction, and due to its special history, it was more or less 'ordained' that it would always remain exactly the same."

As we approached the chapel, my eyes longed to view the crucifix that had been so real to me. To my enormous surprise, in exactly the place where I learned to love the Lord, there was indeed a crucifix, but it could not have been more than two feet in height! Further, even as an adult, it would have been impossible to reach!

I disappointingly asked the sister what they had done with the life-size figure of Christ on the cross that had once graced the chapel. She told me that she had no recollection of there ever being any other crucifix but the one that we saw there now.

At first I was sure that this was impossible. There had to have been another, and if there had, how could she have ever forgotten it?

"How long have you lived here?" I asked.

"Almost thirty-five years," she replied.

"That must be it," I thought, "it was moved just before she came."

"Well then," I continued to question her, "isn't it possible that the crucifix that I have in mind was replaced prior to that time?"

"Oh no," she answered emphatically. "For you see, there are pictures of this original building and you can see for yourself that everything is exactly as it was. Years later, thousands of square feet were added to the Academy. You can determine the various stages of development by the difference in the stone surface on the outer walls.

"When a fire badly damaged the majority of the school in 1938 [at least 10 years before my attending], the original part of the structure, which included this chapel, as if protected by God Himself, had not a mark upon it. The wall of flame stopped in its tracks at the division line between the old and the new.

"It is claimed that it was a miracle as a result of the blessedness of those who performed the dedication."

There was a sureness about her that ended the apparent controversy.

We walked through the chapel and a recollection of tranquility and contentment immediately returned. It was a confirmation that something wonderful had happened to me in this place.

Having now seen all that we had apparently come for, the sister showed us to the door and bid us farewell. She invited us to come again, any time.

Once outside, I could not contain myself.

"What do you make of it?" I asked my friend Lee, who was as curious as I to solve the puzzle.

He began cautiously at first by saying that children often think of things as being much, much bigger than they really are, obviously due to their own lack of stature.

As I was about to agree that that was quite possibly true, I said, "Well, what do you make of the fact that as relevant as that may be, there was no way that I could have touched the feet of Jesus, then or now?"

"That's the bigger question," he added thoughtfully. "There has to be another explanation. Perhaps you only imagined it."

"Perhaps," I thought.

As I considered this point, I could sense a stirring within my soul that I knew would continue until we were convinced that this phenomenon could not be explained away. For to be sure, I had touched Him, and the figure itself couldn't have been more real. The feet felt as though made of flesh . . . the blood, sticky to the touch.

Could it be (I was beginning to think the unthinkable) that the Living God, in His Almighty Power, the Creator of Universes, Worker of Miracles, had enlarged that crucifix to meet a single child's compassion, allowing her to spend a moment in time with the Saviour, Our Lord?

"But how could that be?" you ask.

It is more than incredible!

But wait!

Is it not true that Jesus appeared to the disciples, asking them to touch His hands and feet in order for them to be convinced of His resurrection? Had I myself not heard countless stories of Christians having encountered Christ at a time of deep reverence, or trial? If I were to believe that they did indeed witness what they claimed – and I do – then why could something similar not have happened to me?

There were no other choices for me now; I had come to know that this was truly my first recollection of being with the Lamb of God, through what was, clearly, a miracle!

With this knowledge firmly planted in my spirit, a remembrance of all things past began to rise up before me while an infinite array of experiences that had been critical parts of my life came rushing to meet me. As each memory surfaced, a cascade of revelations overwhelmed me as He shed His Light upon every moment of all of my days. I stood transfixed, enraptured by the warmth of His wisdom as what had seemingly been hidden from me all of these years became totally clear.

A Scripture, memorized in the sixth grade, oddly enough in a public school during those days when such instruction was still permissible, suddenly rang hauntingly in my soul.

> *For now we see through a glass darkly; but then face to face: now I know in part; but then shall I know even as also I am known.*[26]

I felt that 'then' had certainly begun.

What is continuously elusive is the beautiful mystery surrounding His decision to come and meet with such a one as me. I did not deserve such a visit, neither called for nor planned it. It could only have been that the Lord, through His grace and mercy, chose to respond to the heart's yearning of a little child.

In this knowledge I rejoice and praise His Holy Name!!

*****

Today, after such a long and often difficult walk, through boundless blessings in the face of valleys of darkness, I am able to truly appreciate what wondrous things He is prepared to do for even the least of His children who, with fervent heart, simply want to reach up and touch Him.

*****

Go ahead...
　　reach up...
　　　　touch the feet of Jesus!

> *Draw nigh to God, and he will draw nigh to you.*
> ~James 4:8

*****

The Lord's handiwork, like an intricately woven series of incidents that collectively creates our very own personal tapestry of life, provides confirmation time and time again of the dance between the weaver and the cloth, the 'potter and the clay.'[27]

*****

Over many years, and with astonishing regularity, one of my friends would ask me if I had yet read anything by Charles Spurgeon. After a time, his questions began to haunt me. And yet, Spurgeon's work remained 'coincidentally' quite removed from my path.

With a perfection that can only be considered divine, and just prior to the completion of this part of my story, I was introduced to Spurgeon's legacy quite unexpectedly.

While perusing the shelves of One Way Books, a Christian bookstore in Santa Rosa, California, a very distinguished grey-haired lady caught my eye and spoke to me. She was not distinguished in a worldly way. I cannot say that her dress was fashionable, nor her clothes chic, but her demeanour was one of extended grace and there was an unmistakable glow about her. Standing quite near to one another, she felt inclined to ask me if I had ever read Ravenhill's work on revival.

I said I had not.

"Oh," she said, seemingly suddenly filled with determination to share something vital with me, "come with me . . . I'll show you."

She urged me towards the classic section, insisting there was a book that was 'must' reading for me. We moved easily among the aisles, as if we were old friends, though we had scarcely met.

I took quite seriously her suggestion on Ravenhill, purchasing his book *Why Revival Tarries*,[28] which has since uplifted my heart greatly; however, what was remarkably noticeable to me was that sitting right next to Ravenhill were several books by and about Charles Spurgeon.

I knew immediately that the time had come for Spurgeon and I to meet.

As the 'missionary' pursued our acquaintance, it became apparent that her walk had been unmistakably similar to mine.

"I am buying a book today for our pastor," she said.

"He's quite young, you see, and I find the Lord continues to prompt me to help move him along as quickly as possible, due to the urgency of our times."

I did not say anything as I sensed her desire to share something more with me.

"Some servants of the Lord," and she nodded in a way that included the two of us, "spend a great deal of time providing avenues to Truth to those who wish to know it."

She paused as she seemed to reflect on the enormity of such a task.

Turning back to me, her eyes now flashing with childlike glee, she whispered with both enthusiasm and guarded secrecy, "It's quite exciting, isn't it?"

I smiled quietly in concurrence, comforted by the realization that somehow she was aware of our mutual relationship as members of the Body of Christ.[29]

The moment was all the more precious remembering how often the walk had found me, though never lonely, quite alone. She seemed to know that I needed a reassuring word to confirm my bearing. This she was able to do with salient ease and I sensed somehow a shadow of myself in her presence. She handed me one of her simple cards, and we went about the things we had come to do, our purpose for meeting having been obviously accomplished.

With the physical manifestation of one of Spurgeon's books held decidedly in my hands, I was soon to note how once again the Lord had granted me a gift that would fully complete the picture He had guided me to paint with words.

*****

Charles Haddon Spurgeon (1834-1892) is considered to be, by the majority of Christian authorities, one of the greatest preachers of all time.

During his lifetime, Spurgeon is estimated to have preached to 10,000,000 people. He remains history's most widely read preacher, there being more material written by him than any other Christian author, living or dead. His 63 volumes of sermons stand as the largest set of books by a single author in the history of Christianity, comprising the equivalent to the 27 volumes of the ninth edition of the Encyclopaedia Britannica.

Spurgeon enjoyed a congregation of over 6,000 and added well over 14,000 members during his 38-year London Ministry.

In 1865, his weekly sermons were being printed, having a remarkable sale – 25,000 copies every week – and translated into more than 20 languages.[30]

Although I am more inclined toward Andrew Murray's teachings regarding the 'death of self,' there is no question that Spurgeon's understanding of what it takes to rescue a soul from death and hell is the most profound I have ever encountered. Additionally, Spurgeon's preaching is often beautifully picturesque, doubtlessly encouraging and continuously inspiring. It can be, therefore, no surprise, after the sojourn through my past and consequent discovery, that I was moved to a torrent of tears, my heart leaping with joy and great relief on discovering the following words written by this eminent author . . . words through which he poignantly beckons the listener to 'know' the Saviour . . . words spoken more than a century ago . . .

*****

Let the Spirit of God reveal to you the pierced hands and feet of Jesus . . .

Let Him enable you to put your finger into the prints of the nails . . .

And touch the wounds of His feet . . .

And lay your heart to His heart . . .

. . . why, if you have no peace, you would be a melancholy miracle of perverse despondency.

But you must have rest when you have Jesus Christ, and such a rest that Jesus calls it "My peace," the very peace that is in the heart of Christ, the unruffled serenity of the conquering Saviour, who has finished forever the work that God gave Him to do.[31]

*****

And so it was that His Peace had come to me.

*****

The Visit ❧

For I will never leave thee, nor forsake thee.
~Hebrews 13:5

In the early fifties, a great deal of fear could be summoned concerning red measles. Our house was to be no exception when I was found to be covered in little red dots.

As was the custom of the day, I was promptly and securely shut into my room for a period of no less than three weeks. Additional precautions included the use of heavy blankets draped over every window to ensure lasting, utter darkness. There was always worry that severe damage might be caused to the eyes if not properly protected from even the smallest fragment of light. Blindness was not unheard of in cases where insufficient care had been taken.

Considering mother's fastidiousness in matters such as these, it was no surprise to find myself completely bedridden, in seclusion, in the dark.

For a seven-year-old, this could have been a trying experience. I have to assume that for most of the time, I was suffering from either fever or exhaustion, requiring lots of sleep, because, except for the experience that I am about to disclose, the entire illness proceeded along its normal course to an eventually complete recovery.

My grandfather on my mother's side was a prominent physician, specializing in osteopathy, which sides with the theory that diseases are due chiefly to loss of structural integrity. It is maintained that such loss can be restored by manipulative treatments that stimulate the circulatory system sufficiently to assist the body to re-regulate itself. Consequently, this approach was used to deal with family illness of any kind.

Inoculations were always refused.

Whenever the medical unit arrived at our school for the usual needle-giving ceremonies, it was generally assumed that I was spoofing when I stepped up for my turn to inform the nurses that I was not to be given any injections. Their responses would range anywhere from humour to impatience to outright outrage at the possibility.

Once my situation was confirmed through the principal's office, I was eventually free to return to my class. This family tradition afforded me an early acquaintance with marching to the tune of a different drummer. I must have seemed an anomaly, even then although it is my recollection that the whole scene passed, for the most part, usually without incident.

I will say, however, that although I eventually landed an improvident dose of cancer, my childhood, with the exception of this bout of measles, was relatively illness-free. I avoided the mumps and chicken pox. No matter how badly a flu would circulate the class, I continued to escape the absentee list.

What, if anything, this had to do with the lack of immunization, I cannot say.

One would have to assume that a certain dreariness must have encompassed the three-week endurance event. One evening, after supper had been brought to me with cheery good wishes, the tray now sitting quite empty of food on the bedside table, things were about to change.

As evening approached, I could hear my neighbourhood friends calling out familiar baseball sounds from across the street. Although I was forbidden to look out into the daylight, what little there might remain at this hour, it occurred to me that I was content to remain in my bed. In particular, I had no desire, which was itself unusual, to sneak a peak in the direction of the delicious noise now drifting into the hastening dusk.

I was about two weeks into my recovery and had spent most of this Sunday afternoon sleeping. My appetite returning was a sure sign that we were beginning to hit the home stretch. Everyone was noticeably relieved.

I prepared to entertain myself by considering further the elements of my room, which I had come to enjoy over the years, modest though they may have been. Mother had quite a knack for decorating and always managed to find ways to be clever at little cost to the family budget.

Dad had built a desk into the corner with complimentary accompanying dressers on either side. There were matching drapes and bed skirts, which were Mother's contribution.

For my part, there were eight framed pictures that hung along one wall above the bed. Each picture was a different type of flower – geranium, iris, tulips, pansies – and each had been coloured by me. Somehow, my parents must have thought the accomplishment quite spectacular to have gone to all the trouble of framing each piece. As for me, I have only the vaguest recollection of my involvement and barely recall the process of framing and hanging them. Perhaps the lack of memory explains why they were apparently special – I may have been so young that any clear recollection eludes me to this day. All I can tell you is that the pictures were there, and apparently, I was the resident artist.

I managed to prop a second pillow behind my head and, as I looked toward the corner, where there was ordinarily nothing distinctive to report, I was aware that there now seemed to be something unusual...something faintly glistening.

At first, though slightly startled, I sat bolt upright, peering decidedly into the section of light, which seemed to be increasing in size and intensity. When I was convinced that this was no mirage, I thought better of my exposed position, choosing now to slip more deeply under the covers, peering only occasionally and with measured caution up and over the ruffled down quilt lovingly made by my grandmother's hand.

I watched with amazement as the 'something' appeared to be moving slightly. In no time at all, it seemed, there had developed, right before my eyes, the most incredibly bright white light!

I stared in astonishment, my curiosity piqued.

Nothing happened for a minute, or more, and then, ever so gradually, the light began to fill the lower half of the room, spreading meticulously upward and outward until the entire corner was completely bathed in its brilliance.

As the intensity of the light increased, it became impossible for me to look upon it, making it necessary for me to bring my arm up over my eyes for protection. Short, frequent glances were all I could muster.

Time seemed to be standing still.

After several minutes of simply soaking up the sense of something wonderful, my mind began to shift back into reality.

My first clear thought brought the dreaded notion that this must be what they meant about the measles!

I was obviously going blind!

And this was the beginning!

At any moment, I thought, I will have a totally different life.

Although this prognosis should have filled my heart with terror, I found that I was actually quite calm in the presence of so bleak a future. I was experiencing a peace that I could not understand . . . and yet, it seemed to be a peace that was somehow vaguely familiar.

There was no need to call for help.

The light continued to resonate, and as I was trying to comprehend the meaning of all this, I realized that within the light there was becoming a form . . . like the form of a person . . . and slowly, ever so slowly now, the form was becoming clearer. It appeared to be several feet above the floor, seemingly suspended in space and time. I could sense it was somehow familiar.

As the shape's definition continued to present itself, I began to have the suspicion, incredible though it may have been at the time, that perhaps it might possibly be Jesus.

Moments later, I was sure that it was He.

The vision itself was not what I would consider tangible. In retrospect, the appearance was so transparent that it seemed to represent "the body of heaven in his clearness."[32]

Snuggled securely into the bedcovers, I continued to take in as much of Him as I dared. I was more relaxed now as I was sure that He had come for a reason. More than this, it was clear that He was my friend. I seemed drenched in His friendship and love, the warmth of which enveloped me beyond rational understanding.

The enjoyment of this precious time together did not last for long before a sudden melancholy gripped me as, with exceeding dismay, the reason for His visit became painfully clear. I wanted to hide my face from Him.

"The rosaries," I thought. "He knew about the rosaries."

It was about this time I had an enormous quantity of rosaries stashed away in one of my drawers. I had even been such a thief as to go into other lockers and take whatever I pleased. I had this weird sense that everything belonged to everybody and I had no consideration that what I was doing was wrong.

Now, with the appearance of Jesus in my room, I had no doubt that He had come to warn me that things were not the same here, that there was ownership attached to seemingly everything and everybody. Clearly, He had come to tell me that it was time to change my ways.

"That was it!" I thought. "He came to warn me!"

I was very grateful, though somewhat embarrassed, that the King of Kings had taken time out especially to bring this problem to my attention.

The light became easier to bear and I was able to lower my arm slightly, taking in the full ardour of His Presence.

Though I could not look upon His face, I felt Him smile at me ... and, somewhat sheepishly, I smiled back.

He stayed with me for what seemed like several minutes, though an eternity itself had been presented before me. During His visit, the entire room fell into the dominion of a perpetual existence and the past was left behind.

This, my first awakening of how the Lord forgives us completely upon the simple recognition of the error of our ways, made a deep and lasting impression upon my soul.

Understanding the depth of His forgiveness is a must to experience His peace in your life, an understanding that has taken literally years to unfold before me but which it is my hope to somehow share with you.

Having been granted such a peace, I find that though I have committed many sins, I have experienced only moments of guilt or remorse as the wave of forgiveness overtakes me and I understand full well that my intention was without malice and that I had, plainly and simply, been in error. As I am able to forgive my own children for their misdemeanours, I was able to understand then that my Father in heaven looks upon me in the same way a parent must deal with a child.

Too often we find many, even in the Christian community where this principle should be understood, who are unable to release themselves from guilt and remorse. These two partners hold many a soul in bondage today. If you are not able to forgive yourself, then you have taken the place of God, who has already forgiven you, knowing your sorrow. All burdens must be surrendered unto the Lord; any other recourse is merely self-destructive and self-motivated.

I knew right then in my room, beyond a shadow of a doubt, that with the Lord, there was never a need to carry the burden of our mistakes once the acknowledgement of the mistake is made. In our surrender to Him, He promises to make a way for us to "become perfect, even as our Father which is in heaven is perfect."[33]

There became for me, from that moment on, a certain "knowing" that everything becomes history in the Presence of the Lord.

All things are made new.

The significance of the event can, of course, never be truly measured; however, I know that there were words spoken to my Spirit that I am unable to tell you … for I have no way of knowing what they were.

I can only say that I was being taught by Him …

…of His Mercy, His Peace, His Love.

I felt no condemnation, only a gentle chastisement for my misbehaviour of late. I knew that I was completely forgiven and that I was not misunderstood.

The Power of the Blood of Jesus,[34] a short but monumental piece by Andrew Murray, provides an understanding that, when we can accept that Jesus died in our place, we are 'cleansed of an evil conscience,' bringing about an innocence in our lives that we lay claim to through our personal relationship with Him. The capability of action created through dark intention is completely removed from one's life.

To God be the Praise for this incredible eventuality!

The thought of such undeserved beauty in a life defies our most vivid imagination. The greatest feats that this earth has ever witnessed could never become even a particle of the light that is poured out from heaven in such freedom.

As the light subsided, I floated ever so gently into the most beautifully restful sleep, like the laziest summer day when there is nothing to do and nowhere to go.

The event itself was, oddly enough, never amazing to me. It was, after all...the Lord.

I understood completely that He was capable of ALL things, and so, appearing in my room was most likely the very least of these.

I continued to give the incident no particular significance, except to recall His perfect beauty whenever days seemed blue.

Later that evening, I began by making a quiet mention to my mother of having seen a bright light in my room. When she seemed to fall into fear about it, I decided it wasn't wise to upset her, and so the story remained untold for many years.

About to enter my fifties, I have seldom been able to grasp the wonder of that moment, and although the event is so very close to my heart, I cannot fully comprehend it still.

The Lord has many reasons for each of His actions.

One of the things I have come to deeply appreciate is how very hard it is to stay in touch with a miracle, even if it's one of your own. This has provided me with an increased understanding, when circumstances surround us threatening our victory, of the difficulty in surrendering our total reliance upon the Lord. I believe it was His intention to protect me, until much later, from the realization that something extraordinary had occurred that day.

It would seem that in doing so, I was continuously able to experience Him in a perfectly natural and childlike way. Consequently, I was never overwhelmed or threatened by His Presence. I could be totally at ease with Him and have remained so throughout my life.

There was, in addition, an especially unique bonus. I never knew, until recent years, how rare such a visit had been. And delightfully, there had been no opportunity for pride to set in as there was, for a very long time, no one to tell. It was simply a moment shared between a little girl and her Lord.

*****

Although His attendance is no longer presented to me in such a spectacular way, there is little doubt when He is coaching me to make a certain decision, or more likely, to wait . . . and there is absolutely no doubt whatsoever when He speaks an instruction to me.

To be in His presence was then and is now as natural as waking up in the morning…
And I wanted to do it forever…
And I knew that I would.

*****

In the Garden ❧

. . . the garden of the Lord; joy and gladness shall be found therein, thanksgiving, and the voice of melody.

~Isaiah 51:3

From as early as I can remember, my mother played the piano and I would sing.

After teaching me the usual children's favourites, she stretched me to conquer difficult songs from a variety of musicals. Strewn throughout the repertoire of her most cherished hymns were a number of delightful duets, which she and I practised regularly.

Having her A.C.T.M., which was the highest achievement in voice, her euphonious ability could not be questioned. But in addition to having climbed to such scholastic heights, she was gifted with such natural talent you couldn't help but want to listen to her all the day long.

During her high school and college days, she secured the lead in many a musical, including the Mikado and H.M.S. Pinafore. She was a constant guest soloist at weddings and special events throughout the city of Hamilton, which was the center of a thriving industrial area prior to and during the Second World War. It is called Steeltown to this day.

Added to mother's flare for singing, she enjoyed excellence in piano. Clara Mae Giddens, my grandmother, an established beauty and accomplished pianist, had become a teacher at a very tender age. It is no small wonder that it was to her sheer delight to play for her eldest daughter who had the voice of a meadowlark.

As the tradition was wanting to continue, I received voice training in my kindergarten year. My only sister was not scheduled to arrive for several years; consequently, mother had plenty of time that she may not have had otherwise. We had great times together, and, as I myself was quite a ham, we were a pretty good team.

After one year of practice, I was competing for either gold, silver or bronze medals at the Kiwanis Music Festival held in Niagara Falls, Ontario, which was the city to which we had moved when I was three. Well known for its high quality of competitors, talent came from sometimes as far as 100 miles, no small feat in the late 1940's.

Unfortunately, singing was not to be my best suit, as I was particularly disinterested in songs about fairies, goblins and turtledoves, which continued to be the class of selections for competition. I could never seem to get my heart into secular fantasies even then. Consequently, my marks often fell somewhere in the middle of the pack.

About this same time, mother taught me piano basics.

Since this seemed to have a greater appeal to me, I was swiftly enrolled in Loretto Academy's Fine Arts Program, renowned for its scholastic as well as musical tutelage. It was there that I became a budding musician, but most importantly, it had been there that I had experienced my first encounter with the Lord.

My piano instruction continued at the Academy through to a grade ten level, despite the concern already mentioned on my mother's behalf that I was becoming somewhat enamoured with 'religious' things, though she couldn't be sure in exactly what way.

By the time I was nine, I was competing with sixteen-year-olds, often taking first or second place. I looked forward to the events, although something quite extraordinary would persistently occur on the way to each event. With little or no warning, I would feel desperately ill.

As quickly as I could open the car window, I would thrust my head out into the fresh air, take a deep breath, following which I would usually 'upchuck' my latest meal. Consequently, I have a great deal of compassion for those whose careers include performing live, for they tell me that stage fright such as this is very common.

Mother confessed to me some years later that she had always felt terrible about this procedure and often wondered how it could possibly be right to put any child through such apparent agony. But since this seemed to be the only side effect, with no complaints coming from me, she determined to press on as all other indicators were pointed unanimously toward certain accomplishment.

I have since convinced her that I was certainly grateful for all of her efforts, as the competition was an excellent experience that has stood me in good stead over the years.

To prove this point, let me briefly recount a situation that occurred in 1983, when, at the age of 39, I found myself seeking the federal nomination of the Progressive Conservative Party of Canada for a seat in the House of Commons. Known as a 'swing seat', the riding for Saskatoon East was often touted as 'the' pivotal seat in the country.

Not surprisingly, all eyes were upon this event.

The Conservative Party was still reeling from some of the most tumultuous events of its history. With Brian Mulroney established as its new leader, backroom bargains made in the process had left an even darker shadow on a party that was nationally viewed in times past as sporting a relatively dim reputation toward its own.

As public opinion continued to sway, pollsters were having a field day while voters kept a watchful vigil as the popularity of the three major parties rose and fell erratically, seemingly without reason. For a time, the undecided vote was so large that it was unanimously agreed that the election would be 'too close to call.'

As time wore on, the Conservatives began a dramatic rally, and in light of this situation, nominations throughout the country were becoming heavily contested. It is little wonder that the Saskatoon nomination proved to be the largest in the history of that province.

It was amazing to most everyone, including myself, that I had absolutely neither fear of nor attachment to the process, including television interviews that were carried across the country, talk of a Cabinet position, and a growing list of supporters who believed that I would be, without doubt, positioned to become the first woman Prime Minister of Canada. Knowing how Kim Campbell fared, I appreciate all the more having been spared the experience.

Three nights before the nomination, I attended the Saskatoon Centennial Auditorium to give directions to the stage and lighting crew. As I stood behind the podium, looking out into the darkness of the theatre where within hours 3500 excited participants would be waving placards and behaving hysterically, I sensed an inordinate calm that one only experiences when enveloped by grace.

In the thundering silence of that moment, there was a 'knowing' that this was an appointment with destiny that had been set long ago. Somehow, through a variety of avenues, I had unmistakably arrived at the designated hour.

Though I shared my spiritual understanding of these times with no one, I was well aware of the seemingly supernatural events that transpire when involved with episodes of this nature. It can only be compared to having boarded a train that is continually picking up steam with no intention of stopping before reaching its destination.

Knowing that my competitors had been running their race for an entire year before me, compared to the six weeks left for me to prepare for the contest, I should have at least been in awe of the burden before me. However, the extreme contradiction in preparedness proved to be an extraordinary blessing. I had little choice but to turn the entire process over to God.

Each morning, I began my day in this way.

"Lord, it would be impossible for anyone to believe that one's own ability could have anything to do with the outcome of a race such as this; there are too many variables that cannot be controlled. I know that You have placed me in this position for a particular purpose, though I haven't the slightest idea what that purpose might be. I ask only to serve you. Throughout this process, take me wherever You will."

"I accept, without question, the outcome."

This simple prayer allowed me to walk through whatever door opened with no second thoughts. From my perspective, there was little or no concern regarding the results.

A personal agenda did not exist.

The absence of any sign of stage fright bewildered even those closest to me. Of course, they had no way of knowing that I had literally outgrown 'performance panic' as a result of my countless car-window experiences way back when, nor could they have understood the simplicity with which I embraced the eventualities.

73

The fascinating run and climax of this political endeavour was complex indeed, and it is enough said for the purpose of this narrative to point out that I did not take up residence in the nation's capital. However, what is important to note was that our team accomplished exactly what we had set out to do: make a difference!

Much like Gideon,[35] we had accomplished the unexpected and against insurmountable odds. By collecting my supporters together and backing the man who was second on the first ballot, the future Member of Parliament became so because of our being there.

But it was ever so much more than this. Our 'being there' had defeated the backroom boys!

Immediately thereafter, horrific retaliation pursued me relentlessly, the ghastly details of which I will presently spare you.

*****

Mother and I continued our distinguished repertoire several times a week, she at the piano, and I, standing close to her side, my little hands cupped together . . . shoulders back, stomach in, chin up . . . confidently composed while enunciating the story of the song.

Although she is no longer with us, my heart is continually thankful for those precious times. It was on occasions like these, while performing selections from the hymnal, that I came to easily communicate with Jesus in a very personal way, my heart yearning to be with Him at any cost.

*****

At thirteen, the age at which most organized religions declare you eligible for membership, I had decided that I wasn't interested in joining Lundy's Lane United Church, taking a rather dramatic stand against what I considered to be, for the most part, a sanctimonious body of church-goers. Though I taught Sunday school and sang in the choir, I felt absolutely certain that there was something terribly wrong with the congregation as a whole. When asked by my parents to elaborate, I was unable to be any more specific than the fact that things 'just didn't seem right.'

Without anything more than this 'hunch' to go on, my parents suggested that I take the confirmation classes anyway, through which I might change my mind.

My teacher was a lady who had very definite ideas about what was acceptable and what was not.

One evening, after a class, I overheard her laughing mercilessly regarding a fellow member's shabby dress. Several other women quickly joined in the fun. Horrified, I ran indignantly out to the car, where my mother had been waiting to take me home.

"Mother", I said, "It's impossible to learn about Jesus from anyone who doesn't know who He is. I just cannot continue. Please don't make me."

Although this was certainly not the last discussion we had about the matter, not to mention the disagreements the family had regarding my obstinate determination, I have to say that at that precise moment in time, mother not only understood exactly what I meant, she wholeheartedly agreed with me somewhere deep within her soul.

As it turned out, I was not forced to commit to something I could not believe in. Only months following this interlude, the assemblage collectively dismissed the minister because they were bored with his sermons. The way in which the dismissal was handled was nothing short of a lynching party.

Mother herself found this most disagreeable and immediately thereafter left the choir, seeking comfort elsewhere, which, sadly, she never found.

Perhaps the Lord was guiding me even then to recognize the beginning signs of a falling away from the Truth, for recently, the apostasy in that particular denomination is undeniable.

About this same time I began helping out at my dad's grocery store and filling station, and so my time at home became less frequent. Coupled with this had been the recent addition to the family of my only sister, Roslynne, making it necessary for Mom to attend to important maternal matters that beforehand had been non-existent.

The timing for this worked out relatively well as the spectrum of my world became enlarged. No longer in the choir, busy at school and at work, I was becoming an individual separate and apart from my family. The singing of hymns fell farther and farther into history. In just a few short years, I would take another avenue that would lead me to Toronto, where I became a legal secretary at the age of nineteen. More than ninety miles from the peninsula, even weekend visits were rare.

It is an inevitable part of life how too soon childhood experiences come to a close. All that seemingly remains are the briefest shades of recollection that waft through your windows of days gone by. I feel blessed to have such fond memories, barely recalling the various difficulties that we, as a family, endured but prefer to forget.

Years later, after looking for the Lord down a vast number of avenues, I began to witness for Him under a special anointing that I did not understand. Separated from true Christian elements, I had no way of knowing how God's hand was so carefully guiding me, in spite of my mistakes and my somewhat rebellious nature.

Our personal acquaintance when I was just five had made it possible for me to know "The Word."[36]

When answers were genuinely required for those in need, I was often able to expound on the truths and the mysteries of the Scriptures without ever having known that they were already contained in the 'Word' written centuries ago.[37]

This opportunity was never available on demand, but always and only as the Lord would lead. Memories of my earliest experiences with Him would come flashing back to me from time to time, and to my delight, it would be like living them afresh.

On one such occasion in recent years, I was visiting a tiny church in Saskatoon, Saskatchewan, when, taking me by complete surprise, the choir began a familiar refrain.

" I come to the garden alone ...
While the dew is still on the roses" ...

The words began to minister joyfully to my heart.

Presently, as clear as if it were yesterday, I could see myself standing next to my mother while she played and I sang, this wonderful, wonderful tune, which had been for us, our absolute favourite.

And then, the remembrance of something more began to unfold ... a unique excursion that somehow enveloped me whenever we joined together in this song ...

*****

…there is a garden, drenched in an early misty morning. A slowly winding path beckons through the overhanging trees and lush foliage.

As I approach the path, I seem to step up and out of who I am in my physical world. It is as if the garden is situated within a giant movie screen. I move toward what one would expect to be a solid impenetrable wall upon which this fantasy is playing.

When my torso begins to move through the wall, I am not surprised. I know that I am standing at the piano, and yet, I am at the same time moving toward what you might call a daydream. I confidently press in as I pass completely through any apparent barriers. This brings immediately to mind the new bodies the Lord has promised us.

I enter the garden…alone.

I have a sense of anticipation, with the keen awareness that something wonderful is about to happen.

I am now but a shadow of myself.

Though I seem to have lost touch with my physical senses, I am astutely aware of the smell of the moist greenness and the spectacular beauty around me, which I drink in with an enormous capacity to breathe.

Very shortly, I can see an outline of a park bench.

Through the haze, which seems to be lifting, a beam of sunlight pours out upon a small clearing just ahead while miniature rainbows glisten on the dew.

A suggestion of a man seated on the bench begins to form. One can see that he is youthful and kind. It is warm where he is and I am drawn to his presence.

There is no doubt that he is waiting for me.

As I approach him, my heart becomes frightfully still.

I pause for a moment to memorize his countenance; yet the enveloping peace compels me to move closer.

There is a sense of belonging that I cannot describe.

In the heightened anticipation, I am now scarcely breathing and, when I am convinced that I can wait no longer, I begin to contemplate seeking him out.

It is my earnest desire to share who I am with him, though I somehow conclude that he already knows me very well.

Like a recurring dream where you continually forget the ending, I can never be sure until the very last second who this gentle person is, but always, just as I had hoped it would be, it is my wonderful friend … Jesus.

His beautiful white garments flow gracefully around Him. He looks off into the distance to my right, and so at first I see only His profile. He seems not to have noticed my being there, yet I know surely that He has. I tiptoe ever so quietly near and I slip softly onto the seat.

For some time, we do not speak.

With tenderness, He smiles.

He has not looked at me fully, but in spite of this I know that His smile is entirely for me.

Taking my hand in His, we begin our 'walk about' the garden …

*****

"And He walks with me and He talks with me
And He tells me I am His own …"

*****

Oh glorious day!
There is no other garden like this!

A kaleidoscope of colours and heavenly sounds
It is perfectly safe . . .

Gladness surrounds my heart
I want always to be there.

Although I know I cannot stay...
I know this is my home.

The thought of taking my leave of His sweet presence brings a
melancholy moment...
He, too, seems saddened by the thought of my going...
I linger yet a little while...

This time together is brief, and yet not.

Forever is close at hand...
...experience worlds
in the twinkling of an eye.
...and ye know all things.[38]

*****

"And the joy we share as we tarry there
None other has ever known"

*****

"In the Garden"

Song by C. Austin Miles, 1913

I come to the garden alone
While the dew is still on the roses
And the voice I hear falling on my ear
The Son of God discloses…

And He walks with me and He talks with me
And He tells me I am His own
And the joy we share as we tarry there
None other has ever known.

He speaks and the sound of His voice
Is so sweet that the birds hush their singing
And the melody that He gave to me
Within my heart is ringing…

And He walks with me and He talks with me
And He tells me I am His own
And the joy we share as we tarry there
None other has ever known.

I'd stay in the garden with Him
Tho' the night around me is falling
But He bids me go through the voice of woe
His voice to me is calling…

And He walks with me and He talks with me
And He tells me I am His own
And the joy we share as we tarry there
None other has ever known.

In the World ❧

...*the world by wisdom knew not God*...
~*1 Corinthians 1:21*

Returning from the garden to this present time and place, I am surprised to consider a deeper message, which comes back with me from this haven of rest.

As a child, trusting a vision is simple; to enter the garden was easy for me. As each year passes, we find that we are not so easily inclined to believe what may seem to be the impossible. As adults, we become more and more reluctant to get in touch with the child within. To our disadvantage, often after we have been the victim of a single overwhelming event or perhaps some form of continuous abuse, we find ourselves setting up 'boundaries' intended to be impenetrable.

This is tragic indeed, eventually only adding to our dilemma. We must go beyond these barriers, and in order to do so, we must learn to set them aside.

Sadly, many styles of psychotherapy are bent on convincing us that we are in error to let others come into our space if they appear to be harmful to us in any way or if we are being unnecessarily taken advantage of. I beg to differ with such theories, and I do so based on the Word of God.

Whosoever shall smite thee on thy right cheek, turn to him the other also. And if any man will sue thee at the law, and take away thy coat, let him have thy cloak also. And whosoever shall compel thee to go a mile, go with him twain. Give to him that asketh thee, and from him that would borrow of thee turn not thou away.[39]

*****

...Love your enemies, bless them that curse you, do good to them that hate you, and pray for them that despitefully use you, and persecute you; That ye may be the children of your Father which is in heaven.[40]

*****

For if ye love them which love you, what reward have ye? do not even the publicans the same? And if ye salute your brethren only, what do ye more than others? do not even the publicans so?[41]

There is a most relevant consideration that needs to be taken into account here. In order to be empowered to behave in the way described in the three previous quotes, we must first clean up our own act. This, I agree, is often made difficult while others are 'filling up our space,' clouding the issues at hand. But it can be done!

So, in one way I will agree to the aspect that we must be aware when destructive personalities might circumvent our progress; however, and I mean this sincerely, God is fully cognizant of each of our situations, and truly, if we can but surrender our life to Him, He makes a way for our freedom.

I knew a lady who married an alcoholic; she was nineteen at the time. After ten years of continuous abuse, she left and divorced this man. Her second marriage was more of the same: the husband appeared to be great, but six months after the marriage he began drinking and the whole process started all over again. Believe it or not, she divorced and repeated the entire scenario for the third time.

What is it about these patterns that keeps us in bondage? Was it her or was it them?

It was both.

The bonds remain while the 'old life' is still intact.

'New Life' is required for change to take place, for the old ways have a way of showing up, again and again.

Working with street ministers brought to the fore the fact that, often, it was only a matter of time before the reformed person's 'old ways' surfaced once again. If it did not, the one holding the improved life together was in a state of constant self-inflicted pressure. To fail was a frightening concept.

While the twelve steps are still accomplishing much to assist those who want help, there is, in my mind, a vital thirteenth step, the one where a total surrender takes place, where you are no longer required to keep tabs on yourself, where you have become brand new and you are an 'alcoholic' no longer, or whatever the addiction . . . where you have been truly 'made free.'[42]

With the 'surrender' that brings about a 'new birth,' you have become willing to let go of the controls, to turn them over to God. When a new birth takes place, then and only then are you in a position to respond with confidence and authority, as Jesus called us to do: turning the other cheek, forgiving, judging not, able to resist temptations.

If we could look at our difficult relationships, whatever they might be, as opportunities for clearing those dark areas in our own lives, turning the outcome over to the Lord, we would discover some amazing results.

The promotion, through various infomercials, of the fact that you deserve to 'have a life' brings greater frustration for those who are in the middle of working through some difficult relationship, which, lest we forget, God allows in our lives for instruction and understanding.

Creating and controlling our own environment is a form of letting God know that we have decided what is acceptable in our world and what is not. Granted, the Scripture states that we can "ask and it shall be given," something even Christians today lean heavily upon while attempting to determine their own fate. But let's not stop there; consider the remainder of that teaching: "seek and ye shall find," and finally, "knock and it shall be opened unto you."[43]

What if these three offers are three separate and individual 'choices' . . . choices *not* interrelated? Three very distinctive stepping stones to absolute freedom. Three stages of believing that God is real, that miracles happen, that someone 'up there' is listening to you and working *for* you, then *with* you and finally *through* you.

Isn't it interesting that Matthew 7:8, which follows the ask, seek, knock verse, looks like this:

For every one that asketh receiveth;
and he that seeketh findeth;
and to him that knocketh it shall be opened.

It seems quite clear that you are only likely to be doing one of those three at any given time . . . asking, seeking or knocking.

Are there any clues that suggest which of the three is the most important?

. . . seek ye first the Kingdom of God . . .[44]

It has been my unfortunate experience to note that most of us are pretty much stuck on Door Number 1: *Asking*. The determination to take charge of who we are and what we are going to become, without ever considering what God's choice may have been for our lives, will, after often invigorating and successful ventures, eventually leave us in a tired and lonely place.

What we are continuously taught in this modern era regarding a take-charge attitude, combined with the determin-ation to prevent anyone from taking advantage of us, has unwittingly set us up to be incapable of 'surrender.' If we must always be on guard, then surrender becomes impossible! And it is only in this 'surrender' that a 'new birth' happens.

To surrender means letting go of trusting *your* decisions, *your* confines, *your* control. To surrender means that you have dared to 'trust God' to protect you – from anything and anyone that may get too close, so close it might 'cost you,' even, your life.

Cost is sacrifice; if you can bear the cost, there is no sacrifice.

Let's look at the most extreme example of 'loss' in order to really get the point home, in a verse you will find that I refer to often. I do so because in its essence is held the whole point of the question of life and death.

> *He that loseth his life for my sake shall find it: He that findeth his life shall lose it.*[45]

Here it is said another way.

> *For whosoever will save his life shall lose it: and Whosoever will lose his life for my sake shall find it.*[46]

Let's go slowly through this. It can be tricky, but once we get it, we have it for good.

If you (yourself) save your life, denying God's protection, you have only saved your life here (physical) having lost it there (spiritual).

However, if you lose your life as a result of standing on the Word of God, trusting Him to the limit, you may have lost your life here (again physical), but you will have gained eternal life with Him (spiritual).

This is an astounding concept!

It is almost unbearable to comprehend.

In fact, I think it quite impossible to connect with what this means to us, unless the Holy Spirit guide us through it.

Further, the principle is kept far from us when we are still protecting *our* property, *our* family, *our* rights, *our* money, *our* future, *our* safety ... *our* 'life.' We have been conditioned to do these things because we feel constantly threatened by the world around us.

We have not come to realize that we have nothing unless the Lord gives it to us. We came here with nothing and will leave with nothing; all that we enjoy along the way is strictly on loan to us; we won't take any of it with us and what we do with it while we are here is where the trial awaits.

To "be careful for nothing"[47] cannot be exercised without a *knowing assurance* that there is no protection other than that which ultimately comes from God.

We live in a world that teaches the opposite.

The save/lose Scripture can be accurately adapted to meet a wide assortment of situations (perhaps I will do a whole chapter on that in another book). Study the words and ask the Lord to help you; He "will teach you all things."[48]

*****

The intensity of trouble is just beginning to heat up in North America. Dangers abound while the loss of life through violence, pestilence and disaster moves like an ever-tightening noose around those closest to us.

Panels of well-meaning individuals discuss 'ad infinitum' whether television has contributed to the violence in our children's lives and if true, what steps, if any, the media brokers are willing to take to decrease such 'overkill.' Though the well-intentioned of us hold meetings, seminars, conferences and referendums, host call-in talk shows and live debates, the country continues to deteriorate 'moment by moment' while we refuse to 'humble ourselves and pray.'[49]

Believing that we will come up with the answers, given enough time, we do nothing more than listen to ourselves repeat worn out platitudes eventually destined to destroy ourselves and our children. Our lack of interest in the Living God, preferring to read the latest New York Times' best seller, is finally catching up with us.

Time was when to hear of someone you know being involved in a drive-by shooting, a robbery or a rape, was rare.

Wasn't it once the same with cancer? As I look back, I realize that it wasn't so many years ago that those afflicted with cancer were nothing more than nameless faces, too far removed to be personally intimidating. Now, few families have been left untouched by this dreaded killer.

How close must suffering come to our very individual lives before we actually believe that it IS happening and that, in truth, it is happening to US? Isn't it possible that our lack of care for one another is proven by the fact that until a tragedy hits home we really don't feel called to be a part of it?

The protections that we believed we had so carefully set up are falling away, day by day, threatening every aspect of our being. Locked doors, vehicle and house alarms, devices attached to the steering wheels of our cars to prevent theft, enormous hikes in insurance rates, extravagant law suits, carrying mace in our purses to avoid unwanted attackers, buying guns and learning how to use them.

Where will it end?

How blind we must be to not have begun to realize that these atrocities are so close to our innermost core that we can barely breathe. I think it's not so much that we don't see it but more that we hope it's all just a bad dream.

*****

Arm yourselves as you will, there is no safety but the Lord's. We have placed our trust in everything BUT! Our only strength can be found in knowing that it is He who gives life and He who takes it away, thus making room for miracles in our lives.

*****

There was a young preacher in Novato, California. His name was Dan. He was a handsome young man with a beautiful wife, one child and one on the way. Personally, I enjoyed meeting him and found his sermons lively. However, he often spoke in what I call mixed messages ... sometimes the Spirit would be talking through him, and sometimes, it was Dan.

The Lord had directed us to attend this church from time to time and to be a witness to the things that happened there.

Dan had a hefty southern drawl. One Sunday, Dan was preaching when he began to 'mix.' He was talking about gun control, from a political point of view, and I could feel the sermon getting out of control as Dan continued in words similar to the ones following here.

"I'm a Louisiana boy," he began, "and where I come from everybody has a gun. I'm sorry, but I have to say that it should be the right of every American to have a gun in order to protect his family and his home. I'm just gonna tell ya that if some darn burglar comes into my house aimin' to hurt my family…and gets by the Holy Ghost, then I got my gun in the night table to take care of the situation."

I was stunned by these words!

I felt a cold sweat of fear for him because of the position he took that day. Basically, we were hearing a preacher say that the Holy Ghost might fail, and well, if He does, you have the right to take matters into your own hands.

IF the Holy Spirit fails? If?? Not only was he saying this, which would be bad enough all by itself (this may very well be the only time I have heard anything that sounds like blaspheming the Holy Ghost, the only unforgivable sin), but he was teaching his entire flock that this was truth.

First of all, the Holy Ghost cannot fail. The position should be that if the burglar gets to you, then you must do what the Scriptures say: let him steal from you and even give him more. If waiting on God to come through for you costs you your life, so be it.

He that loseth his life for my sake shall find it:
He that findeth his life shall lose it.

My worst fears for Dan surfaced, knowing Mark 3:28–29, which reads as follows:

Verily I say unto you, All sins shall be forgiven unto the sons of men, and blasphemies wherewith soever they shall blaspheme: But he that shall blaspheme against the Holy Ghost *hath never forgiveness, but is in danger of eternal damnation:*[50]

From this account, you can understand my concern for Dan having spoken such frivolously dangerous words.

Shortly thereafter, a woman came to the church to teach about demonic activity and spiritual warfare. Everyone in the church was getting into it – speaking in tongues, lashing out at the enemy, taking 'personal' action to defeat all the 'demons of hell.'

I found this somewhat discomforting, for there was a certain measure of emotionalism surfacing out of these events. There was an underlying fear, and fear prompts irrational behaviour as a result of its being the opposite of faith.

*****

About a week later, we attended another service. At mid-point, we were told to join up in groups of about six or so and pray 'against the enemy.' I was personally reluctant to participate, for in order to do so I would have to take my eyes off the Lord, my source of hope and joy, in order to focus on the demonic realm. Since I was present in order to learn, I moved towards a group to my left.

Attending with us was a young woman named Sonia, who had only recently given her life over to Jesus. As the members began to join hands, Sonia leaned over and spoke somewhat sheepishly to one of the 'schooled' participants.

"Since Jesus already defeated the enemy, I don't really understand what everybody's doing." She raised her shoulders and eyebrows simultaneously, combined with a childlike glee, awaiting their response, if any.

Collectively, everyone in her group moved quickly away. Such truth from such innocence was totally unacceptable.

It seems that the Lord's wisdom is truly given unto 'babes.'[51]

*****

Within the month, the Lord shared with me a few words that I was to prepare and take with me to the church. I wrote them out on a file folder, ready to give, I thought, to Dan.

This is what I wrote.

Dan...

I received a two hour sermon this morning in the Spirit. These are the highlights. I will be glad to share the rest with you any time.

The Lord says...

I have the keys to death and hell and in that knowledge your blessed assurance can be that I have paid the price.

The victory is won.

It is finished.

Resist not evil.

Matthew 5:39

Let thine eye be single (unto the Lord).

Matthew 6:22

Fear not, for lo I am with you always.

Matthew 28:20

My 'armour' placed on you will make the enemy flee!!

There is nothing that you, of yourselves, in all vain repetition or by the power of your own hand, can accomplish.

To stand ... (in majesty, in silence, in honour, in glory, in the fullness of the Spirit, in peace)

What armour?

Truth, Righteousness, the Gospel of Peace, the Shield of Faith, Salvation's Helmet, the Word of God, Praying in the Spirit, Watching for the 'Saints.'
Ephesians 6:13-20
This is 'quiet' power.
Let no corrupt communication proceed out of your mouth, but that which is good to the use of edifying, that it may minister grace (not fear) unto the hearers ...
Ephesians 4:29
Fear not.
If I be with you - who can be against you?
Perfect love casteth out fear.
1 John 4:18
And last, but not least, a fresh word from the Spirit ...
All attempts of the 'flesh' in attacking the enemy states an unbelief that the victory is yours through me and thereby denies your safety.

*****

The end of the service came ... and just as I was about to head to the front, I suddenly 'knew' that Dan was not able to receive the message prepared, especially coming from me ... not a member of his church, and what would be construed to be worse, a member of no church.

I was, in many ways, a foreigner in a foreign land.

I was saddened by this revelation, but I was instead led to speak to and show the writing to an elder who was sitting nearby. The elder glanced at the material only long enough to disclaim somewhat offhandishly that the words "resist not evil" were NOT in Scripture.

I did not wish to argue with him, but I was able to make it clear that I was indeed sure that "resist not evil" was most certainly from the Bible. I apologized that I had not written down the specific verse and did not at that moment recall the reference, but I suggested that if he would like, I would call him later by phone to further inform him.

This was an elder in the church who understood only about *fighting* evil, not a Scripture that said 'not to.'

I was hard pressed to know what to make of the this, for if the elders in the church know not the gospel...then who?

I called the elder as I had promised, leaving a message on his answering machine. He never returned my call.

*****

Just a few short weeks after this incident, a couple of Mexican-Americans decided to rob a number of churches.

In the morning, they entered a church office in San Rafael where one elderly lady was doing some filing. The invaders had a gun and told the lady to give them all the money available. Since there were no church funds, the men commanded the lady to give them whatever she had in her purse. Nervously, she handed over every penny she had.

As the thieves were about to leave, she began to cry quietly, telling them that she was on social security and that if they took this money, she would have nothing until her next cheque. She had no savings.

On this note, oddly enough, the men returned the money to the little old lady.

Their next stop was Dan's church.

They entered the second floor office by the outdoor staircase where Dan was working.

Something went terribly awry during that visit.

Did Dan make it his business to ward off the intruders? Had he defended his property as he had promised he would? Had he begun to speak in tongues as if to defeat the enemy? Did he chase the burglars out of the building with threats?

No one really knows.

But what we DO know is that whatever happened that day cost Pastor Dan his life.

*****

He was found halfway down the outdoor stairs, with three bullet wounds, one of which was fatal.

When I was informed of the tragedy, I was sorely moved.

There were many questions I felt I had to ask myself.

Should I have insisted that Dan hear me out with my message about 'not resisting his enemies?'

Had I listened accurately to the Lord?

What was my responsibility in all of this?

I spent many hours agonizing over this.

While asleep the night before the funeral, the Lord spoke to my spirit. I awoke with the impression of the words upon my lips.

There were no visions, no dreams, no other words but these:

"You live by the sword, you die by the sword."[52]
"You live by the gun, you die by the gun."

On the subject at hand, the words seemed 'final.'

This was to be my answer.

Inevitably, I had to forgive myself for whatever mistake I may have made in failing to speak to Dan in time, finally reckoning that it is the Lord that has all power under heaven, not me. If the Lord had wanted to intervene in Dan's death, He would have, in spite of what I may have failed to do.

There were some very important lessons to be learned in all of this, not the least of which included maters of 'life and death.'

*****

I do not tell you this story to place judgment on Dan or make of him a spectacle in any way.

He loved the Lord deeply.

I believe that his death was not in vain, as it has served many well.

For instance, Dan's wife, who came to sing at the church several months after his death and just weeks before her delivery, displayed such love for Christ that all who saw her could not help but be encouraged by her strength. Her wise acceptance of God's will was apparent in her demeanour of gratitude to the Lord for His kindness and mercy.

There is a purpose in all things.

> . . . *judge nothing before time, until the Lord come, who both will bring to light the hidden things of darkness, and will make manifest the counsels of the hearts: then shall every man have praise of God.*
>
> ~1 Corinthians 4:5

*****

Violence begets violence.

The Lord, wanting us to be safe, has wisely shown us in His Word what is the right way to handle matters of disorder. Can we not see from this lonely example that the more the nation arms itself against 'intruders,' the faster 'we lose the war'?

By so doing, we are at war against…ourselves.

We would do well to take a lesson from this story.

*****

So where do we find our comfort and our strength?

How do we come to the place of understanding that the power is not really ours, and in knowing this, come to know that we can expect protection from the One in power?

There is great solace to be found in the Psalms, many of which were written by David. It is evident from David's writing that he truly knew how to lean upon the 'Rock.' The most famous of these Psalms I have had reprinted for you here.

Psalm 23

The Lord is my shepherd; I shall not want.

He maketh me to lie down in green pastures: he leadeth me beside the still waters.

He restoreth my soul: he leadeth me in the paths of righteousness for his name's sake.

Yea, though I walk through the valley of the shadow of death, I will fear no evil: for thou art with me; thy rod and thy staff they comfort me.

Thou preparest a table before me in the presence of mine enemies: thou anointest my head with oil: my cup runneth over.

Surely goodness and mercy shall follow me all the days of my life: and I will dwell in the house of the Lord forever.

*****

If you find Psalm 23 comforting in some small measure, let me direct you one step further to another look at this psalm through a book called *A Shepherd Looks at Psalm 23*,[53] written by Phillip Keller.

The author, formerly a shepherd in Africa, takes you through each phrase from Psalm 23, leading you on a journey that demonstrates how perfectly this psalm relates to shepherds and sheep, and then, transcending shepherding a flock of sheep, we recognize a flock of lost souls like you and I.

It is refreshing, delightful, insightful and quite frankly, in its simplicity, remarkable.

Another Psalm to bring us to that place that knows that God is with us: Psalm 91, the author Moses.

It is supposed that Moses wrote Psalms 90 and 91 at the beginning of the forty years in the wilderness, the wanderings of which are the subject of what is known as the fourth book of Psalms, beginning at Psalm 90 and ending at Psalm 106.[54]

Psalm 91

He that dwelleth in the secret place of the most High shall abide under the shadow of the Almighty.

I will say of the Lord, He is my refuge and my fortress: my God; in him will I trust.

Surely he shall deliver thee from the snare of the fowler, and from the noisome pestilence.

He shall cover thee with his feathers, and under his wings shalt thou trust: his truth shall be thy shield and buckler.

Thou shalt not be afraid for the terror by night; nor for the arrow that flieth by day;

Nor for the pestilence that walketh in darkness; nor for the destruction that wasteth at noonday.

A thousand shall fall at thy side, and ten thousand at thy right hand; but it shall not come nigh thee.

Only with thine eyes shalt thou behold and see the reward of the wicked.

Because thou hast made the Lord, which is my refuge, even the most High, thy habitation;

There shall no evil befall thee, neither shall any plague come nigh thy dwelling.

For he shall give his angels charge over thee, to keep thee in all ways.

They shall bear thee up in their hands, lest thou dash thy foot against a stone.

Thou shalt tread upon the lion and adder: the young lion and the dragon shalt thou trample under your feet.

Because he hath set his love upon me, therefore will I deliver him: I will set him on high, because he hath known my name.

He shall call upon me, and I will answer him: I will be with him in trouble; I will deliver him, and honour him.

With long life will I satisfy him, and show him my salvation.

*****

As natural disasters bombard the United States, which once was blessed beyond measure, we see the costs of such devastation gobbling up already defunct resources.

An interesting survey, which followed the mid-west flooding in 1993, showed that 18% polled believed that the losses were an "act of God."

I cannot describe my dismay when following right behind this newspaper article was a quote from the Rev. Robert Dugan of the National Association of Evangelicals who disagreed with those believing God had a hand in the recent disasters.

Not only did he not take the opportunity to encourage those beginning to even lean toward a remote contemplation of where God fit into the equation, he flatly denied any such connection. His reason for such a denial was that "there was a time in history when a flood was in judgment – and that was in the days of Noah. But unless God indicated to us in some special way this is a judgment … it's just part of the forces of nature."

(Which, by the way, God Himself controls.)

It is so desperately sad to me when a nation, while seeking some kind of answers, begins, if only for a moment, to ponder upon the significance of God in their life, and someone, who seemingly represents the Christian perspective, brings such thoughts to a crashing halt.

Deborah Simon, of Windsor, in Sonoma County, California, was interviewed for the same article by the Marin Independent Journal.

She appears on the scene as just your average Bible-believin' gal, with no special title or authority, and hits the nail right on the head. Her words follow:

"When the people became godless and corrupt, their land and civilization were destroyed."

How in control do we really believe we are?

Are we truly infallible?

Do we create our own destiny?

Can we eliminate our vulnerabilities?

*****

And which of you with taking thought can add to his stature one cubit? If ye then be not able to do that thing which is least, why take ye thought for the rest?

~Luke 12:25–26

*****

To encounter a solid faith that makes possible a lack of fear, be that the fear that we will have led a life of 'quiet desperation' or be it fear for our own safety, one must come to know the strength of the Creator and the true principles that provide our very breath.

As we have replaced the Bible with a myriad of other teachings, which often provide confusion and self-interest, we can see that our countrymen, from our leaders to our labourers, have no idea that God is prepared to come to our aid if we but turn from our evil ways and return to Him. This 'turning away' we will never do without knowing the POWER, the LOVE, the MYSTERY and the MERCY of God.

These characteristics are, surprisingly, contained in God's Word. I say surprisingly, for I myself was amazed to discover this to be true.

In churches all over America, we say the words "thy will be done on earth as it is in heaven,"[55] and yet it is OUR will that has become the order of the day.

The words are left ringing in the building, but an emptiness remains in our hearts.

Knowing how to surrender is the key to understanding the Father's will. Often, to do His will requires embarrassment or ridicule. At the very least, it requires service. If still holding on to the need to be recognized by man or, to put it another way, the need to have our own life, such an attitude invalidates our ability to operate from blind faith, and "without faith, it is impossible to please God."[56]

To enter the garden where you can commune with the Lord, you must leave the world behind.

This requires faith, the faith of a little child.

The Lord says to be 'in the world, not of it.'

Many ask what this might mean.

It has been my privilege, and I believe there are many going through this process today, in a variety of ways, to have been taught by the Holy Spirit what it is like to be *in* Him, though present here. This is a work in process, and each of us should seek out the ways in which we interrelate bodily, mentally, emotionally and spiritually.

Additionally, there comes with that territory a way to view the world with new eyes, creating thereby a new sense of being, as if one was literally born anew, or reborn, or born again,[57] all of which inevitably leads us to the ability to be in the world and not of it as the Lord has encouraged us to do.

Please, let me caution you here.

There have been many so-called 'born agains,' who, through inappropriate behaviour, have sadly made even the discussion of such an event literally repulsive. Please do not let this deter you from getting to the truth of what 'being born again' is really all about.

*****

When I was a real estate broker in the seventies, I had just listed a house for sale. That evening the lady of the house contacted me to tell me that another broker, knowing that the house was already listed, attended her home to tell her that I had over listed the house and that it would never sell at that price. He boldly suggested that she should contact me immediately and pull the listing, thereby giving him the chance to sell it, and sell it quickly.

Being a broker, there is not a chance that this man did not know that his conduct was against all the principles of real estate ethics, punishable by serious fines, reprimands, and in some cases, the loss of license to practice.

I was quite amazed by the situation.

In those days, I was often surprised by the lack of morals displayed by the various players in the business.

Later that evening, while visiting friends, there was present a couple whom I had known for approximately six months. Let's call them Dianna and Rob. Actually, I had sold Rob's parents' grape farm, which was how I had originally met the two of them. We had become friendly, although I was quite aware of Rob's devious business practices and, since we had developed an open relationship, I was not remiss in telling him regularly that his operation was 'crooked' and suggested that he himself 'needed some help.'

I was unaware of their religious affiliation.

We were speaking about the situation concerning the broker, as I was relatively new to the area and was hoping for some feedback regarding the man and his reputation.

"There is something about this guy that really puzzles me," I confessed to them. "He says that he's a 'born again' Christian.

"And, I might add, this is sadly not the first time that a person claiming to be 'born again' has proven themselves to be unethical, unreliable, untrustworthy and well, just an out and out pirate.

"In fact," I went on with much enthusiasm now, "I would have to say that every encounter I have had so far with 'born agains' has pretty much convinced me that anyone making such a claim is likely to be a liar and a thief."

Rob began to aggressively clear his throat, thereafter jumping right in behind my words as if to defend not only the broker but also himself.

"Dianna and I are 'born again,'" he declared proudly.

"Well," I responded quite matter-of-factly, "I rest my case."

*****

As a matter of clarification. I do not think that all who declare themselves to be 'born again' are necessarily 'crooks.' Up until the time of the story above, unfortunately, all whom I had met claiming to be so had indeed fallen into that category. However, and I make no apology for my decision, I have to say that those who make claims of rebirth and do not back up such claims with 'fruits'[58] are to be seriously doubted.

And so, what are these fruits?

Love, Joy, Peace, Longsuffering, gentleness, goodness, faith, meekness, temperance.[59]

Consider the following sobering words:

> *Not everyone that saith unto me, Lord, Lord, shall enter into the kingdom of heaven, but he that doeth the will of my Father which is in heaven. Many will say to me in that day, Lord, Lord, have we not prophesied in thy name? and in thy name have cast out devils? and in thy name done many wonderful works? And then will I profess unto them, I never knew you: depart from me, ye that work iniquity.*
> ~Matthew 7:21

1 John 5:18 confirms:

> *We know that whosoever is born of God* sinneth not.[60]

This is a foolproof gauge as to whether or not the claims of rebirth are indeed true.

The Lord spoke in parables, giving examples in earthly terms, but the intent was to teach spiritual truths. He did this in order to facilitate our instruction. He also said that many would not understand the true meaning of his teachings.

In one of the most famous passages, the story of 'The Sower and the Seed' found in Matthew 13:3–9 and then explained in verses 18–23 of the same chapter, we find an illustration of what I have just said: the parable is used in earthly terms for our better understanding, but the teaching is a spiritual one, illustrating elements of the spirit world and how it operates to undermine the growing of our garden.

Life too, is a parable; there is a spiritual representation in absolutely everything! If this is so, how can we thus see, from another perspective, what it means to be 'born again'?

To be born in the flesh, we are first conceived, by a seed, in the womb. Many situations might affect this fetus before it is actually born: there may be a miscarriage, an abortion, an irregularity in the growth pattern so that the birth is defective, so that even if the child is born, it may not be fully productive.

The actual birth process is amazing, to say the very least. The baby does not really want to leave its sheltered place of residence, the comfort of its mother's womb. The birth itself is a struggle, accompanied by pain on the part of the mother and strife on behalf of the baby.

The baby's first entrance into this new world prompts it to cry out in anguish in order to take a first breath separate and apart from its mother. The baby is shocked by what it finds in its new environment; it no longer feels safe, and the baby is often ill at ease with its new surroundings; it now feels hunger, and cold, and disarming separation.

Then begins the incredible process of growing: exploration, receiving teaching and ultimately learning how to operate in this new environment. It takes years to understand the rules: of parents, teachers, bosses, government and in particular, God.

How does this equate with a spiritual birth, or being 'born again?'

I have yet to hear anyone describe the new birth in this way, although I would not be surprised to find someone who agrees with me (for which I will be duly encouraged).

First there is a seed. The Scriptures refer to the 'seed' as the 'Word' ... of God, of the kingdom. When first a person receives the seed (or hears about the Word of God) and this seed takes root, this is what I call being 'conceived' in the spirit. Just as you are not 'born' on the day of conception, you are not 'born again' when you first receive Christ.

But now comes a great journey . . . from the date of conception to the time of actually being born ... remembering that this time you are being born 'again' (in the spirit), since you have already been born once (in the flesh).

This journey is extremely precarious; one might be miscarried through 'another gospel'[61] coming along, which will make the rooting of this seed weak and incapable of 'becoming' that which it was destined to become.

An abortion might take place. This could happen if the one with the seed became totally cut off from the truth – through a variety of ways. Perhaps the family denounces the individual or makes fun of them or keeps them from following the path; the pressure may become so much that the one having received the seed turns away from the nurturing of the gardener and the seed dies.

In these two cases, and others like them, no birth will occur.

From the date of the conception, there are a variety of ways in which the one to be born might be defective. For instance, the food may not have been sufficient to bring forth good fruit.

In the womb, the food is physical; protein, fruits and vegetables combine together with other nutrients to feed the fetus ... add to this the lack of smoking, drinking or any other substance abuse.

Being born from 'life to life,' the food required is spiritual. It is the Word of God or by the power of the Holy Spirit; these are the proper nutrients and cannot be mixed with contaminants or death may occur.

The food that best nurtures our spirit is the Scripture. Without it, we may become seriously hampered in our ability to experience the new birth. Now, add to that the understanding that 'the Word of God' is also known as Christ Himself.

Therefore, we might know Him through the Scriptures or through a personal relationship with Him. This comes differently to each person and must be looked at carefully to determine if we are actually in touch with the Living God and not some other false god.

In the beginning was the Word, and the Word was with God and the Word was God.[62]

Note the double usage of the word 'Word.'

At the end of the gestation period, assuming that all has gone well during that time, a 'birth' takes place. The duration of this stage varies with every individual and each birth is entirely its own.

Not without pain, not without struggle.

Just as the baby did not want to leave its mother's womb, we, too, do not wish to leave behind the things of the world that we have learned to 'love'.

This is an arduous task and cannot be accomplished without our constant 'surrendering' to God the things that have caught our interest here.

Know ye not that the friendship of the world is enmity with God? Whosoever therefore will be a friend of the world is the enemy of God.

~James 4:4

When we are first born of the flesh, there are many obstacles between us and our success here. Similarly, once we are born of the spirit, there are many obstacles that will come between us and our God.

North Americans are consumed with eliminating the bonds that will prevent our 'success in life;' . . . we are still caught up in how to 'make it' here on earth, for this is what we are taught from early childhood to attain. We are not even close to the enterprise of ridding ourselves of those elements that keep us away from heavenly things.

Once you are born into the spirit, you follow a similar path, as in the case of being born into the flesh: there is much to learn. We are first children, then young people and then, hopefully, mature adults. At some point, if we are blessed with exceeding grace, we will grow into maturity, able to speak with some authority, as the Lord leads, completely surrendered to His Will.

It is my belief that Christians today have deceived themselves into believing that simply because they believe in Christ they are already born again. I say to them that if they were indeed born again, they would act as did the early Christians, bearing such inordinate love that this world would never be the same.

And who are they that the Lord seeks?

The humble, the poor, the afflicted.

Those who mourn, those who hunger and thirst after righteousness, the meek, the merciful, the peacemakers, the pure in heart.

Those persecuted for the sake of righteousness.[63]

In my counselling sessions with those seeking God, I often describe how we must prepare ourselves to serve Him. A realization needs to occur that the things of this world are opposite to the way in which God's government works. A few examples are provided at the end of this chapter. I suggest you closely examine the comparisons to see what you might glean from them.

> *For my thoughts are not your thoughts, neither are your ways my ways, saith the Lord. For as the heavens are higher than the earth, so are my ways higher than your ways, and my thoughts than your thoughts.*[64]

*****

A familiar statement on the airwaves today is that anyone who has been hurt has a *right* to be angry and to display that anger is an okay thing to do.

But I say to you that we do NOT have a right to be angry and REMAIN angry. The sooner we understand this, the quicker such emotionalism can cease to control the way too many of us have come to think.

Why are we so quickly accepting of whatever this world has to offer up by way of 'quick fixes'?

One of the reasons is that we are far too eager to listen to the teachers of this world, ignoring what has been written for centuries claiming to be the right way to go. We have forgotten over these many generations that it was God's intention for us to become His Ambassadors.

I suppose it's much like trying every kind of diet under the sun before actually coming to the realization that there truly is only one way that is the 'right' way – to eat properly and to maintain sufficient movement for a healthy body. There's no getting around it.

We are always looking for ways to deal with our emotions that have become, without question, out of control.

Anger, Fear, Racism, Hatred, just to mention a few.

These can only be dealt with to the extent of the admission (confession) of their existence followed by a desire to change – admitting that you are powerless to make those changes – then, surrender to The Highest Power.

At this point, it becomes a possibility for the 'bad' habits to be replaced by seemingly 'good' habits. The good habits, however, are not habitual; they have become something supernaturally natural.

Although much of what I teach often addresses how to be lifted from the pit of negative emotions and is not necessarily focused on 'end times' per se, it is important to note the reason for the sense of urgency being felt by many of us today. There is an arousing in the spirit of man that something is dreadfully wrong, and that wrong is summed up in 2 Timothy 3.

This know also, that in the last days perilous times shall come. For men shall be lovers of their own selves, covetous, boasters, proud, blasphemers, disobedient to parents, unthankful, unholy. Without natural affection, trucebreakers, false accusers, incontinent, fierce, despisers of those that are good, traitors, heady, high-minded, lovers of pleasures more than lovers of God; Having a form of godliness, but denying the power thereof: from such turn away. For this sort are they which creep into houses, and lead captive silly women laden with sins, led away with divers lusts; ever learning, and never able to come to the knowledge of the truth.

Although one can admit that such verses may have applied in other times of history as well, one cannot deny that they are without question even more true today.

Luke 21:25 and 26 sheds more light on what we are to expect. How close are we? Who can say? We are, however, told to 'watch the signs.'[65]

And there shall be signs in the sun, and in the moon, and in the stars; and upon the earth distress of nations, with perplexity; the sea and the waves roaring: Men's hearts failing them for fear, and for looking after those things which are coming on the earth: for the powers of heaven shall be shaken.

We wonder why some streets of America are seething with brutal men, carrying weapons with the desire to hurt anyone who gets in their way.

The wicked walk on every side, when the vilest men are exalted.[66]

There is a morbid infatuation with the fiends of this world: rapists, serial killers, kidnappers, pimps. Add to this the way in which we have made idols of movie stars, musicians, athletes, television personalities and folk heroes. We seek out 'familiar spirits'[67] through spiritism, spiritualism, mysticism, occultism and psychic phenomenon. Finally, without the new birth we are continually plagued with the 'lust of the flesh, the lust of the eyes and the pride of life.'[68]

With twenty-two syndicated talk shows we have become nothing less than high-class voyeurs.

Comparatively, there is too little response to the seriousness of our relationship with God. We are failing in our responsibilities to live holy lives, and until we fully understand that we must turn all that we call our values upside down and inside out, we will be denied the glorious opportunity to view each and every situation from an entirely new perspective.

Let me close this discourse on the world and some of its difficulties with this reminder from James 4:4.

. . . know ye not that the friendship of the world is enmity with God? Whosoever therefore will be a friend of the world is the enemy of God.

Considering some of the horrors we witness every day on this planet, is it any wonder?

*****

A Small Sampling of 'the World' vs 'the Word'

The World says, "Let's go out on strike."
The Word says, "Be content with your wages."[69]

The World says, "If a burglar breaks into my house, I have the right to attack or even shoot him."
The Word says, "Resist not evil."[70]

The World says, "I will countersue."
The Word says, "If any man sue thee at the law and take away thy coat let him have your cloak also,"[71]

The World asks, "But what if?"
The Word says, "Sufficient unto the day is the evil thereof."[72]

The World says, "I'll get him back for this."
The Word says, "Vengeance is mine, I will repay, saith the Lord."[73]

The World says, "I hate them because they hate me."
The Word says, "Do good to them that hate you; bless them that curse you; love your enemies; pray for them who despitefully use you and persecute you."[74]

The World says, "That's the last straw."
The Word says, "Forgive 70 x 7 times." [75]

The World says, "Say no to what is asked of you."
The Word says, "Give to him that asketh thee and from him that would borrow of thee, turn not thou away," [76] and, "Whosoever shall compel thee to go one mile, go with him twain." [77]

ON PRAYER
"Use not vain repetitions for they think that they shall be heard for their much speaking." [78]

The Walkabout ❧

...and they shall walk with me in white.
                                        ~Revelation 3:4

During my political days, I was personally telephoned and invited by Canadian Prime Minister Mulroney's office to attend Queen Elizabeth's 'walkabout' in Winnipeg, Manitoba.

I was allowed one guest.

My mother would have loved to meet me there as she considered herself to be an enthusiastic descendant of the British Empire Loyalists; however, her recent strokes prevented her from having the strength to do so. When I informed her that the only reason I would have attended would be for her to have the pleasure of being there, she was horrified.

"You just can't pass this up," she insisted.

"To be invited to be so close to Her Majesty is a very rare privilege." For days she continued to plead with me to make the trip, and although I knew that to snub the invitation would make it unlikely for a second similar opportunity, I could not bring myself to go.

It was impossible for Mother to understand my lack of taste for pomp and ceremony. I had become aware that the highest society of this world was shabby in comparison to the Kingdom of God, with no disrespect to HRH. To be sure, the Lord who chooses all those in power, had placed the Queen in Her position of prominence on the world stage. Nevertheless, the only inner courts I was wanting a personal invitation to were, simply put, "not of this world."

Recalling the precious childhood journey to the Lord's garden, I was reminded of the numbers who do not know how to 'be' with the Lord, and my heart cried out in anguish for them.

There are certain events in our lives we undoubtedly encounter alone!

Two of these are inescapable, each experienced in the flesh.

One is Birth. The other, Death.

And yet, beyond these spectacular occurrences, there is an event that is unlike every other, where you become separated from the flesh…a spiritual happening!

It, too, produces life, a different kind of life, a life 'in the spirit.'

It is 'Being Born Again'![79]

I have been sharing what I understand about this event throughout some of the pages covering parts of my journey through life. This brief chapter is simply to focus more particularly on this factor and upon this point alone.

The concept is easiest to comprehend through the eyes of a little child; for that matter, it is a must that you become so…

Except ye be converted, and become as little children, ye shall not enter into the kingdom of heaven.[80]

There is so much said about this topic, and yet, it is so misunderstood. There is no greater mystery to unfold before you than to walk where I have shown you, not in the world but through the garden; it is such a simple path.

As I have shared before, the first stage in the 'ask, seek, knock' trio is ...*ask*!

Open your heart wide, wide enough to return to those trusting days of childhood, those days when there was nothing more to think about than the moment at hand. Ask the Lord to enter your life, take you by the hand, and lead you the rest of the way home.

> The moment this happens,
> You will come to the garden ...alone.
> It may be like or unlike the encounter described.
> You will be honoured
> To partake of a communion
> In the secret place of The Most High God
> Where, through knowing Him,
> You will learn to abide under
> The Shadow of the Almighty.[81]
> If you have never met Him,
> You may choose to do so at any time
> ...even now.
> Ask the Lord to take you to His garden.

*****

> *Ask, and it shall be given you.*
> *Seek, and ye shall find.*
> *Knock, and it shall be opened unto you.*[82]

*****

> *become as a little child,*
> *enter the Kingdom of Heaven.*[83]

*****

Wanting to See the Light ✎

*For he that soweth to his flesh shall of the flesh
reap corruption;*

~Galatians 6:8

When I was twenty, I fell into circumstances where Ouija boards and crystal balls were considerably fascinating. The mystery and intrigue of spiritualism was frequent drawing room conversation.

After some coaxing, I eventually joined a friend for a teacup reading (which is another story altogether), followed my horoscope daily and took a slight interest in yoga. I became captivated with the meaning of dreams, keeping a dream log on the nightstand, often waking in the night to make specific notations.

After much frivolous indulging (Praise God that He kept pulling me safely back into His fold), I had the opportunity to share with some new-found friends my own personal story of 'seeing the light' when I was just a child, during my housebound experience with the measles.

As I related the incident, those present seemed strangely impressed, so much so that I myself thought back upon the event with more scrutiny than I had ever been inclined to before. As the reminder of that time kept coming forward again and again, it began to become a fixation for me to 'want' to be in the presence of that light once more.

In addition to this, the enormous emphasis that those around me had placed upon this single event seemed to take my own 'want' and give it, so to speak, a life of its own. Though this may appear as if I am willing to spread the burden for what I was about to do, I assure you that this is not the case. I gladly take complete responsibility for my actions.

It was nothing more than my weakness that prompted me to respond to their own infatuations. I fell totally into the pride of the obvious 'specialness' of His visit and I suspect I must have somehow wanted to now prove I could produce it for myself, thereby possibly gaining even greater admiration than I had already encountered.

One night, after long debating the issue in my mind, I decided to make the attempt to do whatever I could to bring the light into my room. With some understanding of the importance of such a moment, I solemnly stretched out on my bed in an attempt to imitate the same relaxed pose that had been present at the original encounter. Slowly closing my eyes, I calmed myself and began to think upon each wonderful feeling that I had experienced when the Lord chose to visit me on that particularly special day.

The following story is shared as a special caution to all of us who have so lightly considered the elements of the 'spirit world.' Do not be fooled; it is active and real.

What happened to me can happen at any time, to anyone, and does with regularity, to be sure. I have since that time counselled many who have suffered impacting acquaintance with the demonic world. For me, even the thought of how easily we are drawn into the dark side of life presents a chilling reminder of what is happening to so many, even today. It is especially startling to witness the children of this hour falling deeper and deeper into the recesses of the occult to a time and place where they might be all but lost.

*****

We have come to a crossroads and it is imperative for us to understand how these snares are created. Though the world provides us daily with the proof that we need only to 'want' a thing to have it, I caution you here that there remain some grave misunderstandings of these practices. When we willingly open the door to any pleasure or desire to gain, we begin to move into the realm of what we will call for this time, 'exchange'.

This practice, I can assure you, you never want to do!

Sadly, such an exchange has become a part of our everyday lives, though we are, for the most part, completely unaware of its occurrence. Our culture has become overindulgent in the 'things' of this world. We teach our children how to get ahead and encourage them to believe in a very long list of what they deserve. As parents, we fear that our children will 'miss out' if we don't provide them with every conceivable opportunity, though we may annihilate both ourselves and them in the process. Such fears bring a certain frenzied activity pressing in on us to chase after our future while we lay victim to a present filled with spiritual inertia.

The fact is that quotes such as 'create your own future' and 'take charge of your life' are part of the most fervently taught philosophies of this generation. Society drives us to 'go towards the light' and to 'seek the light within.' We sense a burden from all sides to believe that these are the things that we MUST have in order to become anything relevant at all; we pursue self-fulfillment at all costs.

Sadly, there are costs at the end of this journey.

Admittedly, the desire to see a light similar to the one revealed during a childhood illness is not exactly the formula of an everyday chase, but nonetheless, the situation, although somewhat unusual in its context, is not very different from our human desires to be someone special, forever seeking experiences that set us apart and above those around us.

This story will hopefully begin to alarm you that moving into the realm of 'want' is where we begin to run into trouble. It is indeed possible to strive for and realize a certain measure of success in this world . . . for a time. There are even cases where the supposed victory may last for extended periods. Be assured, if you become fascinated for any reason in your own experience, you fall prey to the ultimate booby trap: pride.

There is little doubt that the true desires of our carnal hearts can be brought into our lives. It is these very desires of the flesh, with little or no thought of the will of the Father, that I hope to take issue here.

It makes perfect sense that human beings are spectacularly creative. How could it be otherwise when you consider that God, the Creator of Heaven and Earth, created us in His image?

And if that is the case, what, then, was the whole point of being here? Is it not for us to pursue our dreams and become 'all that we can be'?

Or have we, on the other hand, been called to 'deny ourselves and follow Him'?

When teaching others about the Lord, I often refer to my standard response in times of conflict of difficult decision: What would Jesus do? If we were to follow His lead, then our lives would be about *sacrifice*, not *self-fulfillment*.

And God saw that "the wickedness of man was great in the earth and that every imagination of the thoughts of his heart was only evil continually" (Genesis 6:5).

If we saw as God saw, what would we see?

Take a long, hard, honest look.

Child abuse, rape, murder, domestic violence, racism, pornography, the fight over abortion, money and power struggles, economic anarchy, drug and alcohol addictions, prostitution, missing children in the hundreds of thousands, armed robberies, ALL on the increase, and this in supposedly the most civilized country in the world.

Today, we are encouraged to allow our imaginations to be stimulated fully and to bring into ourselves those things that we imagine. We are taught to utilize our gifts to the fullest for our own well-being and benefit, ultimately, we are told, helping the planet by having become 'all that we can be.'

By the majority of accounts, it would seem that Jesus came here to set the example; He was endowed with EVERY gift, EVERY power, but He set aside these gifts, choosing not to seek His own will but the WILL of His Father. At no time did He bring unto Himself that which He desired, but rather used up His time using His power under direction from above, continually for the benefit of others.

He did not even save Himself when clearly He had the ability to do so, but rather chose to 'give up' His life that others might live.

We are asked to do nothing less.

God has given us the opportunity to take for ourselves here and now whatever it is we want; or, and here is where the choice comes in, to "deny ourselves, take up our cross daily, and follow Him."

Now that is a mighty tall order.

We cannot do it without His help. Our human limitations make it impossible to do nothing more than 'the best we can do.' This is still not good enough.

It is rare indeed to find anyone writing this tough a truth, but. there are some. Philip Keller is one. In his book *Predators in our Pulpits* (original title), you will find confirmed the things of which I speak. You may not come across the book under that title any longer, but rather the same manuscript is now available as *The High Cost of Holiness.*[84]

Although this is purely speculation on my part, it would not surprise me if pressure hadn't been brought to bear upon the publishers to change the title; perhaps those 'pulpiteers' who were exposed by the truth found therein were inordinately offended, and well they could have been!

*****

As I lay on the bed, it seemed to me as if some hint of apprehension, followed by a definiteness of purpose, 'entered' my being. I must have surely been pleased by the impression my story had made, as I began to have a very earnest desire to have something happen.

And, just as I had asked, something did.

Within minutes, I felt as if forced to take a deep, desperately deep, breath, almost as if I was sucking in all at once the air from a large balloon. Throughout my chest and lungs there was a swelling sensation like yeast making bread dough rise on a warm afternoon.

The moment passed with no further event.

After fifteen more minutes of waiting and no hint of a light, I became bored with the idea, got up from the bed and basically forgot the whole thing.

*****

The next day at the office, I began to experience an uneasy sense that the people with whom I worked every day had a new look to them. I didn't feel my usual fondness for them, even though some of us were special friends. Granted, there were those who were often difficult to be with, but this had never been a problem for me, as I had always found it possible to overlook weaknesses, including my own.

Today, however, I was experiencing a great deal of annoyance with every word spoken and every move made.

The feeling was brief at first – although it made me slightly confused, I dismissed it by saying that I was probably having a bad day. For two full days, however, this uncomfortable gnawing at my typically good nature continued to plague me. On the third day, while returning home from work, something quite frightening happened.

The subway was packed as usual. Two or three strangers pressed in close to where I was standing. Glancing momentarily at the face of the man closest to me, a thought all but growled within me.

"I hate this man." I thought, staring at him as if he was my worst enemy. "I want to kill him!"

Bouncing as if from one personality to another, my 'other' self did a quick reality check.

I was shocked at the possibility that I could even think such a thing!

No, I was more than shocked! I was horrified!

On discovery, it was most fascinating to note that my own person seemed to be present right alongside these thoughts. It was as if there were two of me living in my body ... or was it me and some 'body' else?

One thing was for certain: these thoughts did NOT belong to me!

So what was happening?

I became suddenly afraid of certain dire capabilities that I might be somehow acquiring, especially since I appeared to be abnormally subjected to voices that were unquestionably foreign. I forced myself through the crowded train, getting off three stops early. I ran up the subway stairs and all the way to my apartment. Out of breath, and literally scared to death, I tried to collect my thoughts as to what this could all mean. Gaining some composure and wise perspective was uppermost in my mind, yet panic continued to surge through me like bolts of electricity.

The presence of evil was indisputable, a presence I had been heretofore spared.

*****

Dale Sutherland was a high school friend. He had married one of my best friends, his high school sweetheart. They had moved to Toronto also, and lived not far from my apartment on Oriole Road. His office was just blocks away and the three of us had kept in regular touch.

Dale was a special person. At 17, he looked 30. He had been bald for as long as I had known him, but in addition to his just looking older, he often seemed to have an ageless wisdom for one so young. His experience in dealing with mystical things was familiar to me, as we had shared frequent and lengthy discussions regarding a myriad of aspects of the 'unknown.' To my knowledge he was not what I would have considered a Christian. Nevertheless, in light of the emergency at hand, he was the first person who came to mind.

Fortunately, he answered my call on the second ring.

Breathlessly, I recounted the horror of the past few days, desperately ending my tale with "What could be the meaning of this?" and even more importantly, "What should I do?"

"Well," he said, "you must have been delving into something lately that has put out a welcome mat to some kind of other 'presence.' Has anything unusual happened in the last week or so?"

At first I couldn't think of a thing.

And so we talked about other topics, which seemed to calm me down.

Then suddenly ... I remembered ... the light! What about the light?

"Oh yes," I blurted out anxiously, "you remember the time I saw the light when I was about seven?" (We held very few secrets from each other.)

"Yes," said Dale. "What about it?"

"Well, some friends were here a week or so ago and I told them the story. They made such a big deal about it that I decided to try to do it again."

"What on earth do you mean?" asked Dale.

His concern was obvious.

I told him how I had laid down on the bed and tried to recreate the experience.

"That's it!" he exclaimed. "Now, carefully recall everything that took place. Don't leave anything out."

Since the whole event was only a matter of minutes, it was easy to recount. I told him about my lungs expanding while my body changed shape under the pressure of some seemingly supernatural force. Again, as if to excuse myself, I found I was reminding him of how badly I had wanted to see the light.

"Well, Suzanne, what you have probably done is taken on an evil spirit ... darkness, a demon, call it what you will. But hold on now," he had obviously sensed my fear as my blood began to run cold, "don't panic! There is definitely something we can do about it.

"About as easily as you have taken it in, it can be removed. Once you are alerted to such a presence, this spirit cannot stay with you without your permission. What happened was that somewhere in your heart you must have been willing to make some kind of a compromise, however small, in order to get what you wanted. That is how these exchanges take place."

I hardly knew what to say. I couldn't believe my ears. "Do such things really happen?" I wondered. What was worse was that it was apparently happening to me!

"What should I do?" I asked frantically.

"Now just calm down. It's going to be fine," he assured me, though assured at that moment I was not.

"The last thing you want to do at this point is demonstrate fear. So, let's take this one step at a time. You know that Jesus has always been with you." He posed this last statement as if a question.

"Of course," I replied without hesitation.

"And you know that He will never abandon you."

Again I admitted that was true.

"The Lord has simply allowed you to see that fooling around with anything that is not of Him can get you into some pretty deep water. What you must now do is command the spirit that is present with you to be gone from your life. And you must ask this in the name of Jesus Christ."

Although I had never heard of such a thing, I seemed to understand him completely.

I agreed and hung up the phone.

Once again, I lay down on the bed. With not the slightest of doubts in my mind, I declared aloud that I belonged to Jesus

Christ of Nazareth, born of a virgin, the Son of God. I commanded all spirits that were present in my life to leave my temple and never return. I stated firmly that they were not welcome here. I made it perfectly clear that I was not afraid, for I knew that each of these visitors, if there were more than one, were under the authority of Almighty God.

Immediately, the last words having barely left my lips, there was an indescribable pressure on my diaphragm. The pressure seemed to force a somewhat foreign clump of what seemed to be just a big bag of air up through my lungs, lifting my chest at least by an inch, if not more.

The 'thing' continued to move on up through my upper body to my throat, into my mouth, finally expelling itself from my body entirely. I made a gasping sound as if I had vomited an imaginary puff of smoke.

Silence.

The return of serenity.

It was over.

I felt extreme relief.

I called Dale immediately to tell him that the deed was now done and that I felt amazingly better.

Before hanging up, he left me with these words.

"You must always remember, Suzanne, you are a child of God. The Lord has promised to protect you, but that does not mean that you won't make some wrong choices along the way.

"God's promise to you includes that He will turn all evil into good for those who love Him, and my bet is that puts you in a pretty good spot.

"So, no matter how sidetracked you may become, I am convinced that your love for Him will keep you always in His care."

Over time, these words have been proven true.

Had I fallen outside of loving Him, I cannot say where you might have found me now; I dread to even contemplate it.

Love for our Saviour...keeps us in His care.

There is no other way, no other protection.

This situation makes it possible for us to get a glimpse of how easily we take such seemingly innocent steps away from God into the spirit world. If we are not brought back quickly, we will have much suffering, for inevitably we must retrace each step to 'unsow' each seed sown in reckless abandon.

I would not be able to speak so sincerely of it had I not personally experienced many interactions with the demonic spirit world, the story contained here being just one of them. I am grateful that my Lord saw fit to alert me regarding the approaching pitfalls, for since that time I have worked with many people who have fallen prey to the lures of power by any name.

The pain of their walk back from...literally, hell...is not a pretty sight.

It is a desperately slow walk, a painful process.

If you can avoid it now, you must do so, for to put off its inevitability will make it that much more difficult. Every day, every hour that you hesitate lengthens the journey home by that much more.

*****

We are all on a journey; we are either going toward home or away from home. Some of us are on our way home now and some of us are heading farther and farther away from our proper destination every single day. The difficulty lies in determining which is which; the journey can seem so long sometimes and there is often no end in sight. How can we tell if we are headed 'to' or 'away from' home?

We require the help of the One who came here to be like us, and who, by and through His obedience, was able to return to the Father in Heaven.

It was Jesus who said "No man cometh unto the Father, but by me."[85]

Do not be deceived; there is no other way.

"He that entereth not by the door into the sheepfold, but climbeth up some other way, the same is a thief and a robber."[86]

"I am the door of the sheep. All that ever came before me are thieves and robbers."[87]

No man has ever made such claims.

He claims without reservation that He IS the only way. We cannot beg, borrow or steal our way home, nor can we earn it, for none of us is worthy. Studying will not make it; good deeds alone fall short. Specifically, the "self" cannot enter; we must actually "surrender" our way in, leaving our shabby selves at the door.

Accept no other passage home, for there are many who would wish to give you a ticket to ride, but when the ride is over, you will find you are a very, very long way from home and there may be no obvious way back!

A destination of choice.

*****

A security, an awesome protection that is able to blanket you whatever the situation, is built out of a relationship that moves and grows and dwells within you in spite of your running away from Him and in spite of your occasional determination to be removed from His influence upon you.

But as in all relationships...

there had to be some kind of beginning
    a moment in time when two parties are determined to
        know one another
    the heart and hand reach out in the hope of
        connecting
    a sign of the desire to bridge whatever gap may prevent
        intimacy.

The Lord is forever reaching out to us ...
    We are the guilty parties
    continually drawn into the world ...
    a world that appears so vibrant and alive
    so full of opportunities, romance and intrigue
    it compels us to live life to its fullest
    to let go of and turn away from
    The King of Kings.

No man can serve two masters: for either he will hate the
one, and love the other; or else he will hold to the one, and
despise the other. Ye cannot serve God and mammon.
                        ~Matthew 6:24

*****

Demons of Darkness ❧

" . . . in my name they shall cast out devils . . .
~Mark 16:17

It was always interesting to me that Jesus spoke of devils causing havoc in the lives of ordinary people. Language that includes such talk is mostly avoided at civilized dinner parties. We are, however, now talking continuously about the 'shadows' in our personality that keep us in various forms of 'bondage.'

In recent days, we might actually hear the word 'demon' used, albeit rather casually, but at least we are beginning to use the word, thereby somehow legitimizing the concept. Not that any intelligent person would actually believe that such a 'demon' is a 'real' entity that can mess with our lives, but rather, nothing more than a 'shadow,' a nameless, faceless idiosyncrasy.

As is always the case, you will find that conversations with children include frank discussions on how demons operate. Clearly, they have no problem 'believing' them to be real; consequently, they have no problem in dealing with them with authority once they know how.

Since children are usually more in touch with the spirit realm and often are able to describe in detail a variety of demons, you do not have to convince them that such a world exists. They know that it does. We like to think that it is merely their imagination, but with adequate investigation, you, too, will find that it is not.

*****

We were called to help out in a household with three young children while the mother underwent hip surgery, requiring three months of recovery.

We had been given a free hand to share the gospel with the children, and indeed, the mother had pleaded with us to turn the entire family situation, not to mention even their house, over to God.

The Holy Spirit went straight to work, and shortly after our arrival, I was working in the kitchen with Rochelle, who, at the age of five, which is an adorable age to begin with, was the most vivacious and fun-loving creature I had seen in a very long time. She was the youngest of the three and currently sitting on the kitchen counter happily assisting me prepare all the ingredients for chocolate cake.

I could sense that she was studying me closely.

"How come you are always so happy?" she asked.

"What a lovely thing to say, Rochelle. Do you really think I'm always happy?"

"Well, you're always smiling or laughing. I want to be like that too."

"Well," I said, "sometimes I have been cross with you when you misbehave."

"Oh, that's different," she said without compunction, "I know you are not really mad."

"You know, Rochelle," I went on, not wanting to miss this spontaneous opportunity, "the only reason I feel happy all the time is because of Jesus. When He comes into your heart to stay, you just feel different, that's all."

"Can I do that?" she asked sincerely.

"Well, let's just ask Jesus to come into your heart and help you to become the little girl that He wants you to be."

"Okay," she said without another thought about it.

When this type of request is made, the Lord begins to work to make the necessary changes required to cause 'deliverance,' . . . to 'make a person free.'[88]

While working with the three siblings, Mark, aged 9, Karen, aged 7 and Rochelle, I began to lead up to the discussion of demons, for the children had had difficult childhood encounters prior to their having been adopted by Ken and Lara.

At first I barely introduced the words.

For example, when Rochelle was being particularly disobedient one evening before bedtime, I merely suggested that *perhaps she may have a demon, as I was sure that Rochelle would never behave this badly.*

She made little or no response and I left it at that.

The next day, during a similar bout of irrational behaviour on her part, I again suggested that her demon must have returned, because I was no longer dealing with that nice little girl, Rochelle. This time, there was the faintest acknowledgement that I had spoken. It was clear that an impression had been made.

For most children, bedtime proves a good opportunity to kick up a bit of a fuss – but this was a child who literally 'flew' around the house, running up and down the stairs at such an excessive speed that it was almost impossible to catch her, should you be so foolish to even try. In fact, the only way to rectify the situation was to sit very quietly in one spot and wait for her to come to you. Paying little or no attention to her activity brought it to a fairly short conclusion. But there was absolutely no question, something was causing her a great deal of stress every evening at precisely the same hour.

One night, as she began to settle down into my arms, she looked up at me and said, "Every night before I go to bed, something always goes wrong. I don't want to be bad every night."

"Well then, let's figure out what it is that we can do to make this stop." I wanted to give her the opportunity to participate in the choices we were about to make. Since we talked about Jesus regularly, including Him in every part of our daily activities, and since the term 'demon' was now becoming familiar to her, she took the next step.

"Could we just ask Jesus to help?"

"Of course we can, honey; that is exactly what we'll do. What a good idea. What would you like to ask Jesus to do?"

"Let's ask Jesus to take away ALL my demons," she said delightedly, with absolutely no doubt in her mind that just the asking would make it happen.

"All right," I agreed with her eagerly. "Since you have asked for this with all your heart, then the demons must flee from you and you will be set free! Isn't that exciting?"

The look of satisfaction on Rochelle's face was a miracle in itself. She proceeded to her room, blowing me a goodnight, see-you-in-the-morning kiss. She had no difficulty in falling asleep that night, though normally she would have to have the closets checked for monsters (demons?) and she would be up and down several times ... for a drink, a pit stop and whatever else she could think of to postpone the inevitable.

The very next day, Rochelle was a *totally different* person, without any coaxing or reminding. She simply got up, seemingly on the right side of the bed for a change. Within days, her teachers were commenting that something amazing had happened to Rochelle. She had become co-operative and helpful, never minding to pick up after others who had been careless.

When she stayed for a weekend at her friend Cindy's house, the mother called to say that Rochelle had offered to clean Cindy's room when Cindy had decided to have a temper tantrum, throwing toys in every direction. Rochelle began to clean up and talk to Cindy about how she, too, could be rid of the demons that were making her bad.

Another fascinating aspect of the procedure was that Karen, who was usually quite distant and cool in her relationships, began to have sudden fits of rage. This was not typical of Karen, and after a few days of Rochelle monitoring carefully Karen's behaviour, she suddenly had an answer.

"Suzanne," Rochelle began rather cautiously, "maybe Karen got MY demons when I sent them away."

"That's quite possible," I said, "for demons always seek another place to stay once they have been 'cast out.' We were paying such close attention to getting rid of yours that we might have forgotten to pray for the protection of others against these who were now let loose. What do you think we should do now?" I asked her, again giving her the opportunity to participate. We were obvious novitiates in the process.

"I think that we should pray to Jesus to ask Him to take all Karen's demons away too, only this time let's make them go far, far away, somewhere that they can never hurt anybody again."

This procedure again took place.

That night while the girls were in the tub, Karen was quiet and pensive. Thoughtfully, she looked up at me and said, "Are we the only people in the world that know about demons?"

"Well, unfortunately, not too many people understand how demons work," I told her. "Why do you ask?"

"Because if everybody knew about them, they could send them away and people wouldn't have to be so mean anymore. Rochelle and I got better and so could everybody else."

"That's exactly true, Karen, and so now we have a chance to help others, because we know how it works."

The girls took me to task. They began to speak Truth to the dark places in their school, on the playground, at the homes of their friends.

*****

One day, Rochelle returned home and climbed quite shyly into my lap. I could tell she wanted to share something with me that seemed to be quite private, very special.

"What is it?" I asked her gently.

"Today when I was in school, Rosemary was saying bad words and I heard someone behind me say 'Teach her what to do ... Teach her about Jesus.' But when I looked behind me, there was nobody there."

"What did you do?"

Rochelle answered enthusiastically, "I told her about Jesus and that Jesus would not like her to talk that way and that He is our friend and if we just ask Him to help us, we learn how to be nice."

"Good for you, Rochelle. And who do you think it was that spoke to you?" I asked her.

Eyes wide with amazement, she answered, "I think it was Jesus."

"I think you're right!" I was so happy for her delight.

She snuggled into me with a deep sigh of contentment. After several moments like this, she perked up as if suddenly remembering something.

"And do you know what else?" she added, somehow recognizing the mystery of the moment, "Jesus whispered so quietly that nobody else in the classroom heard Him but me."

*****

Encounter with the Enemy ❧

...for your Father knoweth what things ye have need of,
before ye ask him.

~Matthew 6:8

I don't believe that all disease is the result of sin (dis-ease), although the majority is, without doubt.

By sin I mean the darkness of the soul, that which has no light, including those elements of being that bring darkness ... guilt, anger, hatred, sorrow, jealousy, unforgiveness, greed, lust, rebellion ... underlying all of which is fear. Our physical well-being, as has been more recently presented in the media, has a definite relationship with the condition of our souls. Where there is darkness, there is dis-ease that can present itself in a variety of ways.

It is important for those who may be looking for answers to the reasons for their own illness or the afflictions of those dear to them to begin to understand that there is an ultimate purpose in all things.[89] Nevertheless, risking an intimate look at our own lives, we can begin to recognize the many times we fail to measure up to the person we were meant to be. It is most unusual that an affliction is not the direct result of sin, but it certainly does happen.[90] In either case, it becomes, as a result of this truth, a great relief to know that no matter what the circumstance, God is in it somewhere. It becomes our job to determine, whether in the midst of adversity OR triumph ...

What is God's intention?

What does He want me to do?

What does He want me to learn?

What does He want me to demonstrate?

In the case of adversity, for example, if our thoughts could be heavenward, taking our eyes off the seemingly unfortunate circumstances, we are promised the opportunity to deal with the situation 'unnaturally,' . . . coming thereby into contact with God's purpose in every situation.

We live in the 'natural', the physical, the human.

And yet, we are spirit and our ultimate aim is to live here, but in the spirit, not in the natural. There is only one way to accomplish this: we must keep our eyes on the things that are spiritual.[91] Perceive all things through spiritual eyes, endure all things with spiritual understanding, overcome all things with spiritual strength . . . but how can we do this when we still live in the flesh?

We are born of the flesh and into the flesh, and until we start a new life in the spirit, spiritual understanding will continue to elude us. This new birth or new beginning is a unique and magnificent metamorphosis, often brought on by unusually difficult occasions of life. Near-death experiences are the most frequent renewal, but there is also a beauty in utter hopelessness, fear, trauma, shame, despair. Each of these or some combination thereof seems to create the necessary heat for purification. Out of brokenness, wholeness.

Unfortunately, what we come up against, again and again, in our world of inventions and cures, is advice to 'fight' the obstacles that come before us in the way that we have been taught in the world. This leads only to more anguish and more destruction, though temporary relief or success may prevail for a time.

It is good to know that we are to be in the world but not of it, and in order to do this, we must connect with some kind of regeneration process, whether deliberate or impetuous, in order to make us free from the flesh, and consequently, in touch with the spirit.

Into two categories falls our decision to live: in the physical, the natural or seemingly the only way that makes sense, the way 'we' might choose; or the spiritual, the unnatural, the way that does not make sense to a man but is pleasing to God.

We require, for our own sake, an understanding of how it is that some appear able to choose the unnatural way to deal with the circumstances of life and others are in ceaseless conflict with themselves on how to respond to matters of conscience. Too often we witness the failure of humanity to respond from the heart, even though continuously similar circumstances present themselves, offering opportunities for change again and again. As a nation, it seems so odd to find that no sooner do we gain ground in one area, we somehow lose in another. The result: an overall lack of 'true' growth. This deception is so great that we actually believe the world is becoming a better place.

Individually, the lie is no different.

This inability to fully change cannot be denied, for the results are reflected throughout a world bathed in ever-increasing fear lurking from every corner, ultimately causing the erosion of all we once believed to be safe. Moral decay, which eats away at every fibre of our being; increased wars, laden with death and pain; the hatred from which springs ethnic cleansing: a famine of body and soul…

…more anguish…

…more peril…

*There is no fear in love; but perfect love casteth out fear:
because fear hath torment. He that feareth is not made
perfect in love.*

~1 John 4:18

*****

The age of twenty-two brought my first encounter with the
threat of cancer.

The morning began innocently enough. The steamy hot
shower preparing me for another challenging day was
exhilarating as usual. As a paralegal in Toronto, city of
unending energy, I was associated with some of the most
prominent lawyers of the day. I enjoyed my work thoroughly
and was good at it.

Added to this picture was my youth and my health. This
combination provided a vibrancy to match a career that
proved exciting and rewarding. The lawyer with whom I spent
most of my free time was known to be one of the most eligible
bachelors in town.

Could I have asked for more? I surely thought not.

I felt blessed in every way, skipping through my days and
nights with heartfelt glee.

Then, in the midst of all this, came a moment in time when
all the stars in the heavenly system seemingly fell out of view.

Twisting the shower head to pulsating massage, I was
nearing the end of my daily wake up routine. Unexpectedly,
with no more than a split second's instinct, I was given the
sense that there was something different about my body, not
that one could even begin to describe their own body in detail,
but it is something you know, something internal, subconscious
. . . you are in tune with it deep within your being.

As the cloth brushed over my left breast, an alarm went off
in my head. I felt suddenly dizzy. I succumbed to a certain

command to proceed no further. I pressed my fingers into my flesh with caution, hoping against hope my senses were wrong.

But no, there it was!

A mass, the size of a grape, told me that this discovery was more worrisome than the regular bouts of cystitis that had plagued me in the past. At the understanding of what this discovery could mean, an overwhelming feeling of helplessness gripped my heart.

Without warning, I was so stricken with terror that my knees buckled beneath me and I fell to the floor. I lay there, as if paralyzed, huddled in a pool of fear and sorrow, the water continuing to rain down on me in relentless tyranny.

From somewhere deep within my soul came the most agonizing sounds as I sobbed uncontrollably. There was nowhere to go and no one to hold me, as I began free falling with no safety net in sight.

The room swallowed me up now, gathering me into itself.

How many minutes passed in this way, I could not say, but after a time, a certain decorum beginning to return, I managed to crawl slowly to my feet. Now that my body tremors were thankfully slowly dissipating, my mind savagely took up the race, catapulting me headlong into my own death.

I had a sense of existing no longer.

Finding the strength somehow to reach up to extinguish the waterfall, I leaned shakily against the marble shower walls, still hoping to gain my bearings. Grabbing my robe, I stumbled into the living room and lunged toward the phone.

"Somebody help me," I thought, "somebody help me."

My fingers failed to dial correctly several times. Though a calm was beginning to surface within, my body continued, from time to time, to display all the signs of an addict in severe withdrawal.

Finally, the telephone began to ring at the other end.

It kept ringing...and ringing.

I sat motionless as I waited for someone, anyone, to answer.

No answer came.

I did not hang up, however, as there seemed to be a safety in letting the ringing continue, as if the familiarity of such an occurrence could somehow provide solace to what was otherwise a situation out of control.

Staring into the room, with the telephone held firmly to my head, warm and convoluted images began to unfold before me. As if to protect me from myself, some kind of shock seemed to take over my reflexes. I fell into a hypnotic state, frozen in time and space, my head slumped lifelessly forward. Eventually, the telephone fell from my hand onto the floor.

When I finally regained sufficient consciousness to get on with the day, I had all but forgotten what had only minutes before brought me reeling to a halt. And then I remembered. I cautiously searched for the lump again, just to be sure.

It was still there.

Although I lived alone, I found myself declaring out loud to anyone who might be interested that there was no point in getting hysterical.

"Let's just take one step at a time and not panic until there is really something to panic about," I continued to coach myself through to sensibility.

And yet, despite my bravest attempts to be strong, there was a gaping hole in my comfort zone that refused to go away. There wasn't any point, I surmised, in discussing the matter with everyone involved with my life. Wisely, I had chosen to confide in my boyfriend's sister-in-law, who was twenty years my senior and sensible to a fault.

I determined to get to the matters at hand as best as I could; I would try Peggy again when I got to work.

As the leisure time set aside for early morning setbacks had all but disappeared, the clock seemed to be racing ahead of me now, so . . . I began to move more quickly. With significant difficulty, I applied color and tone to my lips and cheeks. Pockets of fear that continued to house my countenance peered back at me from the oval mirror above the dresser. The struggle to keep my hand steady reminded me that all was not as well as could be expected on this otherwise beautiful Tuesday in May.

Watching myself bravely move through makeup motions that now had no significance whatsoever proved to be almost as trying as getting into my skirt and blouse. Stubbornness overtook the zipper and the buttons were as hard to handle as if I was still in kindergarten.

Finally donning my suit jacket and heels, I was ready to face courageously a world that had in the first hour of this day disintegrated before me.

*****

The island situated in the middle of two-way traffic, where I would normally begin the first part of my journey to the corporate towers, was overloaded with patrons.

Disengaging from this precarious locale, it surprised me to note that the surefootedness that usually preceded my movements to employ the streetcar were somewhat amiss, my hand barely grasping the stainless steel pole that would enable me to safely board.

Jostling for position was commonplace at this stage of the journey as passengers considered it important to be first out of the gate upon arrival at the station, thus assuring themselves a seat on the subway. It was not typical for me to compete for these positions, though I would move forward with a certain determination specifically geared to arriving at the office at the appointed hour.

Today, my absolute lack of interest in the thrust of the throng caused me frequently to lose my bearings. My arrival at the platform was facilitated merely by the energy and forward motion of the hundreds of commuters.

Once positioned on the train, I looked about to see if anyone could tell that there was something different about me today. However, patterns set by each individual so long ago were typically in place. Some stared out the window as if wondering who they were; others tore furiously through the newspaper in order to be completely up to date prior to the next instalment already in the making; and then there were those whose habit it was to catch one last snooze before plodding headlong into their places of employment.

Not only was there no response to my need, to my surprise, my fellow passengers appeared not to notice me at all. It had never before this day been important to me that they 'see' me, and I questioned if indeed it had ever before been important for me to 'see' them.

It was apparent by now that my morning newsflash had been of little note to anyone else but me. It was my own personal dilemma; it was not destined for the headlines or the six o'clock news.

Amazingly, despite everyone's obvious lack of concern, my whole world appeared to be tumbling down around me.

"Why doesn't anyone smile?" I thought.

"Can't they see? Don't they care?"

I was screaming inside and yet no one could hear me. It occurred to me that even if they did know, would they be moved to any degree of compassion? I sought, but could not find, just one pair of eyes that held anything more than a robotic-like stare. A chill ran through me, not just for my sake, but for ours: theirs and mine.

I made a mental note that day that I knew would stay with me forever.

I would never again assume that just because someone you meet is not screaming, they are not screaming inside. A full flight of fear is not readily noticeable, for two reasons: the one housing the terror smiles bravely; and those of us on the outside never seem to notice due to the innate inability to see beyond our own little lives.

I was learning firsthand that a person can be breaking into little parts right before you without so much as the slightest change in demeanour, something like an implosion. Stepping away from my own situation, I began to long to see deeper into the souls of the people standing next to me.

"Who is in pain?" I thought.

"Whose life has been rendered worthless due to some tragic loss?"

I asked myself, "How is it that we do not see?"

Not only are we blind to one another, we don't even seem to mind.

"Oh God," I pleaded desperately, "help me ... help me to see their pain."

*****

It happens to all of us.

A phone call, one conversation, the wrong turn in the road, glances, corporate restructuring; there are so many moments that can change your life forever.

You can always wonder later, 'if only I'd listened' ... 'if I hadn't called' ... 'if only I'd said it another way' ... if I hadn't taken that street home' ... 'if only' ...

It's fascinating to me how both our enormous good fortune as well as the bad comes in exactly this same way.

Fate.

Destiny.

Kismet ... whatever you want to call it.

It's plain ... it's simple ... it's out of our hands!

Typically, we never thank God for every miraculous breath we take and the bounty continually set before us, but the moment the turn in the road comes, God is the first one we cry out to or against.

It is accurate to say that there appears to be much we can do to determine our own destiny. The market today is saturated with 'how to' books. These do work, up to a point, the point at which destiny finds you and says ...

"Well, you certainly have been doing some interesting things lately – making choices, taking charge – your confidence that you have done this all yourself is getting sorely in the way of your humility. So, what will ultimately benefit you in ways you cannot now know is this unexpected turn in the road; let's see what you will learn going 'round *this* corner ..."

So much for *your* choices, *your* destiny.

Added to this, we must soon come to recognize the Lord's deliberate 'setting aside' of His own life in order to serve others: us – you and I!

By determining and going after the destiny of our choice, I began to wonder, just exactly how is this similar?

IT IS NOT!

*****

150

I reached Peg that morning.

I quietly described to her what it was that I'd found, and where. The conversation becoming quite personal, and not wishing to disturb the other secretaries, I put my phone on hold and went into my boss's office, which was vacant due to his early morning court appearance.

"Well, what do you think?" I asked her with a certain pleading in my voice.

Tell me it's okay … tell me it's nothing … tell me not to worry … make me believe you!

I paced nervously behind the desk.

True to form, Peggy did cheer me up.

"You must try to remember, Suzanne, we are always hearing about the cases with unhappy endings . . . I'm quite certain that there are many, many situations that never come to that, but do we hear about *them*? Not that often."

"There's absolutely no reason to believe that yours won't be one of those that have been nothing more than a little scare." Peggy continued to soothe me.

I was feeling a bit better now … I noticed I was beginning to breathe normally again, having been quite obviously holding my breath a lot of late, as if to do so would stop time from pressing forward.

Her last minute advice was to 'get an appointment with a specialist and go from there.' I told her I appreciated the support and she asked me to count on her if there was anything at all that she could do.

In the meantime, she was on her way out for groceries and the dentist. She would talk to me later.

There was no getting around it …

I was in this thing alone.

My doctor, to whom I reported to determine the need for a proper referral, made an interesting sound in his throat when he felt the area affected. It was an unusual sound ... there was a question mark attached to it ... more than just a slight concern.

It was several moments before he spoke.

"Let's be on the safe side, shall we?" he asked me as if I was in the room.

"I'll schedule a mammogram for next Tuesday and we'll take a closer look."

"What will that do?" I wanted details.

"Well," he began cautiously, "technology today can tell us if there are any cells even thinking about getting fancy. Our tests are now so precise that we can determine as much as three, maybe five years, into future possibilities."

"Any trouble spots will appear as a red glow on the screen. ..what we call hot spots."

That made me feel somewhat reassured – the three-to-five-year part, I mean. If I was clear for now, then I might even have a ticket for the next several years, a sort of consolation prize.

I dressed quickly and left for home.

Dusk was falling; it was damp and cool, chilling to the bone. "Weather to match the mood," I thought.

The next few days dragged hopelessly along. I went about my duties as diligently as ever, but I really wasn't what you could call 'on the job.' A kind of pseudo person was moving about my desk, answering the phone, taking messages, running to court, meeting with clients.

*****

Greg and I spent most evenings together. Combining dinner with mellifluous music was the usual evening fare. We put in long and often hectic days together and there was no better way to unwind than a good meal, a little wine and each other's company.

We were very used to one another by now, so much so that Greg would scan the paper for the first fifteen minutes of every meal. This I never minded and tonight was no different. I was so very far away that the quiet was a welcome friend.

In spite of the drama in progress, it was not my intention to involve Greg in order to persuade him to fawn all over me and feel badly when I knew beyond a shadow of a doubt that there was nothing he could do. This was just about putting in time until the verdict. It would be best to be as cheerful as possible, I determined, so as not to unnecessarily burden those around me.

This was a tactic I had learned from my mom, surely a mentor when it came to 'just getting through everything with a smile.' Thing was about Mom, though . . . she was always genuinely smiling through the adversity, no matter how intense . . . a true expression of longsuffering and exceeding grace.

She wasn't just putting it on.

Thank God for that woman, for I could sense that some of that courage was mysteriously managing to rub off on me now. Lord knew I needed all that I could muster.

As the music began to play, Greg looked at me.

"Dance?" said his eyes, though he already knew the answer.

I began to move away from the table while Greg came around to slide my chair out from under me. We slipped our hands into one another's, moving as if in a dream to the tiny dance floor.

There was no one else sharing the space with us, something that neither concerned nor pleased us. We were simply at one with the music and the comfort of our arms around each other. There was a 'knowing' about ourselves that we shared a solace so special I have never yet been able to find the words to describe it.

This hamlet of safety was better than anything the doctor might order. Here, one might believe that nothing could touch us. Together, we were sheltered from all unpleasantness, belonging simply to each other and to the night, the comfortableness was beyond all reason, melting away every nuance of fear, nurturing my soul.

"In all of my future," I thought, "there will never be a need for medication to tranquilize. I will simply go dining and dancing with Greg."

As usual, we remained on the floor for the entire set. We did not separate between songs, just happy to be together ... nothing to say, no points to make, no egos to stroke ... ribbons of rest wrapping our bodies together, our breathing clearly simultaneous.

The thought crossed my mind that in order for my life to end, Greg would have to stop breathing too, and since this was unlikely, the obvious result added to my consolation.

I was glad I had decided not to tell Greg, at least not before there was actually something to tell. In the course of the day, I had reduced the whole catastrophe to nothing more than a type of annual check-up – a little more thorough this year, perhaps, but nevertheless, nothing to go falling overboard about.

A faint smile of contentment presented itself for the first time since the dramatic discovery, and as the set finished, Greg joined me in that moment as if to say, "It's all just perfect, nothing to worry about."

*****

The nervous bustle about the waiting room was bringing me closer to the horrific reality that I must surely be facing imminent danger. I watched as worried faces left the room to venture down the lonely corridor marked "radiation."

I label that corridor 'lonely' because no one ever seems to walk there with you, as if there was some kind of unwritten law about it. Your shoes clack deafeningly on the uncontaminated tiles while the frigid, eerie and misty blue light of the fluorescents glares high above you.

A collection of ghostlike creatures accompany you, memories of the past racing in and out of focus, and dreams of the future, perhaps now unlikely, your only companions. You're off to see the wizard, only the wizard's not so wonderful, and this surely isn't Oz.

*****

I was naked from the waist up, covered by one of those notorious hospital gowns, only the open side was at the front this time. Disconcerting.

Standing in a room full of stainless steel machines, each as big as the room itself, I awaited my next instruction with considerable trepidation.

Considering this was 1966 and I was scarcely 22, a full acknowledgement must be given that such a combination of expertise, or lack thereof, was well below what was needed to obtain that which was best for my health. I knew nothing of the technologies, the dangers, the threats or the risks involved in what I was about to do. Actually, I'm not so sure that anyone else knew either. We were all just doing our best.

It was not for at least another ten years that concerns were raised over the possible dangers arising from radiation thus received, which concerns inevitably changed dramatically this methodology.

What I was about to experience was pretty much the best that modern science had available at the time. How bad could it be? Besides, one didn't seem to have much choice; best to just go with it.

Indicative of my trusting nature, like a lamb to slaughter, I never wavered; I simply went through the motions as directed, all the while maintaining a fervent hope that somewhere from 'above' my life was being handled.

*****

A door banged somewhere behind me and a black woman entered the room.

"Ah, nah, lessee," she said in a heavy Jamaican accent, "what is it wur hoving to do today?"

She smiled agreeably.

She took the form from my hand, which had been hanging from my fingertips for the past twenty minutes.

"Ah, yase, left braste."

"Come, come wit' me," she coaxed me toward the back of the room.

Here was the biggest machine yet – my eyes begged to devour its details, memorizing its probes and examining its desires on my life – for this was to be my partner in decisions affecting my future.

"Tak' a sate here honny," she pointed at a stainless steel stool.

"Face thot winda there now."

I turned to my left slightly, which placed me directly alongside a very long stainless steel table. While sitting, the top of the table met me just above my waist.

As the technician prepared her plates for x-ray, I heard the words come from somewhere within the room.

"Poot your left braste on the table … awl be rawt there."

It should come as no surprise to anyone when I say that I was not exactly sure how one was to go about this, but I stumbled away at it anyway. Scrunching my body up close to the table, which was surely well below freezing, it took me a moment to acclimatize. I lifted my breast upon the countertop, where it lay there like a dead fish.

From this perspective, I noted, the breast takes on a whole new meaning. For the first time since acquiring womanhood, this now vulnerable breast suddenly seemed to be something quite detached from me, a 'thing,' totally separate and apart from who I was as a person.

Seems most unusual to consider that one's appendages are nothing more than 'things' that can be lobbed off as life directs. The moment cautioned me to understand what it might mean to me to sever my connection with my bosom as a whole. This I contemplated in an effort to prepare myself to face, without fear, any possible unsavoury outcome.

I was completely aware that that which was keeping me alive was somewhere deep within me and that the parts that carried me about this planet were purely temporal.

The concept steadied me.

The technician moved herself into place. She reached up and pulled a giant steel box down towards the table where my breast continued to wait.

The box, also stainless steel, was being brought down tighter and tighter still, pinching the breast mercilessly.

"Ouch!" I couldn't help myself.

"Should it really be that tight?" I asked.

"So sorry, honny, ahm afraid so."

As I waited in this disagreeable position, there were several more adjustments.

Eventually, the technician left the room, telling me as she went that I must remain perfectly still.

*****

I am convinced there are events that weave themselves so deeply into your subconscious that your every waking moment is forever inextricably bound to their memory. These were sure to become so.

"Peggy. Great news! No hot spots!"
Gratitude! Relief! Inordinate Joy!

****

Although life had not provided a way for Greg and I to marry, the spiritual bond developed between us was never denied, continuing to remain for years to come.

*****

1974.
October.
My oldest son, David, was just past two and my second, Michael, was nearing 7 months.

A troublesome lump in the left breast, which I noticed about two months after delivery, seemed to be growing significantly each month. By now, it was definitely the size of a small egg.

It was obviously not related to blocked milk glands, typical of nursing mothers. The little time it had taken to grow this much was not a good sign.

My history of cysts, always with benign results, made it easy to make an appointment the following week to check it out. It had always made sense to deal with this type of threat promptly, for I have never been into needless worry.

This time was no different.

It seemed slightly unorthodox to be seeing a woman doctor, but she was the only one on call at the clinic. Her extraordinary composure, however, quickly put me at ease.

We spoke briefly of my history while she checked my pulse and lungs. Not two minutes passed from the time she first felt the lump before she returned her instruments deep into her pockets. Without blinking an eye, she matter-of-factly advised me that I would be referred to a surgeon whom she hoped would squeeze me in tomorrow.

"Tomorrow?" I asked, shocked at the obvious increase in the pace of events.

"Yes, I don't want to waste a moment having a specialist look at this. I'm recommending an immediate biopsy; the surgeon may disagree, but we'll leave that decision to him."

Her manner was undoubtedly direct. There was nothing for me to say, for I sensed she would hear none of it.

"I'll call you in the morning to confirm an afternoon appointment. I suggest you eat nothing after midnight tonight, in order to facilitate any tests he may wish to take."

"A biopsy?" I spoke the words to her with disbelief.

"But I have had dozens of these things before and not once did it ever come to this. What's so different about this time? "

I wanted to know and yet didn't.

She began to explain something about how the form within my breast did not appear to be interlocking with the body's tissues, and that was apparently the best news.

Nonetheless, she felt that the situation was worth looking at more closely. Just to be sure.

Other details were forthcoming, but I was no longer listening. My head began to spin. This was not what I had expected to hear.

I moved rhythmically in and out of various states of casual anxiety. The events of the past would enable me to grab hold of myself just before falling into dire alarm as I recalled how this same sense of fear had once before overtaken me, but in its time had been ultimately dismissed.

"I have to hold on to that possibility."

I was talking to myself again.

*****

From the first time I met with the surgeon, my life slipped from my control. I moved along a conveyor belt of endless directives, as if comatose.

In a way, I had a sense that I was outside of myself, watching from some no-man's land the procedures that were intent on turning my body, mind and soul upside down and inside out.

Over the years, I have worked with many sufferers of child abuse, from the mildest cases to those involving satanic rituals. What consistently happens in such cases is that children, in order to protect themselves, by some unconscious or supernatural act, become separated, quite literally, from their soul, keeping them temporarily removed from the pain.

In most cases, the pain must eventually be realized (confessed) and unfortunately experienced. This is tragic indeed, and you would have to agree also if you could ever witness this type of 'deliverance.'

Sitting with a dear friend, whose beauty and wit was undeniable, I watched as the nightmare of her formerly forgotten abuse began to unravel in her mind. This exquisite lady disappeared before my very eyes as she became transformed into a frightened, whimpering five-year-old. This having been accomplished, she ran to the corner of the bathroom and, falling into a tiny heap behind the toilet, murmured, "Don't hurt me, please don't hurt me."

I would describe such separation in the same way in which the body falls into a coma in order to protect itself. One does not consciously instruct the body to make the necessary adjustments; it simply knows that it must, proceeding accordingly.

Keys to unlocking the doors to the soul continue to surface and in many ways we are only just beginning to understand what freedoms await us. It is not coincidence that the Lord said you shall "know the truth and the truth shall make you free."[92]

Separation, not unlike the one described above, had managed to take me over. Not surprisingly, I was behaving rather well – not unlike a heavily medicated mental patient – shuffling along as instructed, having lost the capability to question or make any of my own decisions. Now that I had become completely out of touch with my physical reality, I was slipping further and further into the quiet realm of terror.

*****

Lying in a hospital bed less than two weeks from the first visit to the medical clinic, disconnected advice from family and friends fermented in my brain. Orderlies were fussing over me erratically as night-time began to fall, the day having been filled with many additional blood tests, x-rays and medications.

Surgery would take place the following morning.

My last visitor presented me with papers to sign, giving the right to the medical staff to perform any surgery they considered necessary, including the removal of my breast or breasts and any other parts of my body that may have become violated by 'the enemy.'

I deliberated only momentarily as I recalled clearly the doctor in charge having advised me that "considering the size, shape and positioning of the tumour [it was now being called a tumour] we are 99% sure that it is not cancer."

That left only a 1% chance that it WAS. The odds were definitely resting in my favour. With so little going against me, how could I lose?

*****

I signed the papers without another thought.

My mother had arrived to help care for the children, but particularly for moral support. One of her comfort stories was about a mutual friend of ours from back home who had undergone a biopsy the previous year, the end result being benign.

When Mom told her I was about to endure the same, Carol wanted me to know what she had been told and how it helped her.

"The first thing to do when you awake from surgery is look at the clock. If you've been under less than an hour, you're in good shape. If it's several hours, that's a sure sign of trouble. Next, place your hand over your chest to determine if your breasts are intact. On discovering that you're still in one piece, you're home free!"

These were encouraging thoughts, and from all that I had been told, I shouldn't expect anything less.

*****

I was glad for the sedative. I didn't like to be awake these days, though I'd had little choice with two small children and a home and husband to manage.

Slumber was welcome indeed, and I began to slip away easily in the hopes of escaping possibilities too bitter to bear. As I fell off the cliff, the sensation that always comes to me from sleeping pills, the oddest picture came clearly to my mind.

I saw a very small clump of cells. They did not appear to be dormant; no, they had life, but it was life that rang strangely untrue. The cells seemed to be moving . . . growing . . . actually doubling . . . not all that fast, but fast enough that I was able to discern their so doing.

At the moment I finally disintegrated into sleep, I recognized an ever-so-slight sense of foreboding.

*****

There is possible an alliance of body, mind and soul. When such a merger takes place, you may 'know' everything about your own body, allowing you to become so in touch with all of its domain that you are able to travel freely to each of its counterparts.

The thoughts I experienced prior to my surgery had not come from 'fearing' what might be discovered while under the knife – I had already decided my 1% chance to be a good one. What I know took place within me was like a message on the internet: one part of my being simply and clearly informing another of what might otherwise be hidden details.

*****

They wheeled me into surgery at ten in the morning.

And when I awoke, the clock said three.

"Five hours."

The weight of this fact began to descend.

"Oh no," I thought frantically, "it can't be, it just can't be."

For some time, I lay as if frozen. I was quite groggy, and yet mindful of the concept that sooner or later, I must apprise myself of the outcome.

I tried to look upon my chest, but I was unable to lift my head off the table. My mind was working but my body was not yet up to speed. I could sense there was extensive bandaging wound solidly and tightly around the entire chest area, making it difficult to take a very deep breath.

"Well, I might just as well get this over with," I thought bravely.

My right hand began to move slowly, first across my abdomen and then up ever so slightly across my chest to where my left breast would be normally found.

The area seemed to be completely flat, but I was not yet shaken. It was possible that the bust was flattened by the containment.

This seemed to be a reasonable consideration.

Moving my hand now to my right breast, the flattened theory was shattered completely.

Was it true? Was it really true?

I looked around drowsily. There was no one near, no one to ask, no one to share the grief, the pain, the fear.

Rendered mute, sounds that I would have wanted to make did not surface.

I felt empty and cold.

I closed my eyes, hoping against hope that time would forever stand still. I fell asleep again. The next time I woke, I was in a regular hospital room. There were several people there, apparently waiting upon me to join them in conversation.

*****

"And so, how are you?" The doctor asked this in such a way as if there could be no reason for me to be anything other than fine.

"Okay, I guess." I was hoping to avoid discussing the subject on everyone's heart.

"Well, let me get straight to the point."

No bedside manner here.

I was barely functioning, still mildly sedated. As a result, the surgeon's thick German inflection prompted me to think I was somehow the star in some ridiculous 'B' movie.

His next words, however, alerted me to the necessity of getting my wits about me.

"You have two beautiful children, yes?"

The doctor's voice was coming in clearer now.

"Boys, yes?"

Having considerable sales experience, I was somewhat concerned at his insistence on prompting me to agree with him on matters so obvious. He was headed somewhere with this line of questioning and I was pretty sure I wasn't going to like it.

"My recommendation is that you begin radiation therapy next week, which will continue daily for five weeks . . . weekends off, of course."

He strained at a chuckle over this, but there was no laughter in the room.

Without skipping a beat, he continued. "Our major concern is hormonal imbalance. Your recent childbearing makes it difficult for us to guarantee that these hormones are not completely out of control. You may be in worse danger in the coming months. Consequently, during the last week of radiation, you'll be sterilized."

I did not respond to the sound of his voice, for his words had quite probably sentenced me to death. Prisoners scheduled to die rarely protest their fate, having already lost hope.

"The good news is," he went on, now more cheerfully, "you are 'otherwise' healthy. You have a family worth saving and worth living for; you need to take every step necessary to maintain that."

What 'other . . . wise' was there? Didn't cancer eliminate how good everything else might be?

He tapped my foot gingerly, smiled magnanimously and strode mercilessly out of sight.

Silence stormed the room.

What could anyone say?

The tears held in check thundered in our souls.

"I must be brave," I thought, "not just for my own sake, but for them . . . they seem worse off than me!"

A second glance about the room confirmed this.

I have no recollection of who spoke first that day, nor what was said. I do know that we got through it, though at the time I knew not how.

The effect of the drugs was beginning to wear off; pain was returning, increasing. More medication was hopefully on the way.

*****

There was no way of knowing exactly how much of what the doctor had said had actually sunk in.

What I understood beyond a shadow of a doubt was that this was the same doctor who had said the words '99% unlikely.' Accordingly, these latest words were less than comforting.

Awaking late the next morning, I was alone in my room. Flashbacks were occurring . . . there was something about having no more children . . . I had often said I wanted seven . . . well, I at least had wanted more than two.

*****

While dozing on and off throughout the day, I had come to sense that there was someone holding my left hand at the side of the bed. For a time I had no interest in who it might be.

Eventually, I turned to notice my mother sitting there, a broken heart mirrored in her face. Keeping my hand in hers, she stroked my fingers gently, kindly, mindlessly examining every bone and ligament, like you do when you first take your newborn into your arms.

I heard her whisper, as if to herself.

"You have always had the most beautiful hands."

A single tear slid over her cheek.

*****

Struggling out of bed the second day wasn't easy, but the orderlies were insistent: "Get moving quickly to prevent clotting." Very consoling.

I was no sooner out the door when I happened upon a woman about fifteen years my senior. It was apparent from the way in which she was nurturing her arm that she was in about the same shape as me.

"Hi," I smiled brightly at her, sensing she was very upset.

She all but growled at me, although I knew not to take it personally, for it could be nothing I had done.

"This your second day too?" I asked.

"Third."

"How're things coming along?" I felt the need to press her to open up.

"I just wanna die, if you must know."

"Oh, I'm sorry." I wasn't sure where we were going with this.

"How long have *you* got?" Her tone was very angry.

The question shook me quite hard . . . I hadn't yet begun to think about 'time left' . . . wasn't even sure if there was a need to.

"Well . . . I don't know . . . they haven't told me. But even if they had, I don't think I'd want to be depressed through whatever remaining days I *did* have." I couldn't believe I was saying this. It was like I was admonishing this poor defenceless woman, whom I didn't even know, while at the same time advising myself.

She looked somehow straight through me. She didn't speak.

I was trying to get words out of my mouth to apologize, but nothing was coming.

Several minutes passed somewhat awkwardly.

Finally, the woman spoke.

"You know, you're right! What am I doing? Maybe I have two months and maybe I don't . . . they could be wrong!?"

She was asking me and telling me both in the same breath. She was very excited by the possibility.

"Thank you . . . thank you so much. I'll talk to you later . . . I'm going to call my husband."

Without saying another word, she quickly disappeared into the room next door, leaving me totally baffled.

Years later, I would come to discover that incidents such as these, which had not been unusual in my past, were mysteriously significant in affecting change in people's lives.

*****

Supper had come and gone and I was getting ready for the evening guest list. There would be Mom, of course, my husband, my mother-in-law and several friends. I was actually feeling quite chipper by now, the fourth day after what could have been the beginning of the end of my life.

Fran, the lady next door, with whom I was fast becoming friends, suddenly popped her head around the curtain, presently in place for evening 'meds.'

"Hi, you!" she piped in happily.

"Wanted to catch you before your gang arrived. I'm going home tomorrow . . . I guess you knew." She paused for a moment, appearing to miss me already. "Will you come and see me after you get out of here?"

"Of course," I answered sincerely. "Let's keep in touch."

With a smile of gratitude, she left the room. Moments later, she was back. I could tell she wanted to add something important to the conversation.

"I really want to thank you . . ." she spoke almost sheepishly.

"For what?" I said, somewhat surprised.

"You gave me back my life," she said, as if I should have known this for a fact.

"I ... I don't know what to say."

"Just say 'You're welcome,'" she said winsomely, as if that was all there was to it.

Then she lightly slipped out of the room.

*****

On my release from the hospital, a mere five days after surgery, the totally unexpected happened. A complete collapse occurred.

I had no sooner walked through the door, glad to be away from the antiseptic atmosphere, when I began to shake, although slightly at first. As night approached, things became diabolically worse.

The quaking was feverish, violent.

It wasn't long before I knew beyond a shadow of a doubt that this was a special kind of fear, nestled not in the mind. It was as though the information that had been pouring into my brain over the past few days had somehow finally filtered down into the body and now it was the body's turn to react. I knew it was out of control; I instinctively understood that every fibre within me was involved in this. I had a sense that this could very well be what might be called a 'nervous breakdown.'

I was not familiar with the kind of behaviour that distinguishes a true nervous breakdown from some other types of mental or emotional anguish. I did know, however, there are any number of ways one can 'fall apart.'

In this case, I can only describe what was happening as a 'snapping' of nerves – every precious, normally functioning-happily-away nerve in my body.

Quite literally, my nerves were gone. There was no reaching them; they had fallen under some 'thing' or some 'one' else's command, leaving me a virtual basket-case of bodily jitters, teeth chattering as if exposed to a sudden howling arctic wind in the dead of winter.

My body shook incessantly, almost convulsively.

Hours upon hours passed in this way. Finally, I could take it no more. Asking my husband to drive me to the hospital, he bundled me up in coats and blankets in the middle of the night.

"I need some help to beat this," I confessed. "Just let me get a shot of something to stop the shivering. It's wearing me out; I'm exhausted and yet the tremors continue." I was unable to sleep.

Registering at the hospital was like a bad joke.

"What seems to be the problem?" came the curt question as if they were annoyed to have me back so soon.

My husband answered this time. "She just can't stop shaking. We were wondering if perhaps she could have some kind of sedative … something to relax her … maybe even spend the night."

"Well now, let's see. Checking you in's a bit of a problem. Gynecologically, you're ok … surgically, you're fine too … so, the only place I could put you would be, say, on the fifth floor …"

"Isn't that the mental ward?" I was astounded that this might be my only option.

"Yes."

Unable to speak it, an uneasy thought plagued me. "How on earth would I be able to relax and get some sleep *there*, with a bunch of 'loonies' walking around all night?"

I wasn't making this up.

I had a friend who worked on the fifth. I knew full well that there were more than just 'some' situations where the inmates ambled about, without restriction. There had been stories of patients waking up, on floors other than the fifth, only to find a total stranger standing over them, just looking at them.

No, this was definitely not going to work for me.

Finally reaching my doctor by phone, the intake nurse informed me that I would be given a shot and sent home with some heavy-duty tranquilizers.

"Perhaps we should book you an appointment with the resident psychiatrist." She was waiting for me to confirm.

I took a moment to think about this, and I sensed that it probably wouldn't hurt to actually talk to someone – preferably a stranger – to speak the words "I've lost a breast and I'm going to be sterilized . . . I may even die . . . possibly soon."

It would be important to share this with someone who would not be destroyed at the thought of it, someone far enough removed that it mattered not to them what I had to endure and how it might affect me and, ultimately, them.

"Yes," I said expectantly, "that would be fine."

"How about tomorrow at one? Might as well get right to it." She smiled reassuringly.

"I'll be there."

*****

The psych room was probably less than six feet by six. There was nothing more in the room than two chairs embracing one small desk. No resident couch.

"You wouldn't want to be claustrophobic," I thought.

"How are we doing today?" asked the kindly man behind the grey beard and bushy eyebrows. A veritable Santa Claus.

Wanting to cut right to the chase, I answered immediately. "Actually, I think I must have had either the start, or hopefully, the finish, of a nervous breakdown last night."

"Well, that's a mouthful!" He just smiled.

Having little difficulty communicating, I jumped right into the process, figuring I might as well pack into an hour as much as possible, thereby getting through to the problem resource-fully. I knew I was there to talk and I didn't disappoint.

At the end of the hour, the doctor said quite interestingly that he had been very 'delighted' to have met me and that perhaps we could do it again sometime … as if we were merely renewing an old acquaintance. It occurred to me that he had actually enjoyed the meeting.

"You've had quite a fascinating life," he said. "Come again, if you like."

"Should we make it later this week?" I asked curiously. He gave no indication that the situation was urgent, and yet I wanted to 'complete' as quickly as possible.

"Whatever you think," was his response.

"This Thursday?" I asked, pressing the issue.

The doctor seemed whimsical, as if he was wondering what I needed to come back for anyway.

"Oh well," I thought, "probably just the way they do things. A casual attitude probably keeps us from actually 'suspecting' how bad off we are."

We met once again.

And once again, the doctor was 'delighted.' At the end of the session, he took my hand warmly and said with deep sincerity, "Perhaps I can come to *you* to talk sometime when I get low. I think you'd make an excellent counsellor. If everyone was as well-adjusted as you," his assessment continued, "we wouldn't have the problems in our world that we do. I must say, you are the *least* disturbed person I have ever had the pleasure of meeting. It has given me cause for great hope."

"You mean … I don't have to come back?" I was slightly stunned, and I'm sure that it showed.

"Not at all, unless of course, you feel you must … or would like to. Why don't we make it a coffee sometime?…no need to unnecessarily burden the appointment book when there are so many others who desperately need to be here."

I took this as some kind of compliment, although I was not quite sure how I'd earned it. I wondered, in spite of his obvious generosity, if being the least disturbed of his disturbed patients was anything to write home about. He did otherwise encourage me, however, through nothing more than his genuine friendship.

I had to admit, I was feeling fine … and the shakes had not returned after that first night. Granted, I was taking tranquilizers every other day, but even they were well on their way to becoming redundant.

I determined I must be out of the woods.

One more hurdle jumped.

*****

Radiation began as scheduled.

First stop, outline the areas requiring treatment.

This did not sound threatening, and so, still buoyed by my 'psychiatrist's' commendation, I was feeling quite 'up' today. The procedure itself, however, brought my 'up' swiftly 'down.' The instructions entailed lying stark naked, on my back, on one of those steel slabs I'm sure you've all seen in movies covering stories not unlike mine.

There were two robed persons inspecting me – one man, one woman – on either side of the examining table. They continued to press and probe the areas most recently obliterated. These were still exceedingly fragile and a certain vulnerability began to return. I was at their mercy. There was none to be found.

I caught glimpses of their faces as they went about their investigation. My body didn't appear to them to be anything more than one of those corpses they'd practiced on during med school. I guessed that this was proper, for it wouldn't be wise to get 'personal' with the one lying there, especially being naked and all.

"I am going to be making some marks on your body; the dye in this pen will allow the design to remain beyond the time required to complete your treatments. This is necessary for accuracy when lining up the machine with the affected areas."

I didn't speak as it didn't appear to be expected that I do so.

This protocol continued for about thirty minutes. I was freezing . . . and still naked. Was I becoming used to the humiliation of my exposure? I thought not.

Now they were placing lead blocks over my lungs and heart to protect them from . . . 'frying,' which would instantly end my life. Nothing casual about this day!

Several instructions were given me about the importance of making absolutely no moves whatsoever, due to the fact that these very vital organs might be jeopardized beyond repair should I sneeze or cough or in any way rock them loose from their positions. On this note, my heart picked up speed.

There was danger awaiting me here.

"So," the man spoke abruptly now, "do you have any questions?"

I couldn't think fast enough. Again, no answer.

"Fine then, we will be leaving the room shortly. First, we're going to position this machine about an inch from your body," He now brought down from above me a huge piece of equipment that literally enclosed me, like a metal coffin.

"That looks good, Frank," said the woman, who appeared to be the one in charge.

The two encircled me, checking every inch of the body in question...were the blocks okay, were the markings positioned correctly...was the machine adjusted to meet the markings... searching, searching.

Casually shrugging their shoulders as if they'd done pretty much all they could do, they joined one another at the foot of the table, preparing to leave me behind.

"We'll see you shortly."

Suddenly, they were gone.

Stifling isolation! Clocks ticking somewhere in time!

These were fast becoming the longest few minutes of my life.

Humbled beyond recognition, every control annihilated. I was alone and dismantled.

Slowly, painfully slowly, sorrowfully wet tears were working their way to the surface. For now, a solitary drop was sliding, deliberately, out and over the side of my face. I imagined myself wrapping my arms about me, tenderly holding me, like you might a little girl orphaned through some catastrophic event.

At that moment, I was feeling so sorry for every one of us who has ever endured such tragedy, I could barely endure the pain of it. I was overwhelmed by the incredible compassion consuming me. It was as though I had become in touch with every unspeakable horror from every corner of the globe that strips us unmercifully of our dignity.

What tragedy humankind seems forced to suffer . . . the loneliness, the pain, the terror.

Surely the Lord's healing practices were nothing like these! This could NOT be HIS way! I do not recall His ever removing body parts in order to 'heal.' This was surely nothing more than man's way: hopelessly inadequate!

What was I doing here? Why couldn't I go home? Tears continued to fall, sliding into and inconveniently tickling each ear.

"Don't move." I reminded myself.

Perhaps an eternity passed before anyone returned to my side. There were no comments made to me as each of the lead blocks were carefully removed. Finally handing me a gown, the woman told me I was all through for the day.

Slinking to the change room, I felt that I had somehow been stripped of everything I ever was or even thought I might be.

As predicted so aptly by the surgeon, this procedure continued daily, with the exception of weekends, for five long weeks.

For a time there seemed to be no reaction to the treatments, although I was continuing to lose weight. I was drifting ominously close to a hundred pounds my third week into the program. Considering my height to be five feet, six-and-a-half inches, this was already thirty pounds below what would be considered a normal weight, which I had not been since before my last pregnancy.

Although I had gained less than fifteen pounds while carrying David, I had soared to 185 pounds with Michael. By the time of the operation, (seven months after his birth) I had probably not yet reached one-fifty. With the onset of the illness, the pounds had come off quickly…too quickly.

One afternoon, Mother took me to the mall, thinking an outing would do me good. There had been an endless array of hospital appointments, treatments and assessments in addition to the never-ending 'thinking' revolving around all of it.

My lack of strength shocked me; I wasn't able to walk more than fifty feet without needing to rest. At home, this factor had not been so readily apparent.

We stopped soon at a pleasant restaurant for lunch. I had only just swallowed my first bite when suddenly, and without warning, the food seemed to become lodged, it seemed, somewhere in my esophagus. There was a tremendous pressure coming up from my abdomen that refused the food's further passage and there was no way for the food to come back up.

I stood up, my eyes registering panic, although somehow (do we ever know how?) I had the good sense to remain calm everywhere in my body. I began to walk away from the table but I didn't know where I was going. It was as if by moving away from where the threat had originated I would leave it behind, something we all do in so many ways.

The agency of pacing was keeping me focused; there was an obvious requirement to use every ounce of my strength to hold onto my life – life without breath. I had no thoughts, my mind was clear ... calm ... though I still had no idea what was happening.

Mother immediately jumped up, moving close beside me.

"What can I do?" she asked. Her concern was apparent, and yet, she met me in the eye of the storm and we walked steadfastly through the terrible moments together.

Pain seized my chest, the food still refusing to move.

I made no attempts to dislodge it. My inability to breathe could not continue this way for much longer without grave consequences. We both knew this.

Mother and I held firm. It was as if we were waiting, not knowing for what. I think somewhere deep within us we were resigned to nothing more than prayer.

Slowly and with noticeable precision, the pain was easing. I could sense a passageway beginning to open, if only slightly. Peace flooded my body and the food began to slowly move to its original destination.

When the threat was over, I as much as gasped my first words. "What was THAT?" I looked at Mom in disbelief, anticipating some kind of answer. She didn't respond. She, too, was dumbfounded.

I tried to explain the content of the experience.

"It was as if I knew I was completely helpless . . . the situation hopeless . . . and that there was absolutely nothing for me to do . . . except rely on God."

"There was this feeling, like there was a vice grip around the food keeping it from going down or up . . . it was held firmly . . . there was no budging it. It was frightening."

"Well, thank God, it's over," said Mom, offering by her kindness a welcome sympathy.

On that day, we had no idea that this was to become a regular occurrence, one that continually placed me at the edge of death, time and time again. This incident only needed to happen twice more before I made an appointment to discuss the problem at the clinic.

"It's possible that you are having a side effect from the radiation." The male attendant was morbidly disinterested in the prospect that I might have dropped dead as a result of the experience.

"Side affect?" I asked, amazed at the thought.

"Nobody told me about side affects. What exactly do you mean? Is there anything else I should be expecting that I haven't been told?"

"Well," the female alternate added cautiously, "we cannot really know for sure. Everyone is different. You might become sick to your stomach; some experience swelling of the limbs, most notably the arm associated with the surgery; or perhaps the skin might become burned in varying degrees."

These prospects were not soothing.

"Well, what about my not being able to swallow? Is this a common thing?"

"Please understand" ... she was closing up on me now ... almost patronizing ... "you are receiving radiation in the area of your esophagus and stomach. It's only natural that their functioning would be altered in some way."

"Okay," I added carefully, "then perhaps you can tell me: How long will these problems occur? Is this a temporary thing? Is it going to get worse? Help me out here, I just want to know."

"Again ... I must repeat ... there is really no way of knowing what your particular problems are going to be."

"So, it's just a guessing game on your part and a pay-as-you-go situation on mine ... is that it?"

"I'm sorry." She shook her head ever-so-slightly from side to side, indicating to me beyond any shadow of a doubt that they didn't know what to tell me.

I wondered to myself, "Does *anybody* know *anything?*"

*****

About the third week into the series, I began to experience pain. Mostly in the chest area. It felt like my lungs were on fire. My body was screaming at me to 'stop the insanity,' but that was impossible as there were still two more weeks to go with the last week to be the heaviest doses yet.

The swallowing dilemma was becoming more frequent now and I began to resist taking in food and even water, the resulting experience having become too terrible to bear.

More weight loss.

There was now a handful of drugs to be taken at a time. I was never a great pill taker even in the days when swallowing was a normal procedure. It was now a gruelling scene; often the pills would lodge halfway down. I became good at waiting . . . one thousand and one . . . one thousand and two . . . one thousand and three . . . trusting that I might stop counting eventually and the pills would make their way to their final destination without further adieu.

During this stage of the treatments, it became important to be removed from the area frequented by the children since I was now too weak and too tired to respond to them. Our home was a bungalow with a finished basement and so I took up official residence underground. The family room area became the bedroom, which was not at all unpleasant, although to this day I would be unable to describe the room to you.

Such positioning may have added unnecessarily to my further loss of health, for I was able to hear every sound the children made: laughter, running, falling, crying. I was unable to reply to their needs and yet I most desperately wanted to . . . needed to.

The fifth week. Sterilization.

New markings. Longer stays under the focus of the beacon. Increasing pain . . . reduced strength . . .

*****

"Look at the bright side." I was offering advice to another 'one of us' while waiting at the clinic for yet another assessment.

"If we'd lost an arm or a leg, everyone would know, making it all that much more of a continuous topic of conversation. We're the lucky ones. With a prosthesis, we can just put our clothes on and no one is the wiser. Unless you offer up the information, who would ever know?"

Apparently, and I frankly remember little of this, several nurses came to visit me at home after my stay in the hospital because they had been so encouraged by many of these 'recommendations.' They admitted that after years at the clinic, they appreciated such optimism over lives inundated with devastation. They had learned a new way to view what might otherwise appear hopeless.

Having always been unwilling to waste time on fruitless matters, destructive self-pity was way down on my list of priorities. I take no credit for this aspect of my character and I ask you not to mistake my speaking of it as a symbol of self-esteem. I include this as part of my story only because it so prominently figures in 'walking with the Lord.'

To Him goes all the credit, the honour, the glory; for without Him, I would have remained severely disadvantaged. It was this same guidance and protection that kept me from feeling the need to incur secondary surgery in order to secure an implant.

Considering the numbers of criminal complications I have witnessed as a result of such choices, over which I personally agonize, again I can only thank God that I did not feel the need to 'improve' the way my body 'looked.' I was able to accept the situation as part of the hand dealt. "Best to play with what you've got."

*****

During these fourth and fifth weeks, it became obvious that I was not doing well. I had now been told that it was possible I might have less than six months, and it was starting to look like this might very well be the case.

I was throwing up continuously, so often that I began to lie on the floor in the bathroom, often resting my head on a pillow that I placed on top of the closed toilet seat. I was too weak to keep returning to my bed, only to find the need to return to the 'bowl.' I didn't like to have a barf bucket beside the bed because then the bed itself became a place of unpleasantness.

The 'wretching' was increasing day by day and the pain was indescribable. The assistants at the clinic were somewhat encouraging; they assured me that the worse I felt the more effective the treatment.

Reality continued to spin in and out of focus. The various medications did not seem to be compatible. There were pain killers combined with anti-depressants, and then there were uppers for an added 'boost.'

With this combination going against me, I was less utilitarian than when I first entered this maze.

About this time the Lord began to intervene. He miraculously gave me the insight to deal with the drug situation head on. One day, for no reason at all, I announced that I was going to go off all the drugs.

"How can you possibly do that, Suzanne? You can barely stand the pain as it is." Mom was visibly concerned.

"I know, Mom, but I want my head to be clear. I can't think in this condition, so I'm just going to risk it. I want to be able to 'feel' how bad it is; I want to 'know'; I need it to be 'real.'" These were my reasons to validate such seemingly drastic action.

Not being one to make frivolous requests, Mother knew beyond a doubt that my decision would be unshakable. Her concern was legitimate. For at least two weeks I had been unable to get through even four hours without p.k.'s (pain killers).

The next day, I stopped all medication, cold turkey.

The first twenty-four hours were hell on wheels.

Following this, I was practically unconscious from the delirium, which likely surfaced as the body's way of escaping the pain. Eventually there surfaced a clarity of mind that was beyond my wildest expectations.

My wits returning, the pain was something I understood . . . and it wasn't bigger than me, it was just there. I could hardly bear it, but at least it was authentic.

The concept was highly enlightening. How many people, I thought, have ever had the opportunity to discover this? What we normally do is grasp at any immediate remedy for a 'quick fix' for our dilemmas, thereby denying ourselves an essence of reality that can have revelatory consequences.

Can physical pain really be all that much worse than some of the emotional or psychological pains we have endured over time? The truth is, it's not. For me, all three were in play at once.

Two-and-a-half days passed in this way.

On the third day, the bottom dropped out. I was wretching every five to ten minutes, and although there was nothing at all to 'throw up,' I spent the entire day on the bathroom floor. I was writhing about in constant pain, reduced to nothing more than an animal. I had not eaten in almost a week, nor had I had anything to drink.

Late in the evening, Mother came to me; she'd had an epiphany of sorts.

"There's something in this house that's killing you," she said. "I don't know what it is, but if you stay here another week, you'll most surely die."

I trusted Mother's intuition, for she had been known, on several critical occasions in her own life, to have received revelations, without which, the course of several lives would have been drastically and unfavourably altered. "I'm going to have to get you home somehow," she said.

Home, to Mom, was some 3,000 miles away.

"Mom, I am so sick and so weak, I can barely get up off the floor. But if you can figure out a way to get me home, then do whatever you think you must."

Mother left the room to provide for the necessary flight arrangements.

I had a sense of something spectacular awaiting me, something eternal…immortal.

At precisely that moment of becoming so totally in touch with all there is, responding from the fetal position that had recently become the norm, I was inspired to reach out to God…

*****

"Lord, I can tell that I'm dying. I can't say that I understand, what with those two small children upstairs and all, but Lord, if that's what you want, then I'm okay with it."

*****

Falling into a deep, deep sleep, I did not awake until morning. Upon opening my eyes, I suspected something was different.

By morning, Mother had everything organized. Waking me early, she had me carried upstairs and out to the waiting car. Everything was packed; I did not see the children.

It occurred to me that there was unbelievably no sign of pain or discomfort of any kind. 'Everything' was somehow changed.

And then something even more amazing happened. From the moment we drove out the driveway, I never threw up again!

Dad was anxiously awaiting our arrival at the Toronto airport. As soon as he saw me, he took both my hands in his and said, "Suzanne, you do not have cancer. Whatever the doctors have told you, they've made a mistake; whatever they've done to you, you must put it behind you. Now, we're going out for dinner, you're going to eat a full meal and you're going to get well."

"Okay, Daddy . . . okay." I was saying this for him as much as me.

This having been said, life unfolded exactly as spoken. There was miraculously no further difficulty in my swallowing. It was wonderful to actually 'experience' a meal for the first time in months. I couldn't fathom how the day before I had been so desperately ill and today there was not even a trace of the tortures previously endured.

If it were not for the missing breast, it would have been possible to believe that the whole thing had been nothing more than a terrible nightmare.

The following day I ate three full meals, within two weeks I'd gained fourteen pounds and, at the end of the month, you would have never known that I'd ever been sick.

I was completely well! It was a miracle!

Upon my return to the clinic in Saskatoon, pens dropped and mouths fell open the moment they saw me.

"What happened to you?!?" they exclaimed.

"I guess it just wasn't my time to die," was all I could say.

They would surely never believe that I'd been **healed**!

I hardly believed it myself. Today, I would be far more capable of explaining how this had all come about, but at the time, I was unable to fully appreciate the enormity of the "gift."

*****

Never underestimate our glorious God!

*****

Let's look carefully at the way in which this 'healing' occurred, ...a 'healing' which took place more than thirty-four years ago. Add to this the fact that there is not alive today even one person with whom I had come in contact at the clinic, having the same problems and prognosis as myself. Not one of them lived past five years; most barely survived even two. Taking this into serious account, it seems reasonable to admit that my 'recovery' was nothing less than spectacular.

My 'healing' occurred without any 'formal' prayers spoken on my behalf, although it is highly likely that prayer was continuously on my mother's lips. There were no elders 'laying on hands,' for there had been no particularly Christian elements in my life, no healers, new age or otherwise, no meditation, no ritual, no health foods, no healing 'brews' ...

All that it took, with no instruction, no previous experience to relate to, was a simple discourse with Jesus, the Saviour!

There was no premeditation on my part to 'get what I wanted,' no motive, no personal want. I only wanted what God wanted, and with childlike faith, I presumed that He knew what was best.

For your Father knoweth what things ye have need of,
before ye ask him.[93]

I wasn't angry about my predicament, nor had I ever asked "why me?"

Never having heard personal prayers spoken, I knew not what to speak[94] ...I hadn't ask to be healed...no 'naming and claiming' . . . merely submitted to the Lord's will, in full agreement with His authority, His ultimate choice, even if that choice might cost me my life.

Without knowing the Scripture at all ... through nothing more than an act of surrender...I had given up my life, for His sake, and in return, he gave it back to me, just as His Word promises to do.

Recalling this experience may hopefully prove important during similar critical stages you may have to face in your life. It is unnecessary to fear that you must locate a 'healer' or someone who knows how to pray for you. You needn't run from coast to coast in search of some 'miraculous' cure, some great medic who can 'save' you. Your welfare needn't cost you money, or time or penance, for...

The One
The Only
The Great Physician
       is always available
             with just a word
                    a cry of the heart.

*****

For whosoever will save his life shall lose it: and whososever will lose his life for my sake shall find it.
                            ~Matthew 16:25

*****

The Path ❧

*And straightway, they forsook their nets
and followed him.*

~Mark 1:20

The call had come subtly at first.

Eventually, though I'd had no real comprehension of the process at all, I found that I had left everything behind.

As the world and all that I had held dear became more and more strangely dim, I felt increasingly in touch with a heightened awareness, a 'knowing' that the world and all that was in it was part of a finite plan, a destiny that would unfold despite a growing global desire for it to do otherwise.

There were a variety of stages, each containing its own meticulous history. A thorough analysis of each frame, in order for the specific dimensions to be fully understood, is undoubtedly required. By and by, through a collection of essays, I expect the highlights of the journey to have been completely disclosed.

In this way, an outline will be developed unveiling the incredible number of incidents which have continued to knit themselves, the one to the other, over the period of time that I have come to know as 'my walk.'

Having decidedly left behind links which bound me continually to the world, there had been nothing more than the sheer faith that I would be taken to those places that would forge out for me the life I had come to this earth to live.

189

I did not have to take a deep breath, or tighten my resolve; I didn't think about the 'faith' part, really.

It was just there…a 'gift.'

At the outset, I drifted through a collage of situations that appeared to make little or no sense to the untrained eye, but which I can see now on looking back, were each intrinsically a part of the colour and depth of the affianced result.

There was a six-month contract as a Management Consultant in Vancouver that set me among five partners, each vying for their own identity within the enterprise, some connected to more ego than others.

My instructions were to present an overview of what was 'wrong' and, having done so, make recommendations to make them 'right.' My experience had long ago made it possible for me to easily discern pitfalls, and so this was not difficult for me. It wasn't long before I discovered certain improprieties that had to be eliminated for the good of the company and their investors. Calling them on their 'stuff' was the easy part. Convincing them that the whole was only as good as its parts, and that the parts in their current condition wouldn't make the grade, would be a horse of a different colour.

For a time, they demonstrated an element of commitment – like a smoker giving up his smokes – and, as is often the case, only temporarily. In the same way as the smoker suddenly breaks his own promises to himself, they quickly returned to their old ways with an even greater fury.

Sadly, the addiction of ego is gigantic.

In the end, in spite of the warning they had hired me to give, they inevitably chose to return to their own vomit, the company thereby falling into ruin and disgrace sometime after my departure.

From this magnificent west coast location, a succession of adventures followed, taking me from shore to shore, covering much of the United States and Canada. Years before this, my life could be reviewed as a series of flutterings, like a butterfly skipping from one flower to the next, never staying in one place too long . . . job to job, city to city . . . enjoying the 'newness' of every situation. Travel was a welcome companion; it provided a feel of the land and the people who walked it.

This personality trait was likely the reason I'd always enjoyed contract work, problem solving, management and marketing consulting: get in, get the job done and get out, then on to the next. I cared about the people and wanted to see them do well at their chosen vocations.

During my third year of freelancing as a paralegal in Toronto, at the age of twenty-three, while serving eleven prestigious firms, I often worked until the wee small hours of the morning. This ridiculous timetable would continue for about six months. Then, having no employer to answer to, I would simply become 'unavailable' for a couple of months.

During any self-imposed hiatus, I rarely took trips to soak up the sun in some tropical paradise, although I had not been unknown to do so. What I most loved was visiting . . . old friends and associates, casual acquaintances and family. I would spend long hours with those who were struggling with some problem or relationship issue; I just liked to be there for them. It never occurred to me that I didn't know anyone else who hired themselves out as some kind of social worker. I was oblivious to the norm.

At the end of the year, you might find that I had actually worked through only half, maybe two-thirds of the calendar. While working, I necessarily outdid myself, thereby piling up the dollars required to carry me through a few months of non-production in the business community.

Things are quite different today, although I am surely still very much an anomaly to many. In those days at least, and even today sometimes, in spite of the position I currently hold in the community, I am frequently considered to be somewhat of a 'flake.' Having won the Saskatchewan Order of Merit in 2004 certainly encouraged many to change their minds on these various derogatory opinions. The point is, that in spite of these allegations and the inability for the average person to really 'get' me, I always simply continued on, quite oblivious, for the most part, of any disapproving remarks.

How could I have known that these were but 'practice runs' for a vocation yet to come?

*****

Meticulous job performance had long been important to me. This work ethic had come about through a variety of influences. One of those influences included long hours working for my dad at his grocery store and gas station over a period of six years, beginning at the age of twelve.

While at the store, I found that a simple task such as dusting shelves became a mental and personal challenge to perfectly remove every speck of dust, returning each of the canned goods to rows of faultless alignment.

Later, working in a highly stressed environment for an attorney of dedication and precision made it impossible for me to present him with any work that was less than perfect.

For these opportunities, I will remain forever grateful.

He that is faithful in that which is least is faithful in that which is much: and he that is unjust in the least is unjust also in much. If therefore ye have not been faithful in the

*unrighteous mammon, who will commit to your trust the
true riches?*[95]

Throughout these proceedings, I began to seriously drop
the 'things' of the world that I had gathered up over time,
selling them bit by bit at flea markets or to friends, as the need
arose to buy groceries or gas. Finally, after another brief stop in
Vancouver, I felt directed to head to San Rafael, California,
where this story picks up once again. The supply of money was
sufficient only to maintain daily food requirements and some
travel. Lodging, however, was often somewhat precarious.

As contrary as the following statement may at first appear,
'coming out of the world' meant an overabundance of
restaurant meals. Having no certain dwelling place year after
year, there was often nowhere to prepare a meal. Fortunately,
California weather lent itself readily to a cooler filled with a
variety of picnic-type lunches kept on hand in the trunk of my
ten-year-old Dodge. In this way, a roadside stop could be made
quite spontaneously. Complimenting the many picturesque
settings was a bright plaid tablecloth with matching placemats
and napkins.

On a moment's notice, a meal could become the most
delightful opportunity for a special outdoor occasion.
However, for the sheer sake of diversity, including the need to
associate with other members of the community as a whole,
restaurants became the only alternative to these pleasant visits
with nature.

In order to maintain some kind of variety, it had become
my habit to take note of restaurants we might pass by
throughout the day, with the thought to patronize them at
some future date. My ear was always ready to pick up a
comment about good home cooking or specialty pies. In

retrospect, I would have clearly done better to pay closer attention to establishments known particularly for salads.

My compiling of dining data eluded the dimension of becoming a fetish or anything even close to it. In truth, it was nothing more than a passing mental note; sometimes I would remember and sometimes I would not . . . a position of 'want' was not part of the equation.

This point is emphasized due to its specific relevance to the situation that would ultimately unfold.

*****

We first visited Novato, just 30 miles north of San Francisco, when a couple responded to my ad placed in the Pacific Sun for housesitting.

By the time I responded to the message left on my friend's answering machine, I was told that an author from Britain would be taking the house, but if there was any reason that he didn't, they would get back to me.

Sometimes, when housesitting possibilities arose, I would be inclined to drive by the property to see if it was worth considering further. I compared the name and number left on the machine with those in the telephone directory, hoping to find the address.

Lazy Summer Drive had a special ring to it, so that evening, we took a leisurely excursion to evaluate the house in question. We proceeded north from San Rafael up Highway 101 for less than ten minutes in order to reach Ignacio Boulevard, the exit that would take us west toward our destination.

The location was extremely convenient to the hospice work that was recently consuming the majority of my time – a precious 42-year-old 'girl' named Sonia, whose cancer was fast approaching terminal.

Making our way past a large number of army barracks, the roadways began to wind up and through the rolling hillside. We very quickly came upon a house of special appeal, nestled in a naturally wooded environment surrounding the Novato Golf and Country Club.

*****

Since housesitting days had begun, you couldn't possibly imagine the wide selection of houses that had surfaced from which to choose, from living in the 'wilds' of Mt. Tamalpais with a full sized teepee on a deck suspended high above a plunging valley below, to a house full of show bull terriers – seven, to be exact!

Needless to say, some we turned down.

With the exception of my favourite Sausalito abode, where I have regularly 'sat' for my now-good-friend Gail, most houses had been more of a challenge than a benefit. The challenges were met with enthusiasm and interest, enabling in the midst of these an advancement of maturity and a certain innate wisdom. Clearly, the situation with Gail had been a blessing from the start, with the Lord's fingerprints very noticeably all over it.

We were first introduced at the San Francisco Psychic Fair, an annual event displaying all the latest discoveries, supernatural and paranormal, self-improvement programs, self-styled gurus and personal indulgences connected with the secular and/or supernatural world.

Anyone having been there can tell you that there is no place on earth better equipped to update you on the current trends in mysticism, cults and the new age movement than in this eclectic environment. I sensed an enormous opportunity to acquaint myself with just exactly how 'conscious' the world had convinced itself it had become.

Although two days hence I would be without accommodation, this was of little concern to me, for I was becoming well-schooled in the teaching that "sufficient unto the day is the evil thereof."[96]

This principle having become one of the most valuable in my life, I had no difficulty refusing to concern myself regarding appropriate shelter, knowing that the Lord would somehow inevitably 'provide.'[97] I have learned to expect a constant rebuttal from many of my 'Christian' acquaintances for this belief. They often counter with "God helps them who help themselves," as if God Himself had, somewhere, somehow, pronounced these words. They are most often astounded to be informed that this well-known phrase is *not* from the Word of God, but rather, Benjamin Franklin.[98]

Though I myself had, for most of my life, believed this saying to be one worth banking on, I have come to realize that, on the contrary, God delights in particularly helping those who depend solely upon Him.

The old saying "Be careful what you ask for, you just might get it" fits nicely within this topic. If you help yourself to the potatoes on the table, you get them. God will not deny your taking what you want, nor giving you what you ask for, but if you want HIS help, you must WAIT upon Him, after which He will come forth. It should not be surprising that His choices for us are always the best, though they may not always seem so. Like good parents who will comply often with their children's requests, knowing full well that there is a better way, the parents wait for the child to make the mistakes necessary for instruction, patiently waiting in the hope that the child will ask for the guidance most needful in order to save themselves from a more difficult response.

The friends with whom we were visiting were expecting a large group of people from France who were involved in presenting 'Est-type' seminars under another name. Members of the group would be manning a booth at the fair. The lady of the house, abused as a child, had been drawn very deeply into the process. It was apparent that the group was very powerful in its persuasions.

We had thoroughly enjoyed our stay thus far, but with the French team arriving shortly, requiring every spare bed in the house (there would be 13 visitors in all), I had planned to explore the Bay area on my own. This would take some doing, considering I had barely twelve dollars to my name.

This no one knew and I had no intention of making it known. To depend solely on the Lord is to risk assuming that He lives and desires to make provision for those who will trust Him. To learn this completely, one must be willing to 'hang out over the edge' of what might otherwise appear to be 'safety.'

There are two approaches here that must be considered, which I will but briefly entertain for the purposes of this commentary. Waiting on God is an exercise in discipline and faith. Sometimes, one IS prompted to 'ask' for help, especially from those who declare themselves followers after Christ. The results are copious: perhaps for our own further instruction through 'being denied,' ... perhaps to offer up an opportunity for the giver to be blessed or for the one denying to fail a test.

No matter what the combination, God is nevertheless the orchestrator, and it is always for us to assume that there are heavenly reasons for ALL things . . . this assists greatly in sponsoring the position of 'judging not.'[99]

Departing from my friends' home was sweet sorrow. It would be a trifle lonely without them, and yet, looking forward to exploring this magnificent scenery held a certain excitement for me.

Having spent most of our several weeks together talking about God with hearts uplifted and revelations abounding, our hostess, experiencing a briefly faint understanding that this was, without doubt, 'our work,' she handed me a thank you note as we left. There was a fifty-dollar bill in it with the regret that she "wished it could be more."

With no immediate means of earning a living, no government subsidy, no family or friends in support of my lifestyle (at this point in time it was not considered a 'ministry'), I would be sleeping in my car by Saturday night! This did not prove to be a problem for me, as I had become used to 'making do' whenever supplies were scarce. The California climate was a monumental improvement over Canadian winters, where my first experiences in 'car camping' had taken place. Bearing that in mind, you might better understand how I might have little or no complaint with the situation at hand.

Tobie, a French Interpreter for the American Government who worked by monthly contract, accompanied me to the Fair, he being currently unemployed. We had met through friends in Marin and since I was relatively new to the area, I had eagerly accepted his offer to be my guide for the day.

We had been at the Fair less than 15 minutes when Tobie noticed Gail, one of the friends he'd met through volunteer work at the Center for Attitudinal Healing in Tiburon. We were lined up for a cold drink, as it was an unbearably hot day. After the basic introductions had been made, Gail asked me quite directly, "And what do you do?"

Without skipping a beat, I said something that I had never even considered before this moment, but which seemed to literally 'leap' out of my mouth.

"Oh, I just roam around the planet as the Spirit leads me," I said cheerily.

"You're kidding!" She was obviously intrigued by the notion.

For several moments neither of us spoke. Much to my amazement, and I'm sure to hers also, her next comment began for us a journey of continued friendship. "That's exactly what *I* want to do," she exclaimed. "You simply must tell me all that I need to know so that I can do that too."

And then, as if prompted by some brilliant discovery, she all but blurted out the following words.

"Hey! I'm going to Greece for six weeks. Would you like to housesit for me?"

"Why...I'd love to," came my almost immediate reply. We smiled agreeably at one another, quite pleased with our instant camaraderie.

Determined to get to the details, she began searching through her bag to locate a pen and paper in order to provide me with her phone number and address.

"I'm leaving in two days," she said, digging deeper as she spoke, "I hope that's not too short notice for you?"

"Oh, no, quite the contrary, that will be just perfect."

It was marvellous to watch the Lord at work.

Gail was continuing... "If you don't have time to come by before then, I'll leave the key under the mat. Use whatever is in the cupboards and fridge. I'll shop before I go so you'll have plenty to eat. And...make yourself completely at home and have a wonderful stay. I'll leave a note regarding garbage pickup and the mail."

In that brief a moment in time, the deal had been struck!

Interestingly enough, this was my first knowledge of the common practice known as 'housesitting,' which would inevitably provide more than adequate accommodations throughout our stay.

Gail's obedience serves as an example to confirm that there is no timing like the Lord's. What's hardest to get used to is that you will always be down to the wire before He will move. He will always give you time to choose your own way out. Then, if you have stated absolutely by your actions that you are going nowhere without Him, He provides.

Though the only prayer that Jesus taught, known as The Lord's Prayer,[100] includes the request for nothing more than our 'daily bread,' you will find that the Lord provides in abundance, more often than not.

*****

The house in Sausalito was wonderful. I could have easily chosen all of the furnishings myself. There were three bedrooms, two baths, wall to wall windows overlooking the port and on out to the Bay. A large round 'bay window' (the term for which I am told, and not surprisingly, comes from this part of the world), protruded from the front of the building.

In its alcove was a huge round ottoman and two large tub chairs that swivelled around to meet your favourite view. From this vantage point, you could watch a variety of water craft as they left for points unknown, not to return until late in the day. At night, the city lights sparkled mystically as the sailboats bobbed up and down in the harbour, anxiously awaiting their next adventure.

The master bedroom was huge, with a king-sized bed dressed in a billowing comforter and pillows galore. The bedroom furniture was so enormous that it had to be brought into the house in pieces. The entertainment credenza, also located in the master suite, sported state-of-the-art stereo equipment, television and VCR. More than a hundred CD's were cradled in special compartments, with a variety of classic videos on hand. Speakers were located throughout the house.

From the moment of entry, I felt completely at home, with the result that the entire stay passed charmingly. When Gail returned, she was so busy taking several quick trips we had little opportunity to become properly acquainted, although I think we both sensed a desire to do so. With the passage of less than a month, however, she had decided to return to Greece for yet another five weeks.

"Since my house was so lovingly cared for the last time I was gone, I was hoping you would come and stay again," came her request by telephone.

There was not a moment's hesitation to my response.

Upon her second return, we became fast friends. As she discovered how I lived from day to day, she recognized similarities to the process that she had come to deal with in her own life.

A former IBM Executive who had traveled extensively throughout the world as a top selling agent of mainframes, she had left her position, took an early retirement package, negotiated a costly divorce settlement and decided to take a rest from her previously hectic lifestyle. From this new vantage point, looking from the outside-in, it was her hope to become better acquainted with 'what it's all about.'

As a result, she had an innate understanding of the values that had become important to me. Instinctively, she would know when I might need a few days off from the constant care that one labelled a 'missionary' is required to supply while tending to the many broken lives about us. Responding to her call, I would move into the guest room at the back of the house for a much-needed hiatus. These brief interludes contributed greatly in assisting me to maintain my optimism and good cheer in the face of the enormity of the task at hand.

Sadly, out of the hundreds of people we had met along the way, including professed Christians, and aside from those who understand as a result of their hands-on work in mission fields, she was one of merely a handful of persons conscious enough to look beyond her own life's needs and recognize that someone other than herself required something that she was able to give . . . and then, going beyond that, finding herself able to give it. This is not to say that there are not countless individuals who give much, but merely to note that we had not run into many of them during this time.

More importantly than this, she gave without ever being asked, confirming yet again that to 'live' the Scriptures is more a matter of heart than of instruction. Growing up in Georgia, she had, not surprisingly, received Bible instruction as a child. Although she had long since stopped attending church, she was better able than most to demonstrate through her actions . . .

. . . freely ye have received, freely give . . . [101]

This is, tragically, where many of us fail. I cannot begin to enumerate the times that those who should have known how, and worse yet, having ample ability to contribute, simply turned their backs on others, thinking that it would be better for the one rejected in the long run. There were those who USED the Word of God in order to secure their own position, incorrect though it might have been, becoming thereby deaf to the Lord's words. [102]

My heart would constantly go out to such as these, for I understood only too well how they were inadvertently depriving themselves of the richest of blessings.

The apostle Paul demonstrates in his communication with the Philippians that he has learned how to endure all things and that his asking for a gift from them is "not because I desire a gift: but I desire fruit that may abound to your account."[103] His understanding was such that he knew that to refrain from giving was to deny access to God's gifts. Paul is saying here that as a teacher he was providing them an opportunity to add treasure to their account in heaven, for to seek a return in this life will inevitably bring upon you this pronouncement: "You have your reward."[104]

Our generation has a very long way to go to get to this place, but once clarification might arrive on this spectacular truth, we might become "doers" of the Word, not just "hearers" only.[105] Praise God that the disasters besieging this planet in massive numbers, the rampant starvation and pestilence increasing hour by hour and the onset of the fear that one's future may not be as safe as previously expected, have all contributed to the tugging on the heart of God's community to begin to reach out to a crying world.

And the crying is no longer thousands of miles away, merely to be viewed on a television screen – the cries have come home to haunt us ; it is the cry of our neighbours, our friends, our family…ourselves.

Records indicate that a large number of employed Americans give at least one hour a week to service organizations, totalling in labour dollars more than one half of the national debt. Just think where we would be if we were truly responding as the example was set by the Son of God.

This new phenomenon, however, will eventually break into a forked road. One will be the humanist philosophy that "WE can do it, if we all work together, coming together as one." To be sure, at its base, the desire to co-operate globally has merit. However, working together in the flesh supports the New World Order. Working together in the spirit supports the Body of Christ.[106] We will be given the option to choose, but how will we properly choose if we lack understanding about the choices?

Consider this. It was Jesus who said "I do nothing of myself."[107]

When "WE" become the achievers without relying upon the intercession of Christ between us and the Father, we do indeed become that generation that will "have a form of godliness, but deny the power thereof."[108]

Except the Lord build the house, they labour in vain that build it: except the Lord keep the city, the watchman waketh but in vain.[109]

There will become less and less doubt that America must return to its founding principle: "In God we trust." In our prosperity, we have turned our backs on our Creator. With the cry of desperation beginning to rise from the lips of old and young alike desiring to know what it is that is causing our children to carry guns, to hate authority, their parents and one another, wasting their talents and destroying their future, I can only say this:

Blessed is the nation whose God is the Lord.[110]

What will it take to put America on notice that the blessing that was once poured out upon that great nation has been removed? Lest we repent, there is nothing to stop the downward slide into a pit out of which there will be no return.

It is clearly a commandment of The New Testament to respond to our brothers and sisters, whatever the need, knowing that whatever we do for them, it is as if unto the Lord.[111] Our selfish desires convince us to 'look out for number one,' but in so doing, we must put others behind us. If we cannot do for others until we are complete in ourselves, we will never be ready to care for another, for there is no satisfying man's "lust of the eyes, lust of the flesh and the pride of life."[112]

These cannot be quenched. Loving the world in place of God has brought us to a terrible fate.

Forget waiting until you are complete to 'give back' to the world; it is the very 'giving' itself that brings completion.

It is relevant here to look at how directly the Scripture deals with this issue during the judgment at the second advent when the separation of the 'goats' from the 'sheep' takes place. The Lord will speak the following words to those who have chosen to tend to their own needs, overlooking those doing without who are all around us:

> "I was an hungred, and ye gave me no meat:
> I was thirsty, and ye gave me no drink:
> I was a stranger and ye took me not in:
> ...naked, and ye clothed me not:
> ...sick, and in prison, and ye visited me not"
>
> And they shall ask the Lord in bewilderment when it was that they saw Him in these conditions and failed to minister unto Him.
>
> And He shall answer unto them saying:

"Inasmuch as ye did it NOT to one of the least of these, ye did it NOT unto me. And these shall go away into everlasting punishment:"[113]

Tough words.

Many of us have come to believe that there will be no such judgment. But if you look around, that judgment is here and it's happening now.

I leave this debate for your own conscience to consider, knowing only too well that the understanding of this topic is imperative to your spiritual health. There is much to say to spark relevant controversy; however, I must leave this discussion for another time.

The most fascinating thing to me through all of this is how so many quote the Bible, actually USING the Scripture to serve their own choices (lusts). For just one example, whenever the issue arises about whether or not we should be caring for the hungry and those in need, a common misunderstanding prompts some to argue, "the poor will always be with us."[114] There is a finality to this response that remains so if we have failed, through our own lack of diligent study, to know the context here of the words of Jesus.

Upon a review of the several verses both before and after Matthew 26:11, you will find that Jesus was not saying, "Since the poor will always be with us, you don't have to deal with it." Rather, he was referring in this instance, being a very particular moment in time, to the use of the expensive oil to anoint Him as being a worthy cause.

We cannot afford to allow others to interpret for us the Word of God, for "they be blind leaders of the blind. And if the blind lead the blind, both shall fall into the ditch."[115]

Once we come to a place where we realize that we are missing something without the knowledge of God, we begin to call upon Him to show us who He is. As He begins to draw us nigh unto Him, we come to recognize that Jesus Christ is, without a doubt, His Son. At that precise moment, we receive our own teacher, The Holy Spirit. As we yield to the ways of the Lord, the Holy Spirit begins His work to remove our 'old nature of sin' to become a 'new creature in Christ.'[116]

I know this seems impossible for most of us to comprehend, and though I refer to this event often in a variety of ways, from a collection of perspectives, it cannot be 'learned,' it must be 'received.'

It is a mystery of God.

*****

"Lazy Summer Drive is headed for the top ten range of most desirable houses to sit, if only for its name alone," I thought as we passed slowly by.

A slight edge of disappointment began to gnaw at me when I realized that my missing the original phone call probably cost me an obviously more-than-pleasant stay. However, I was quick to remember that the Lord has reasons for all things, and mine was simply to await His next move.

From time to time over the next several days, I was prompted to think about the house, since a five-week stay was called for as part of the job. This clearly added to its appeal.

One of the toughest parts of the assignment of learning to lean only on the Lord, had been the constant moving, never knowing where a bed might be offered from one day to the next. In addition, becoming enabled to "be careful for nothing"[117] was a most monumental task, considering the extent to which such an instruction applies.

Packing and repacking with only the rarest of opportunities to iron clothing and keeping them tucked away neatly so that the ironing would keep; organizational difficulties due to the absence of drawers, closets; laundry perpetually falling behind; the feeling that you are on a 'forever' camping trip; sometimes sleeping in the car – all this and more can be understandably taxing.

These were but a few of the smallest of ways of becoming only slightly familiar with the true walk of a disciple of old. Please understand, if you will, that I am not asking you to consider me to be called such a one; however, I would dare to point out that the Christian world has come to use the term 'discipling' with regularity, and since it is my earnest desire to experience a closer encounter with my Saviour, thereby choosing to be 'discipled,' the possibility does exist for me to become exactly that.

What I have learned is that there is no other way to understand the walk of one of these than to "deny myself, take up my cross daily and follow Him."[118] That is where my life's path had been progressively leading, and it became my constant desire to follow it with diligence and consequent tribulation.

Many doubt that the most dedicated follower of Christ should live in such a way. For those who share this concern, I always suggest they consider several things.

First, those known as disciples who became "fishers of men" "straightway left their nets and followed Him."[119] They had been willing to forsake "all"[120] and Jesus tells them of their reward for so doing. He further goes on to say that, beyond His disciples, "every one that hath forsaken houses, or brethren, or sisters, or father, or mother, or wife, or children, or lands, for my name's sake, shall receive an hundredfold, and shall inherit everlasting life."[121]

Second, the Lord makes it clear what kind of a walk is in store for those who would choose to make their life entirely with Him: from rejection to hatred, betrayal and mocking, to denying the self in order to serve, to the giving up of "everything" to "press toward the mark for the prize of the high calling"[122]…but then, to life eternal with the King.

Third, let us not ignore the apostolic life of Paul, who demonstrated over and over again humility and suffering. There are those of us in this day that know this walk, and it can be gruelling indeed. It goes something like this:

> *For I think that God hath set forth us the apostles last, as it were appointed to death: for we are made a spectacle unto the world, and to angels, and to men. We are fools, for Christ's sake, but ye are wise in Christ; we are weak, but ye are strong; ye are honourable, but we are despised. Even unto this present hour we both hunger, and thirst, and are naked, and are buffeted, and have no certain dwelling-place; And labour, working with our own hands: being reviled, we bless; being persecuted, we suffer it: being defamed, we intreat: …we are made as the filth of the world, and are the offscouring of all things unto this day.*[123]

During a discourse with certain scribes and disciples regarding the testing of discipleship, one of the men spoke to Jesus, saying, "I will follow thee whithersoever thou goest."[124] Jesus, as if to point out that the man in question should look very carefully at the cost of such dedication and as if to give him a deeper understanding of only one of the difficult outcomes of his decision, responded thus:

The foxes have holes, and the birds of the air have nests;
but the Son of man hath not where to lay his head.[125]

There follows no further discussion after this statement; it seeming to be quite final in its impact. The Word does not offer what the man felt or thought. We can only surmise that he may have been somewhat shocked or dismayed.

I count it no small matter that our Precious Saviour had nowhere to be born and nowhere to safely dwell throughout most of His ministry, though He was the ...

... *"King of Kings"* ...[126]

He had no earthly home, because He was not of this world.

He was in the world, and the world was made by him, and
the world knew him not.[127]

There are some in this world, as the Word confirms, who are commanded to walk after Him in this manner. It is most unfortunate that such a walk is so gravely misunderstood.

Did the Lord not also leave us with the understanding that " ... ye shall be hated of all men for my name's sake"?[128] Walking His walk was to consist of moving from place to place: "But when they persecute you in this city, flee ye into another."[129]

Words for another time? I think not, for I myself have experienced this, and though these are but the earliest days of thus 'walking' I am confronted with responses identical to those outlined as our 'destiny.'

It became very clear to me through these of learning why it was that the Lord was often without a proper dwelling place.

Those who wanted Him continuously in their presence were rare indeed. Jesus explains why when He said:

> If I had not come and spoken unto them, they had not had sin: but now they have no cloak for their sin.[130]

It is the greatest comfort for me to see just two verses earlier that " ...the servant is not greater than his lord. If they have persecuted me, they will also persecute you."[131] In other words, as servants of Christ, if we are indeed to be considered His servants, we are to expect the same treatment that was given to Him. Praise God that such condemnation comes as a result of our dedication to His truth, though certainly it comes not often enough. It also follows that, as servants of Christ, the 'world' will 'know us not.'

Although I was often considered 'homeless' during those times, I considered it nothing less than my opportunity to allow the Lord to provide whatsoever He would. I wanted to, needed to, know firsthand of His excellent provision.

And oh, how He has provided!

But let us not kid ourselves, as M. Scott Peck has said in his opening statement in *The Road Less Travelled*, "Life is not easy."

Let me add to this if I may. The life of 'waiting on the Lord' is more difficult still. We were never told that it would be easy. However, one of the plusses of the stacking up of the smallest inconveniences is that special time when, after passing through a channel of what might have otherwise amounted to total frustration, you find yourself coming up for air and out the other side. There you find unspeakable patience, not of the kind that we, as mortal men and women, might demonstrate from time to time, but an everlasting patience, which is given as one of the "fruits of the spirit."[132]

This creates a shift in the weight of the load, as the Lord lifts from you that which you have endured with love. Be assured, another gift will now begin to move your way.

Throughout this process, tests of endurance are brought forward and, as a result, whenever a place of rest looms on the horizon, it is looked upon as a special blessing.

*****

And so, in contemplating the likes of Lazy Summer Drive, after moving continuously for several years, I knew what repose could be provided by staying for five weeks in just one place, especially recalling the wonderful experiences in Sausalito!

Five weeks gives one ample opportunity to actually 'settle in'...to catch your breath. With the needs of so many pressing in so strongly of late, my exhaustion had pushed me to a point of requiring some serious quietude.

I had been waiting on the Lord to fill this need.

In addition, right in the middle of that 'possible' stay, I had consented to deliver an eight hour seminar called "Forgiveness is Freedom" to a group of new-agers in Marin. The proper environment for rest and preparation that such a home might afford seemed likely to enhance such a performance.

Sitting quietly one afternoon by the duck pond beneath the Court House in Terra Linda, a Scripture came to mind... "You have not because you ask not."[133] This I had always recognized to be seemingly in contradiction to "Thy will be done," unless of course what it is that you want is within His will.

I had often pondered over these teachings, as it was quite apparent to me that Christians have a great deal of trouble deciding which is which. As yet, I have heard no one tackle this comparison, although I have been to more than 200 churches in recent years, covering more than 30 denominations plus those having no denomination at all.

My bout with cancer in the mid 1970's had taught me that there was nothing for which I *needed* to ask, as God was already completely aware of any predicament I might have fallen into. What I learned back then was that, having come directly to Him, asking nothing for myself, submitted entirely to His will, He had instantly handed me back that which I was willingly about to lose ... my life ... and He gave it back in fullness of measure.

Needless to say, that incredible experience taught me that it was possible to allow the Lord, in His infinite wisdom, to make ALL of my decisions, without concern or anxiety. Of significant note is that resulting from His sparing me in this way, it is rare for me to put in any request on my own behalf. I say this not to commend myself, but to demonstrate fully the 'knowing' I have come to enjoy that the Lord's hand is over us at all times.

One too often will hear the argument, sometimes vehemently, against this attitude of submission; some say it is a sign of weakness, though I am reminded of Paul's words: "My strength is made perfect in weakness."[134]

Many Christians rely heavily upon the 'name it and claim it' theory, though I have held discussions that lasted for hours on precisely this issue, which have thankfully caused many to rethink this point of view. On the down side, such discussions have, from time to time, brought upon my head intense anger mixed with the nastiest of accusations. But the bright side is that naming and claiming is allowing the participants to watch God answer their requests. And in the days to come, we are going to have to know that He comes through. A greater level of faith is the next step, waiting on Him to decide, when, where and how.

I find it interesting that when Jesus prayed in the Garden of Gethsemane the night before his crucifixion, he made a request to allow the difficulty He was about to face, to pass. However, He went on to say...

...nevertheless not as I will, but as thou wilt.[135]

My attitude as a result of this example is this: if it was good enough for the Lord Himself to submit to the will of His Father in Heaven, then it is surely good enough for me!

On the specific night in question, the Lord spoke honestly and stirringly about His plight, so much so that he literally sweat blood.[136] He, knew, however, that He would not refuse to carry through with that which He was sent to do, if there was no other way.

In all situations that oppress or confuse me, it is my hope that my first thought is ever this: "What would Jesus do?" If the solution is not immediately forthcoming, I search the Scriptures with diligence until the answer is clear. With such singleness of purpose, inevitably, light must come forth.

*****

From the moment I was healed so miraculously I am sure that it will come as no shock to you that my talks with the Lord unfold in what some might think a 'peculiar' way and why, while seeking God's will with respect to the house on Lazy Summer Drive, my discussion with the Lord would go something like this:

Lord, you know everything! And you know my every need. You know the extent of my exhaustion as a result of constantly moving. You know that the house in Novato appears to be very pleasingly comfortable and possibly has the necessary elements to provide a substantial rest.

But . . . you also know what dangers or difficulties would ensue if we were to take that house . . . difficulties that are hidden from us. And of course, it is You who knows the road You prefer us to follow . . . it is You who has a perfect design for each life.

And therefore Lord, I commit, as always, my life to You, for I cannot know what lies before me and I must trust in Your guidance always to remove the stumbling blocks that would impede my work for You.

If, for any reason, it is necessary for me to make a special request about the house in order to receive it, I am making that request to you now.

And Lord, You know how foolish I feel speaking these words out loud, as it is clear to me that You know, beyond my own ability to know, the desires of my heart. This request of mine, as you well know, is not intended in any way to preclude Your will.

*****

I know that this is a most unusual way of praying, and many have argued that such a prayer demonstrates a weakness or lack of belief. However, I thirst always to take my examples from Christ Himself.

He only taught us one prayer.

It did not include making a shopping list of worldly goods. It did, however, include the supply of 'our daily bread,' to ask for 'forgiveness in the same measure that we were able to forgive,' and to pray to let 'Thy will be done.'

In order to obtain the ability to do 'His' will, one must 'lose' their own life, taking no thought for the desires thereof.[137] Only in this way do we have any hope of becoming a vessel of honour. And only in this way do we stand the hope of discovering what it is that the Lord delights to give us. Surprising His children with joyous moments is His very heart's intent.

*****

After a week of receiving no inclination whatsoever as to what path to take regarding the house, a quiet unction of the Holy Spirit caused me to call the owners back.

As it turned out, Ted, the man of the house, answered the phone. We had a wonderful chat. Within minutes, he was telling me that he had the feeling that the man from Britain was not going to be able to take the house and that it was a good thing I had called as they had somehow misplaced my number.

"My wife, Jean, usually makes these types of decisions," he said, "but since I have you right here on the phone, I might just as well decide here and now. As far as I'm concerned," he added, "the house is yours."

We made an appointment to meet a week or so before their trip. As with most homeowners, there is a certain care and routine that is generally hoped will be followed in their absence. In the case of Lazy Summer Drive, there was an additional task of dogsitting – a beautiful, mild mannered Irish Setter named Tammy. Tammy loved to chase raccoons, and the raccoons were happy to comply. It would be important to learn certain tactical manoeuvres to prevent general havoc as a result of such encounters.

Ted turned out to be none other than Ted Van Kirk, one of the illustrious crew members who flew with the Enola Gay, the oft' noted infamous aircraft that dropped the atom bomb on both Hiroshima and Nagasake. I had always heard rumours that each of these 'flyers' had been given up for dead as a result of their exposure to nuclear fallout. Our visit to Novato proved that nothing could have been further from the truth.

Here sat the navigator of that very plane! And what a tale he had to tell. He and his wife were delightful, sharing countless stories about their life and times together. Jean was from Georgia with a marvellous southern drawl.

We took a detailed walk through the house, stopping for an hour or more in the den, where thousands of items of memorabilia regarding that most famous-of-flights were displayed.

The story behind the story was fascinating and, since Ted, the pilot and the co-pilot made it a practice to attend speaking tours and autograph signings throughout the country (their upcoming trip was another such venture), he had a regular routine prepared, providing a provocative account of the events of that time.

Knowing the casualties of some of those involved in the inventing, preparing and administering of such a horrible fate for so many innocents, I wondered what, if anything, might be hidden behind that jovial countenance that might prove to be depression or despair over his part in such a monumentally historic moment in time.

Casualties such as Robert Oppenheimer, the talented physicist came to mind.

Later in the day I had the opportunity to ask him.

"Ted," I said carefully, "did you ever experience remorse or any kind of depression as a result of having been on that fateful flight . . . the lives, the destruction, the inheritance of death to the survivors?"

"Suzanne, I count it merely a great blessing to have been available to serve my country well. I have never thought that what had to be done was anything less than our duty to the lives of my friends, my family and the future generations of every country around the globe," he answered with a definite strength of conviction.

"You see," he went on, "we were all very aware that the Japanese and the Germans were only moments away from discovering the secret themselves. We knew that whoever got to the answer first would win the war. And it was vital to the lives of all of us, even today, for such a win to be obtained by the Americans. However, you can know this: no member of any of the armed forces looks forward to the loss of innocent lives, but when duty calls, duty comes first."

The years had been kind to Ted. He was still very charming and pleasant to the eye. His upper body, over the years, for he would be a man in his mid to late sixties, had become somewhat slumped over and his neck had all but disappeared into his chest.

On the topic in question, however, it was clear that a certain strength returned to him somehow as his back began to straighten and he became almost tall. His shoulders took on a new form, his eyes brightened and his chin lifted high as he reflected back to those frightening, yet exhilarating flights.

I could sense his own personal awareness that he had simply done his job and done it well. He had no regrets.

*****

The tour of the yard was splendid.

The grounds were wonderful. There were fresh tomatoes and a good selection of vegetables. Many varieties of apple trees dotted the land, bearing more fruit than you could ever eat or cook up. The property was about a quarter of an acre, with an outdoor inground heated pool.

Extensive concrete decking joined the house to the pool with lots of umbrella tables and lounge chairs, not unlike an exclusive health club. Just south of the pool area, the yard rose into the Novato hills and the house was actually nestled tight into the hillside laden with ivy and wild flowers. Deer, one of my special California memories, roamed freely throughout the hills and, in particular, loved the little creek next to the front door.

It was sublime! The privacy created a longed-for-peace and tranquility. I couldn't help but feel that it had been the Lord's desire to present this gift. He knew only too well how difficult 'coming out of the world' had been. Moving to sole dependence upon Him, if you have some familiarity with the Scriptures, is not something that anyone does easily. In fact, it is clearly what each one of us fights.

I was beginning to feel rested already.

The tour and subsequent visit went so well that several hours drifted easily by. Finally, as evening was approaching, we got up to leave. As we made our farewells, Jean said, "Gosh, I had so much fun that I think we should just stay home and housesit with y'all."

We had indeed enjoyed our time together.

With the last 'good nights' having been spoken, Ted, as if struck with a wonderful idea, nearly lurched out the front door toward me.

"How about calling me a couple of days before we leave? We would love to show you around the town and finish by taking you out for dinner."

I was so startled at his casual familiarity that I made no immediate response.

Noticing my ever-so-slight delay in finding an answer, he began to attempt to persuade me.

"You'll have a much better stay if you know where everything is … the deli, the cleaners, a good service station … you know, all the things that make this little town tick."

Recovering quickly, I happily complied, "That sounds terrific!"

My enthusiasm having obviously returned, I added, "I'll call you on the Tuesday and we'll plan to get together late in the afternoon."

The appointed day came soon enough, and, as it happened, on my 47th birthday.

The tour of Novato proved to be fairly short, as the town itself is, as Ted had hinted, relatively small. Within minutes of leaving the house, we passed a very attractive building, which housed a beautifully appointed Italian Restaurant.

"That's Dalecio's," piped in Ted, "fabulous food, quite expensive, great ambience. Be sure to take that in sometime before you leave the area."

Right then and there, I made one of my 'mental notes' to put Dalecio's on our restaurant waiting list.

"We had considered taking you there tonight," said Jean, "as it is actually my favourite. I just love their homemade bread pudding with caramel sauce. But we opted for a romantic view overlooking the rolling hills of Novato and the town itself.

"The Hilltop Cafe, appropriately named, sits up high enough to provide just such a view and the cuisine is one of the finest in Marin. From its vantage point, you will become more quickly familiar with the lay of the land," she contended.

The dinner was spectacular; the specialty items were dishes that were completely unique. Having discovered that it was my birthday, the Van Kirk's graciously insisted that we hold nothing back on our order. They were charming and celebratory. Their hospitality matched Jean's southern accent, which was simply, in a word, hearty. The cost of the dinner, they insisted, was theirs alone.

Taking nothing away from their generosity, it was clear they were appreciative of our willingness to house and dog sit 'at no charge.' Housesitters in Marin can make a fairly decent income, not to mention having great places to stay. Charges range anywhere in those days from one to five hundred dollars a week, depending on the responsibilities included.

We, on the other hand, in spite of the need to care for the dog, were more than grateful for such fabulous accommodations.

Without sitters, for example, Tammy would have spent her time at a kennel, at tremendous expense and, more importantly, in less comfort than if she were able to stay at home. In the past, she had been known to become very depressed when this had been the only option.

As the meal progressed, the evening shades absorbed the embankments surrounding this quaint little town. Warmly wrapped in a kaleidoscope of purples and gold, there is nothing to compare to the California slopes, which smoothly unravel themselves right out to the sea.

Despite the fact that there are mountain ranges worldwide that can literally take your breath away with their spectacular beauty and austere splendour, what makes Marin so special is the way in which the landscape gently wraps you up and tucks you in for the night.

Throughout the day, the unending sight of voluptuously rolling land is ever-so-easy on the eyes, posing as a nurturing backdrop to your every waking moment. It surprises me no longer when I hear tales of this famous county's ability to create in you a yearning to return.

Could I have ever planned such a wonderfully perfect birthday surprise, with great company, stunning cuisine, sublime sunsets? I think not.

Winding our way back to the Van Kirk's home, we passed Dalecio's once again. And again, the mental note. My senses confirmed that there registered no special 'need' to go there, but simply that it would be an especially nice thing to do.

*****

Two days later, our stay began.

The weather that fall was extraordinary. The inground pool served us well as we were able to use it almost every day. The grounds were professionally maintained, so there was literally nothing for us to do with respect to the property. We relaxed, having company just one of the many weekends. Tammy was thrilled, for she enjoyed frequent walks through the hills.

Twice each day, I had occasion to drive by Dalecio's, as it was situated on the main artery to the highway that took me into San Rafael. If I happened to glance in that direction, or think of it at all, it became, after a week or so, nothing more than the fleetest of thoughts. The kind of cost involved in fine dining was not something that we sought to enjoy, but rather allowed the Lord to surprise us whenever He deemed it appropriate, and so, for the most part, I put the thought completely to rest.

The stay progressed without considerable mishap, although there was an exciting skirmish with raccoons invading the garage when the side door was inadvertently left ajar. After much broom handling, they finally became discouraged and fled.

Late in our stay, Tammy was plagued with eczema due to allergies, a situation with which we were unfamiliar and unprepared, and so she was sadly a little under the weather when her owners returned. After a quick visit to the vet for her regular shot, she perked up in no time at all, much to my relief.

I had thoroughly enjoyed the advantage of the serenity offered, enabling me to complete the finishing touches on my one-day seminar, which went extremely well. All in all, the time passed in the most congenial way.

Ted and Jean were happy to be home and asked us to keep in touch. They were hoping to make a trip at Christmastime and asked if we might be willing to return. As it turned out, Ted came down with a terrible case of shingles and their trip had to be postponed.

From time to time, we have spoken over the phone but never seemed to secure a reconnection. I did run into Ted at the supermarket shortly after his recovery. He still seemed a little weak, however, and so we took little time to chat. Having later returned to Canada, where this report was written, our communication was all but severed. It is my hope they will like my story, of which fondly they have become an important part.

*****

June, the following year, found me in San Rafael once again. This time I was helping my friend Jeff decide if he should be looking for a new location for his law office.

One weekend, I had agreed to drive his car to pick him up from a Christian men's retreat that he was attending several hundred miles north of Novato. On the way back, upon approaching Ignacio Boulevard from the north this time, Jeff suddenly turned off the highway, stating that he had seen an article in the local paper about some very nice offices that were renting at a more than reasonable price.

Apparently, the owner of the two office buildings in question was a restaurateur. It seems that running businesses other than his well-known eatery was not something that he could easily manage. He had to give up the buildings, one on either side of his restaurant, to an owner more inclined to operating leaseholds.

Although it was a Sunday, Bill, the grounds keeper, was out and about. When he saw that we were peering vigorously in all of the windows, he asked if he could help us. Upon confiding in him of our interest in renting, he suggested we call the owner, who lived just blocks away. We were hesitant at first, but Bill insisted that they were anxious to acquire good tenants.

Tony showed up within minutes. He was exceedingly eager to work with us and asked us to write up an offer as quickly as possible. He would even provide leasehold improvements that would greatly enhance the already pleasant decor. Without going into the details, suffice it to say that we were packing boxes within days.

A hub of activity followed, with Jeff taking up space in two of the offices while walls were being constructed adjacent to him according to our liking. I had little time to consider anything else as I was doing my best to help smooth out the transition, including dealing with the trials of construction, which was going to take the better part of a month.

French doors and windows presented a flattering touch to the environment. Three of the offices overlooked the neighbouring restaurant, complete with a grand outdoor patio, smartly dressed waiters, and gigantic planters of both dreamy impatiens and brilliant begonias. This setting was spread out beneath an umbrella of one of the oldest oaks I have ever seen. Italian opera continued throughout the day, convincingly mirroring an exclusive European diner.

A few weeks after completing the move, I found myself sitting beneath the gracious oak, now a frequent companion, at a little table covered in a sweet red and white checkered cloth. The weather was especially balmy, with an air of romance hidden softly in the day.

I was meeting 'Sausalito Gail' for lunch, and, as she was unusually late, I found myself luxuriating over a cafe latte.

As I looked around at the beautiful setting, a certain familiarity began to blossom. And then, slowly, it began to dawn on me. At first a quiet smile crept over my face, and then, as the amazement of what I was comprehending began to become clearer, I simply had to chuckle right out loud.

Coming back to me in a series of flashbacks was the realization that here I sat at Dalecio's, the van Kirk's favourite Novato restaurant that I had so often thought about when driving by last fall. Surprisingly, I had long since forgotten it. (Constant traveling allows you to leave ideas and trends behind more quickly – a necessary part of worldly detachment – and Dalecio's had been a casualty of exactly this sort).

On the surface, discovering the mystery of finding myself on this glorious patio may not seem to be particularly significant. Not only was I sitting at Dalecio's for lunch that day, but as a result of the convenience of its location, clients were prone to bidding us join them for a quick bite; consequently, this was already my third visit this week!

It was Dalecio's that befriended our daily activities now, and it was Dalecio's that had become 'almost like home.'

Home cooking, bar none! Absolutely delicious!

Until this very moment, it had not once occurred to me that this was precisely the great Italian restaurant that Ted and Jean had spoken of so highly and the one that had been quietly noted on my 'restaurant list.'

The way in which the Lord so subtly gives us the desires of our heart came flooding into my soul. Not only had my little thought come to pass, but it had come in greater abundance than I would have ever imagined.

*****

As I continued to celebrate the wonders of the Lord and His blessings so great, in total appreciation of His ways, my eyes were opened to see yet another aspect of how He works. Revealed to me at that moment was the following little scenario.

*****

It's like I'm this little girl, playing in the sandbox with a friend in my back yard. And while we are playing, I'm telling my little friend that when I was downtown the other day, we walked by the bicycle store where I saw the most beautiful bike.

Now be sure to understand what I'm telling you here. I was not coveting the bike. It was an appreciation. I was simply telling my friend about its 'specialness.' I knew that I would not be asking my dad to buy it for me, because I already had a bike. I felt no remorse about this, nor loss at doing without. It was more or less an acknowledgment that such a bike existed and I would have been happy for anyone to have it.

As we were playing and talking, my dad had been weeding the garden not too far from where we were sitting. And although I didn't know it, he had overheard how enchanted I had been about the bike.

And then the Lord asked me,

"Do you not think that your dad, after hearing you talking about that bike in such a way, wouldn't be delighted to surprise you with the very thing that would make you squeal with joy?

"Even though you hadn't asked for it?

"And especially because you hadn't asked for it.

"That is exactly how I feel about my children," said the Lord.

"Just as it is my delight to give you the kingdom, it is my great pleasure to surprise you every step of the way . . . if you'll only let me."

For the heart of God to be revealed in such a way was, I believe, distinctly rare and beautiful.

*****

There is also a critical teaching here.

We have lightly touched upon some of the world's teachings on 'getting what you want,' and you are no doubt aware how the world encourages us to go after the things that will make us happy. In fact, the world will even go so far as to create elaborate ways to convince us of what those things should be. There are constant reminders about positive thinking and bringing into your world exactly what you desire.

Would it surprise you to know that these practices DO work?

I know, because I have often taught these very principles and many have successfully followed the instruction. Once the Lord brought to my attention a better way, His way, I came to understand how "old things are passed away."[138]

And this is the better way.

Our Lord came to be among us. He had all power given to Him under heaven. And yet, He set aside ALL of his gifts in order to do the will of His Father.

This is precisely what we are asked to do also, if we are to follow in His footsteps. This is why He said, "I do nothing of myself."[139]

Let's make an important distinction here.

Yes, I could desire a bike. I could visualize it until it becomes very real to me. And within days (this also works within hours and sometimes even minutes), I could have the thing that I have chosen. And for that, who would get the credit? In reality, it would be me, although I might try to improve its credibility by praising God for the gift.

There is no doubt, however, that I would have strongly participated in bringing that bike into my life. And, had I chosen to do this with Dalecio's, it would have seemed to be ME who had brought such fine dining to my doorstep.

Having completely forgotten about the restaurant – I had simply thought about it as nothing more than something I'd enjoy – there was no 'desire' built up within me, no 'naming and claiming.' The very fact that it came to me, with no effort whatsoever on my part, makes it absolutely obvious that the glory belongs only to God.

Here lies an important issue, which demonstrates what I believe to be the central theme as to why we are having so many difficulties in the world today.

WE want the credit for creating our own destiny and bringing into our lives the very desires of our hearts.

Isn't it fascinating to note that such a desire was precisely the reason for Lucifer's fall in the first place?

HIS wants, HIS desires, HIS dreams.[140]

That same need – to be equal to the Creator, to be, in effect, some kind of 'god,' – is the noose that is tightening about society's neck today.

Prophesy is clear about the apostasy that shall be a sign of the Lord's return. One of the signs is noted as "having a form of godliness, but denying the power thereof."[141] The Word tells us "from such turn away."

It matters not how good your works may 'appear,' if the glory is not God's, the works, when measured, will amount to nothing. Likewise, it matters not how successful our life may 'appear'; if we have not lived for God, it amounts to nothing.

Everywhere you turn, there are psychologists, philosophers, entrepreneurs and even religious leaders who tell us that "You can do it!" The power of positive thinking has permeated everything that we do. And yet, none of these methods include any mention of what it is that God wants us to do or to become.

Waiting on the Lord, which was something that Abraham, David and Moses (to name but a few) HAD to do, has become, in our day, all but obsolete. We want everything NOW!

In addition to this, do you not know that the Lord *wants* to perform for us? He wants to do it all! We need to simply get out of the way and let God be God.

This may seem to some to be a radical point of view; however, I can assure you that there is something extremely important that we keep missing in the concept of 'losing your life.'[142] You can only 'lose your life' by 'giving it up.' This includes 'giving up' what YOU want.

Let me recount an event that brought this to light for me. As always, the understanding came not by reading, not by receiving instruction through someone else's teaching, but by revelation in the heart of experience.

*****

A business friend, known to be the marketing genius behind a highly successful multi-level corporation, enters as part of this story. Let's call him Bryce.

I had spoken to Bryce at length over the course of one full week in the fall of '85. This was at a time when I understood, better than most, the ability to bring into one's life those things that we would choose.

Bryce, on the other hand, who had been experiencing enormous ups and downs throughout his volatile business career, had a reasonable grasp on the process but seemed to be unable to get a tight enough grip to enable him to remain free standing.

Having been friends for years, with an interconnecting weave between our lives, it was comfortable for us to be together. We agreed to meet at the Constellation Hotel in Toronto, where he was presenting seminars to very large audiences as one of the top ten producers in an MLM that sold health and weight loss products. However, the company had been recently experiencing a massive reduction in support. From what I understood, top producers were dropping from monthly earnings of $25,000 (plus) down to $5,000 or less.

This factor was about to figure greatly in Bryce's production, and although we spoke little about it, I sensed that it was weighing heavily upon him. It was likely that Bryce figured me for a sponsorship, expecting me to be either inspired or convinced that the company was worth a closer look. I should have been an excellent candidate, since I was probably thirty pounds overweight at the time.

As it happened, it was Bryce who apparently became inspired. We met each morning; I went with him everywhere: to his speaking engagements, to his one-on-one's, for meals.

The first couple of days, my input was minor. As the days passed, I began to interject into our private conversations, first a word or a thought every now and then, and eventually, what I would call 'mini seminars.' We spent the fourth day at Toronto's Harbourfront at the edge of Lake Ontario. We had a perfect table at the outdoor cafe. It was a spectacular day . . . slight breeze, sun glistening on the water, sailboats gliding by.

I suspect Bryce was feeling relaxed for the first time in days, possibly weeks. We spent hours there and I spoke at length about what it really means to 'believe.' My sincerity in wanting to help him understand prompted me to perform what is known as 'intercessory prayer.' At the time, I had no idea that I was able to do this; I have since come to know more fully how it works.

If your heart is right and you are truly seeking to 'help' someone, knowing that 'of yourself, you know nothing,' something quite wonderful occurs. The truth has a way of coming forward, allowing you to become an 'instrument of service.'

I was aware that this had a way of happening to me, often with incredible results. Even so, I was completely unaware of the methodology involved. There is much to cover on this topic, which is a spiritual form of communication. Intercession is a most remarkable and indispensable aspect of prayer, something we need much more of today.

As a result of that afternoon at the harbour, everything that Bryce needed to know to take him to the next stage of his life . . . how to 'believe,' was made available to him. It had long been his desire, you see, to be rich beyond anything he had ever dreamed.

I do not make this claim lightly, for Bryce himself wanted to credit me with having taught him these principles. In the early '90's, at a very large (taped) conference, he did indeed do so, mentioning me by name. He must have spoken of our association often, for once when I called his head office to locate him, upon giving my name, the secretary with whom I had never previously spoken, knew immediately who I was.

I had offered Bryce the keys to obtain the desires of his heart; it gave him what he wanted and he is a wealthy man today.

'Belief,' however, as I was soon coming to learn, was only the first part of an amazing triple header:

Belief ... Trust ... Faith

I have since written and made many presentations about these three most precious, yet basic, elements of life taught us through the Scriptures.

Believing that something will occur can happen even without acknowledging God. What then occurs is quite mystical. You might begin to sense that there may be truly 'someone' out there looking over your shoulder, somehow helping and guiding you. This may then lead to a search for the understanding of heavenly things.

Belief is a first step to encountering God.

Once you first believe that 'God is' and take the opportunity from there to allow your belief to be strengthened, the results can be astronomical. At first, this may seem to require a tremendous amount of work, but it needn't.

However, it has been my experience to witness that most people have difficulty accepting 'belief' as a reality and have often spent literally years listening to 'power of belief' tapes, attending endless seminars and workshops.

Most don't get it even then.

If you look carefully, you can see for yourself how quickly the world is moving into understanding the way to 'make things happen.' Anthony Robbins, Robert Schuller, Kenneth Copeland – these are just some of the names that come to mind. Two of these men run under a Christian banner. One has no religious affiliation, being clearly 'new age.'

We have become a society bombarded with how to get what we want and get it now. We must move way beyond the 'I wannas' if we are to become pleasing to God.

There are few television programs, stage plays, movies, talk shows, infomercials or books where you will not find this continual infiltration of lust and greed, often subtle, mostly blatant.

Sadly, one can often be led astray by those in the limelight who have allowed their teaching to suggest that these are the only principles to live by. While our hearts lust after the 'things of this world' the Lord waits, ever patient, for someone, anyone, who might have a heart like David, a heart after Him.

That the Lord is our provider, I have no doubt.

He maketh his sun to rise on the evil and on the good, and sendeth rain on the just and on the unjust.[143]

In other words, God, being 'no respecter of persons'[144] provides all – that which seems good and that which seems bad. From this, you should also recognize that it is impossible to determine who is 'good' and who is 'bad' simply by the bounty being enjoyed … or denied.

The Lord's desire to provide life 'more abundantly'[145] fools many of us today into relishing in the abundant things 'of this world.'

How could such a misunderstanding occur?

The Bible is a spiritual book and although there are without doubt principles to live your physical life by, the teachings are ultimately spiritual, describing spiritual rewards, providing access to what is known as the 'gifts of the spirit' – 'abundance' in 'spiritual' things.

If 'abundance' of the worldly things was the way to rate how we are doing; if a peaceful, successful and well-organized, well-balanced life were methods of examination; if the measure of your worth was related to the things you had acquired; it would be clear that the apostle Paul would not have rated so well.

Are they ministers of Christ?
(I speak as a fool) I am more;
in labours more abundant,
in stripes above measure,
in prisons more frequent,
in deaths oft …
…Of the Jews five times received I
forty stripes save one.
Thrice was I beaten with rods,
once was I stoned,
*   thrice I suffered shipwreck,*
a night and a day I have been in the deep;

In journeyings often,
*   in perils of waters,*
*   in perils of robbers,*
*   in perils by mine own countrymen,*
*   in perils by the heathen,*
*   in perils in the city,*
*   in perils in the wilderness,*

in perils in the sea,
in perils among false brethren;
in weariness and painfulness,
in watchings often,
in hunger and thirst,
in fastings often,
in cold,
and nakedness.

~2 Corinthians 11:23

Consider the implications of what Paul is saying!

We have seen that, in spite of this accounting, attacks are continually made in the name of 'Christianity' (by those calling themselves 'Christians') against anyone not experiencing 'success.'" If one should fail, if one endures hardship, suffering illness, suffering abuse, being attacked by the heathen, or false brethren, helpless, thirsty, hungry, broke, cold or naked, I have heard it said that if such is the case, then those enduring such difficulties 'must be out of the will of God' or these things would not be happening.

In 1991, I created the Community Resource Network, a matching program of goods and services between donors and recipients established on a computer database, an early dawn of today's Craig's List, if you will. Participants called in to a radio program and the information of needs and items available was entered into a computer program that sorted and matched givers and receivers. By today's standards it would be a dinosaur, to say the least. However, the idea had been birthed and it worked! A California non-profit organization utilized the program and we took to the airwaves on KFAX, a Christian Radio Network out of Hayward, California. The results were phenomenal.

On more than one occasion, we had people call us who were just about to hit the streets, with kids in tow. They had been down and out for some time, finding that their church/minister had told them to simply 'get their life in order and get right with God.' Time and time again, it was found that the 'Christian' community was not coming through for these people, having clearly turned their backs on them.

The Scripture does not say ... when someone asks you for something, give them something YOU want them to have, and it doesn't say you have the right to turn them down, after praying about it, or just because you want to.

Specifically, here is what we are told to do.

Give to him that asketh thee, and from him that would borrow of thee, turn not thou away.[146]

Nowhere in this statement is there any reference to trying to figure out how to respond to the one asking, nor does it say that you have the right to 'deny' anyone because 'you think it to be in their best interest.' The mandate is clear: GIVE and DO NOT TURN AWAY, no matter what the request might be.

Whenever I hear stories of a person's unwillingness to help those in need, whenever I have to listen to excuses justifying their turning away, whenever I hear false accusations hurled at those who are down and out by saying that 'they are out of the will of God' or 'they must be living in sin' ...

I think about Paul.

*****

The first stage of one's operation as a believer is, more often than not, stuck in 'self'-service.

I think that it is not without merit to experience 'naming and claiming' in order for one to understand just how potently such 'asking' works. Once you know how to *make* it work, things can get pretty exciting. You can ask for the car of your choice, the home of your choice, a fabulous career, money, mates, and it can all come effortlessly to you.

You may be climbing 'seemingly' higher and higher up the ladder of success. The goals become bigger. Is there nothing you can't have?

My question to those chasing such dreams has always been: "At what point are you prepared to stop?"

When will you have accomplished 'enough?'

During such quests, does it become important to ask the Lord what *His* wants are for our life?

Or, are we filled with the prospect that we have somehow come upon some magic formula, creating within us greater and greater desires for achievement – *personal* achievement?

'Wanting,' as we have earlier touched upon, prevents us from moving into the area of 'true' gifts, gifts that come only when the heart turns its desires over to 'serving others.'

The matter of understanding how to believe comes through little successes at first. Then, as your confidence builds, you understandably might begin to ask for the materialization of greater and more complicated desires.

These, too, you may find, begin to surface.

After a time, the wait period gets shorter. Such success can be, without question, an exhilarating experience. What follows is most difficult to avoid. You may begin to exercise an enormous 'reverence of self.' Over time, one can become drunk with one's 'own power.'

After a season, you become familiar with the process. This allows you to begin to move towards a state of Trust. What you first trust is that the operation of 'Belief' is real.

You now begin to operate from a newer perspective. In the 'Trust' mode, you simply state certain things and, through 'believing,' those things which you have stated come into being. Soon, you no longer require determining 'if' you believe or not; you just know that you do.

You are likely still, however, operating from a personal perspective. You continue to ask for the things that YOU want to have happen to you. What you formerly thought was all that you needed in your life has now become but a shadow of the list that grows daily. Breaking free of this chain of bondage becomes increasingly more difficult. However, take heart, it can be done!

You may hopefully soon find that you wish to move to another step – asking on behalf of others. To your delight, you may find that what you have asked comes to pass. You may find that you have acquired a healing touch, you might be vicariously responsible for another's blessing and you may even cast out demons.

Throughout this process, it is only fair to ask yourself, even when the request is to support another, whether the things that you have asked are what YOU want to see happen or whether you have consulted with your Father in Heaven with respect to the things that He would have you do.

It is wise beyond words to critique yourself continually, for these sobering words spoken by Jesus and recorded in Matthew 7:21 are written not without reason.

> Not every one that saith unto me, Lord, Lord,
> shall enter the kingdom of heaven;
> but he that doeth the will of my Father which is in heaven.
> Many will say to me in that day, Lord, Lord,
>   have we not prophesied in thy name?
>   and in thy name have cast out devils?
>   and in thy name done many wonderful works?

And then will I profess unto them,
   I never knew you:
   depart from me, ye that work iniquity.

Always there remains the danger that we have sought our own glory, our own desires, for ourselves and, even, for others. As Bill Hybels, in his book *Descending into Greatness*,[147] so beautifully lays out biographies of individuals seeking less instead of more, we must continually respond to the Scripture "He must increase, but I must descrease."[148]

Only when we can move into the third stage ... Faith ... do we truly begin to seek His will for our lives. Sadly, even our participation in the greater good – be it peace, feeding the homeless, tending suffering children, serving the blind, the sick, the lonely – often comes from a place of pride in our hearts and the desire for others to know of "our good works."[149]

*****

"Anything the mind of man can conceive and believe, it can achieve."

This quote is much used in conjunction with multi-level marketing incentives, positive thinking plans and the general 'restructuring' of lives. The idea is that a person can decide exactly what his desires are, make a list of the those things, then build upon the desire, finally coming to believe that the things desired will be received.

If these principles are so often successfully used, and they are, consider this. There is virtually what I would call a media blitz on 'fear mongering' in America, through which a belief is building that we need to become better equipped to 'protect' ourselves. This result is coming from an increased fear of the environment, our neighbourhoods, our economies, our cities – a fear that we may be unsuspectingly attacked, that our houses are no longer safe – the belief that we are no longer able to trust ANYONE.

Having therefore CONCEIVED this concept, moving well into BELIEVING it, the process is now well underway to being ACHIEVED.

Welcome to the future.

To cover just one example alone, the frequent TV topic of women buying a gun and learning to shoot one often includes close-ups of a woman pointing the gun in preparation for her actually pulling the trigger.

Quite a visual imprint.

As fear is building throughout America, everyone's nerves are getting a little more frayed each day. There are more and more incidents of people being shot inadvertently because of misjudging the situation through overreaction.

We are becoming so heightened by fear that eventually we will shoot at the least little disturbance.

Conceiving houses, careers, Cadillacs, well, that's one thing. Let's look carefully at all those other things we are conceiving every day: new morals, new values, new fears, new ideas, new horrors…

Conceiving doesn't just happen with the good things, it happens at the lowest end of the scale as well. The media is producing a feeding frenzy of the macabre, the bizarre, the violent.

To be sure, every once in a while we have a Forrest Gump. This uplifts us and inspires us to consider that, well, everything's not so bad after all.

Let's compare weights – one Forrest Gump to one hundred suicides, murders, rapes, affairs, violence, racism, fear, horror. I'm sorry to report – on the Gump side: one pound. On the side of the despicable: one hundred pounds.

Frankly, it just doesn't add up.

We can't keep kidding ourselves. Things are way out of balance, and in spite of any 'light' derived from a show like Forrest Gump, which might for a time convince us that the 'darkness' emanating from every other corner of our world isn't that much of a problem, there just is no getting around it.

These are the seeds that are being planted throughout our great land. We reap what we sow, and there is a new harvest growing. GOD HELP US!

So what is the antidote?

We must learn to trust God!

The simplicity of the method of recovery will not be well received, for we have indeed learned to trust no one, and when we trust no one, ultimately what we have learned is that we do not trust God.

*****

Trust.

Trust means not needing to ask.

Trust means understanding what the Lord meant when He said "... for your Father knoweth what things ye have need of, before ye ask him."[150]

Trust means waiting on the Lord for your security, your safety, your salvation.

*****

I first discovered this glorious revelation after my healing in 1975. My heart began to understand the first steps taking me to a walk of 'faith.'

Why would I have to ask for anything when my Father knows about it already? Isn't it true that He would prefer me to leave my welfare entirely up to Him?

"Isn't this confirmed through the following beloved Scripture, which many in the Christian community accept as nothing more than delightful prose, failing to acknowledge its literal possibilities and further, direction?

> *Take no thought for your life, what ye shall eat, or what ye shall drink; nor yet for your body, what ye shall put on. Is not the life more than meat, and the body than raiment? Behold the fowls of the air: for they sow not, neither do they reap, nor gather into barns; yet your heavenly Father feedeth them. Are ye not much better than they? Which of you by taking thought can add one cubit unto his stature? And why take ye thought for raiment? Consider the lilies of the field, how they grow; they toil not, neither do they spin: And yet I say unto you, That even Solomon in all his glory was not arrayed like one of these. Wherefore, if God so clothe the grass of the field, which to day is, and to morrow is cast into the oven, shall he not much more clothe you, O ye of little faith?*[151]

*****

> *Seek ye first the kingdom of God, and his righteousness; and all these things shall be added unto you.*[152]

*****

Faith.

Faith means 'knowing.' It goes beyond trusting. Trusting works closely with hoping, but Faith, well, Faith has no room for doubt.

Only when falling into the purest state of Faith is it possible to comprehend that each statement taken from Matthew 6 above is exactly as the Father would have us live.

How close we are to these concepts can be answered by looking at those principles in operation today that have become for most of us, a way of life. Life Insurance, Registered Retirement Savings Plans, IRA's (taking thought for tomorrow?), Shopping by the Case, Savings Accounts, Financial Portfolios ... art, stamp and coin collections ... fine jewellery, furs, antiques - storing up treasures?

Lay not up for yourselves treasures upon earth, where moth and rust doth corrupt, and where thieves break through and steal:[153]

Consider the S & L scandals and US bank failures of years gone by, insurance companies such as the Lloyd's of London's bankruptcy, leaving previously fat investors holding the bag. The warning was evident. And now it has taken us to a staggering debt load with no way out but on our children's backs. And what about today's financial disaster, which is a worldwide phenomenon? Are we finally becoming aware that 'sure bets' are not infallible? It's interesting, too, that the more expensive our toys, the more loss and theft protection required.

But lay up for yourselves treasures in heaven, where neither moth nor rust doth corrupt, and where thieves do not break through nor steal: For where your treasure is, there will your heart be also.[154]

No man can serve two masters: for either he will hate the one, and love the other; or else he will hold to the one, and despise the other. Ye cannot serve God and mammon.[155]

...choose the world or choose God...

There is no way any of us can serve both. The Lord asks us even more specifically when he tells us to "get hot or get cold."

If our service to Him is merely "lukewarm," He has promised to "spue us out of His mouth."[156]

Our greatest difficulties arise when we resort to taking matters into our own hands, simply because we become impatient waiting for the Lord to come through for us. We have become, over and over again, totally reliant on our own devices.

When one takes it upon themselves to risk the wait, obvious misunderstandings take place. In this fast-paced, success-oriented society, those who may appear to be getting nowhere fast are looked down upon with disdain and annoyance.

Those whose hearts are truly after God might fall prey to accusations of 'laziness,' 'fear of success,' or 'irresponsibility.' Sadly, the higher road of 'judging not' is usually the one 'less traveled.'[157]

*****

In the fall of 1988, I was suffering a severe financial loss for a number of reasons. Two of the reasons I will outline to apprise you of the difficulties, none of which could have been avoided.

First, the franchisor with whom I was working, without provocation, broke his contract with me within weeks of my opening a passive reducing salon. This tactic made it impossible for me to pay the many thousands of dollars owed to the contractors who had completed the leasehold improvements on the salon. The franchisor held back some $16,000, which he had agreed, in writing, to pay. This situation seriously jeopardized my success, not to mention that I was forced to struggle to find funds to pay the workers.

Second, my mother suffered two strokes, then broke her leg, all within a two-month period just weeks after my opening the salon. A substantial amount of my time was now required at the hospital, as I was the only member of the family living in town. My only sister, who had two small children and lived at least an hour's drive away, was naturally unavailable for emergency visits. This made it very difficult for me to pay the kind of attention necessary to make a new business venture successful.

The connecting point here is that Bryce had always told me that anytime I needed anything, I was to call him. In fact, the previous year he had actually called me to say hello and to ask if everything was going well and, did I need any money?

At the time, things were fine, but he clearly informed me that I would always be able to count on him in any kind of an emergency, that this would be his way of thanking me. He acknowledged that he was extremely grateful and that his life had been totally 'changed,' all for the better (from his financial point of view).

With the difficulties building, I decided to get in touch with Bryce to ask him if he would place a lien on my condo for $10,000, the amount that would enable me to get back 'in the game.'

His reply took me totally by surprise.

"Suzanne, you, of all people, should be the richest woman in the world. YOU know how to make these things work; YOU taught ME. Why don't you stop helping everybody else to get what THEY want and use your skills to help yourself?"

In simple language, he was saying No.

Not only was I speechless, but I was incapable of understanding why I was unable to explain to him about why I simply could not do as he suggested. I could not account for it, but I knew that what he had asked me to do would be impossible for me!

The very thought of his suggestion felt like it would be a 'sin.' Somehow it would be unethical, immoral.

For the remainder of the evening and well into the night, I was gravely perplexed by his accusation. A part of me knew that what he said was true, but then there was another part that screamed inside that the reason for my doing it that particular way was the way that it HAD to be.

But I couldn't say why.

It's important to understand the timing here. It was 1988, just prior to the time of my coming to read the Scriptures, while I still had no idea that somehow His 'Word' had been supernaturally planted deep within me. This incident with Bryce would become a veritable signpost, one which so illuminated my relationship with the Lord that I was never the same.

I went to bed that night somewhat upset but mostly confused. About three o'clock in the morning, I awoke with a start. I went to the dining room table, took up paper and pen, and began to write very quickly.

I had no idea what I was about to write.

In essence, what followed was a letter to Bryce as a result of our conversation that day and, to my amazement (since I was not accustomed to speaking in this way), it began like this:

The answer in Christ is:

When Jesus was on the cross, his torturers mocked Him, saying to each other...

"He saved others; let him save himself, if he be Christ, the chosen of God" and "If thou be the king of the Jews, save thyself."[158]

"If he be the King of Israel, let him now come down
from the cross, and we will believe him. He trusted in God;
let him deliver him now, if he will have him: for he said, I
am the Son of God"[159]

Suddenly, I knew why it was that I had been able to help
others and not myself. And yes, it was exactly as it was meant
to be! Praise God! For I knew that "flesh and blood had not
revealed this to me."[160]

For the first time in my life, I understood my obviously
strange modus operandi. And I felt comforted in the
knowledge that the Lord's way is consistently the opposite of
what we find here 'in the world.' I was exceedingly grateful for
the opportunity to 'know' this, although I had no idea why this
might be happening to me.

*****

Yes, Bryce had turned me down.

Nevertheless, I consider the outcome of his decision to be
immeasurably valuable to me. I am grateful for his actions, for
it forced me to seek an answer from the Lord and thereby
receive one.

Bryce may have missed his own opportunity to be blessed
through helping me, however, and for that I am sorry. For my
part, I feel no animosity, no judgment, nothing to forgive.
("Judge nothing before the time."[161])

There are reasons for all things.

The outcome became an amazing blessing to me, for
although Bryce did not come through for me, I was forced to
be reliant totally upon the Lord. I had been mistaken in
thinking that Bryce had been my last resort. There was a
spiritual hope awaiting me, one that never fails.

I cannot conclude this story without letting you know exactly how it was the Lord and His faithfulness that brought me through this difficult term.

*****

The $10,000 came cleanly and...just in time!

The gift was prompted by the Holy Ghost, proving yet again, "though men fail you, the Lord is faithful."[162]

During those days, some friends had asked me to make myself available to share with them insights that the Lord had given me regarding forgiveness, faith, patience and unconditional love. I had complied by making it known that my home would be open each Monday evening from eight o'clock on, to anyone wanting to talk over difficulties they might be experiencing in these areas.

I made it clear that if no one came, I would not be disappointed, nor would I be contacting anyone to attend.

I would do it simply for them.

Over the course of many weeks, there were regular attendees, and often there were those who popped in only from time to time.

One such lady came and went without much notice. The first time we met, she asked if I would say a healing prayer at the end of the evening. Though I was fully unaccustomed to doing so, I said that I would try my best. When the prayer ended, she commented to me that it was the most beautiful she had ever heard. We spoke little more than this.

The next time she came to my home, there was again little exchange. She watched me carefully and I was aware of her desire for understanding. She portrayed a certain inner strength that does not come from words.

I had not seen her for some time, likely several months, when she called me by phone.

The conversation came just a few days after my discussion with Bryce. I was sitting in my office, looking over the books, contemplating the morbid state of the finances. Christmas was soon to be upon us and both my sons were staying with me. From the looks of things, there would not only be no money to meet the bills, but it would be worse than bleak from a celebratory point of view.

I thought to myself, "Well, the Lord knows my finances, and that's pretty much all there is to it." This was no more than a state of observation and understanding. I was calm in spite of the situation.

And then, the phone. It was the mysterious lady from the home meetings. She told me that she had been somewhat burdened to call me, for more than a week.

Upon asking me what was happening in my life, I briefly filled her in regarding my mother and the difficulties at the shop.

"How bad is it?" she asked me straight out.

"Oh, nothing that about ten thousand dollars wouldn't cure," I replied rather comically.

Without hesitation, she replied immediately, "I can give you $10,000."

I was totally surprised by her outlandish statement. I quickly responded by apologizing for my comment, explaining that I had in no way intended for it to be a request, but simply a joke.

"Seriously," she said, "Would $10,000 make the difference you need to keep going?"

"Yes," I said, "but please, you mustn't concern yourself about it."

"But I want to," she was becoming insistent now.

She told me that she wanted to meet me for lunch, at which time she would be delighted to give me a cheque for $10,000. I had no difficulty meeting for lunch, but I assured her that to lend me $10,000 would not be wise from her perspective, for things were now beginning to deteriorate so rapidly I could no longer be sure when, and even if, I might be in a position to pay her back.

We met for lunch that very afternoon. More than two hours passed. She asked what seemed to be a hundred questions regarding my healing and subsequent encounters with faith. I came to know that she had had cancer twice herself and was facing yet another bout.

She told me that she had been married to a very wealthy man who had died and left her a rather substantial income. She was a world traveler in constant pursuit of 'healers.' She surprised me by saying that in all of her travels, she had concluded that my miraculous experience of deliverance from breast cancer in 1975 was the most extraordinary story she had ever heard. She said she had been truly inspired.

As we were about to leave the restaurant, she reminded me that she wanted to give me the money that I needed. Again, I sincerely suggested that I would rather not.

Her reply to me made it impossible for me to reject her further.

"Suzanne, I have watched you do things for others, through your teaching and your kindness, for nothing in return. You have given to others truths so few of us have heard. I cannot do the things that you do, nor do I know the things that you know, but I do have what you lack and that is money. Please, let me give you what I have so that you may continue to give others what you have – the understanding that they need."

Her argument changed my position.

She wrote out a cheque on the spot. Her final words on the subject were that she never gives money unless she does not mind if she never gets it back. "If you can, repay me sometime; if not, then consider it a gift."

Having been treated unbearably by Christians during her childhood, she was never able to accept the name of Jesus as anything but diabolical. She did, however, relate to the kindness those of us who knew her shared without measure.

She died less than a year later of bone cancer, before I was ever in a position to repay her.

*****

Later, I came to know of a Scripture that aptly fits this situation...

If we have sown unto you spiritual things, is it a great thing if we shall reap your carnal things?[163]

These words provide a clear demonstration that carnal blessings should be readily sacrificed in return for spiritual truth.

True sacrifice is equal to service...
...serving others, not ourselves.
Jesus came to serve.
We can do nothing less.

In serving the Lord, the things of this world fade quickly away. Our carnal self says, *I don't want to give up the world*, but if and when you choose Him, God gives you the courage to accomplish what is necessary for victory. Without anguish or remorse, those things that we previously loved, we love no more. It then becomes easy, for He fills us with a desire to seek and follow Him.

Heavenly intervention, from the incident at Dalecio's, the home in Novato, the gift of $10,000, and literally hundreds of others throughout my own life, are part and parcel of God's continuous confirmation that He participates in the very least of our thoughts.

The Lord has, thankfully, shown me that once I had 'no wants of my own,' allowing Jesus to bring to me whatever was HIS desire for my life, He was waiting, prepared to give me 'everything' though 'everything' no doubt appears to be drastically different from the things which those of us still 'of the world' have come to treasure.

'Everything' He has to offer includes Himself; if we give up 'us,' He gives us 'Him.' This is not a fair exchange from any perspective, but it is we who are remiss in not seizing such an opportunity. Here we find God's generosity displayed in its totality.

To replace the things of the world with the things of the spirit is a 'deal' we should not refuse. Unfortunately, most of us cannot endure the loss of those things we consider too precious to surrender. In spite of how we 'dress up' the Scripture, 'doing without' is what has been asked of us.

...deny yourself, and follow Him ...[164]

Andrew Murray (*The Best of Andrew Murray*) says it well.

See these Apostles, Peter and John, penniless in their earthly poverty, and yet by virtue of their poverty, mighty to dispense heavenly blessings.

"Poor, yet making many rich."

This points us back to the poverty which Christ had enjoined upon them, and of which He had set them the wonderful example. By his holy poverty He would prove to men that a life of perfect "trust" in the Father is how the possession of "heavenly riches" makes one independent of earthly goods, how 'earthly poverty' fits the better for holding and for dispensing eternal treasures.

The inner circle of Christ's disciples found in following the footsteps of His poverty the fellowship of His power. The Apostle Paul was taught by the Holy Spirit the same lesson.

To be ever in external things utterly loose even from earth's lawful things is a wonderful – he almost appears to say, an indispensable – help in witnessing to the absolute reality and sufficiency of the unseen heavenly riches.

To have no certain dwelling place, sleeping in a car or someone's spare room or living room floor, being denied compassion, friendship and help or being persecuted and falsely accused are none of the things we might consider 'abundance,' and not something supposedly sane people would choose. For these situations, I am comforted to know that Jesus warned us that this was indeed to be expected if we were following in His footsteps.

> *The servant is not greater than his lord. If they have persecuted me, they will also persecute you ...*[165]

*****

I fear that the 'abundance' of which the Scripture speaks is a far, far cry from what most believe it to be. If it were not so, why did Jesus not live in material abundance, and why not James, or Peter, or Paul after Him? No, the abundance of which the Word so mightily speaks is of *heavenly* things, deceive ourselves as we may.

As you begin the process of relinquishing those things (blocks) that keep you bound to the world, a displacement begins to take place while the world about you 'decreases' and the spirit of the Lord within you 'increases.'

Let us get out of the way of the Lord, letting Him have His way with us. When we can stop needing to 'do it ourselves,' then we give Our Father in Heaven the opportunity to provide for us like no other Father we could ever imagine, the culmination of which is the opening of our spiritual understanding, that we might 'know all things.'

> If we want really to understand what the imitation of Christ means, we must go to that which constituted the very root of His life before God.
>
> It was a life of ABSOLUTE dependence, ABSOLUTE trust, ABSOLUTE surrender…
>
> Until we are one with Him in what is the principle of His life, it is in vain to seek here or there to copy the graces of that life.[166]

Christ surrendered His life for us. Would we not give our all for Him?

> *Present your bodies a living sacrifice …*
> *… which is your reasonable service.*
>
> ~ *Romans 12:1*

*****

Though the leap of faith looms frighteningly large before us, we have no other choice; for the return, not given in earthly rewards, awaits those of us willing to pay the price.

*****

Fear not, little flock; for it is your Father's good pleasure to give you the kingdom.[167]

*****

The song "No Place to Lay my Head"[168] on Sandi Patti's album *LeVoyage,*[169] provides reasonable support that *nights in the car with no home of my own, standing 'outside' the world and all that it had to offer, was a good place to be.*

*****

Foxes have holes, and birds of the air have nests, But the Son of man hath not where to lay his head
~Matthew 8:20, Luke 9:58

****

In Conclusion ❧

There has been only One who came to this earth without spot or blemish. Prior to their conversion, His disciples were weak, erring often in their ways. There is no one who will proceed otherwise, and we are foolish to seek any other perfection than our giving up of ourselves to Christ.

*****

I do not claim to be pure or perfect. I am far from holy, although the Lord has promised to make me so. My life is filled with grim reminders of weakness, backsliding and foolishness, to name just a few.

It would serve no particular purpose to list all of my sins here, for in so doing, provision may be made for some to judge me too harshly. If whatever good that might have come through the relating here of these simplest of tales were to be lost in the process of exposing 'the shadow,' then the whole point would be missed entirely. There are enough gruesome exposés available in the marketplace today without my having to contribute to their sordid collection.

I have no difficulty discussing all elements of who I am as a person; however, some of the people who have participated in this journey are not the least bit interested in becoming a topic of public information. I have been cautioned by this thought in order to prevent personal injury to anyone involved as a result of this exercise.

Experiences of my life are shared here without hesitation and with little elaboration, being, for the most part, as true to my 'remembrance' as possible. Names and places have sometimes been changed where protection has been deemed appropriate.

The intention of the communication laid before you is to lift the hearts of those readers who are able to receive something fresh, to comprehend the sweetness of the moments of joy as well as the sorrow and, in particular, to appreciate the revelation of truth, where applicable.

By sharing a glimpse into my own personal walk with the Lord, it is my hope that those who either know Him not, or who may wish to know Him more intimately, will somehow benefit.

*****

What I hope you will find in these pages is a confidence that I am "washed, sanctified and justified"[170] in the name of the Lord Jesus, and as such, continue to experience His grace and His blessings, although my life, like all others, "comes short of the glory of God."[171]

My desire is to share some of the supernatural experiences that have occurred throughout my life as a result of my willing submission to the Power of God. Anyone who tastes such sweet surrender is provided access to the mysteries of heaven, according to His promise.[172]

If yours is a tendency to find fault in others, I ask only that you be kind when reviewing these contents, which can never be fully understood without having walked every step of the way with me, moment by moment. More importantly, I ask you to comply with our Lord's direction to "judge not."[173]

There are some situations where it appears that I may have been involved in the occult – inadvertently, I was – my point in sharing is not to become a target for condemnation but to prove beyond a shadow of a doubt that the Lord has pulled me out of trouble time and time again…as He has done for others and is prepared to do for you.

Praise His Holy Name!

The nature of certain individuals may cause them unnecessarily to equate some of the things that have happened to me with 'the enemy.' Because of this, some may wish to discount the experience.

Two keys are relevant here. First, an attempt by the reader should be made to connect with the innocence and the purity of heart conveyed. Second, let us recall that the apostle Paul zealously murdered Christians, and yet, became the most often quoted and decidedly effective servant of the Lord.

It is not unknown to me that innocence and purity are of little interest to the powers of evil. In fact, when these two exist, the enemy becomes all the more anxious to destroy. I know this very personally, for I have been a target of the devourer for many a year.

However, for some reason, and I cannot say that I understand it at all, it has become apparent to both myself and others that I have been rescued by my Lord to serve Him. My only guess would be that perhaps I paid little attention to the snares before me, having kept my eyes forever heavenbound.

This, I can assure you, happened not without grace.

I am content to allow those who may wish to criticize my work to use the following guideline: "You shall know them by their fruit."[174] To those who may be my critics, I beseech you to examine only the strength of my conviction and the degree to which I risk following the Word of God.

Although I have a long way to go, as do we all, it is with fervent heart that "I take up my cross daily and follow Him."[175] Though I may stumble and fall, failing often as I journey home, I am willing, in order to speak to but one heart through this manuscript, to come before anyone wishing "to cast the first stone."[176]

Because I am not denominationally associated, representing no church other than the "called-out ones,"[177] daring to assume that the covering of the blood of Jesus is sufficient, I have been continuously monitored, often with bitter scrutiny by those whose desire it is to seek the slightest opportunity to discredit my testimony.

My position tends to rattle some church authorities, which is the reason for some organized religious groups to feel justified in their condemnation of the context of my beliefs. However, I have found many Christians, comfortable with who they are in the Lord, to remain unthreatened by my confidence. The result has been a welcomed challenge to grow in the spirit, seeking both edification and exhortation.

Christ's words from the cross, "Forgive them for they know not what they do"[178] is a major clue that those who do evil, no matter how despicable, are unaware of their own behaviour.

Hence, how can we condemn them?

His words are pleading with us to this very moment in time to diligently review what is probably His most important teaching. Even in His darkest hour, the demonstration of His unconditional love was overwhelming! We are personally unable to even begin to walk like Him without the assistance of His Precious Holy Spirit. Our lack of wisdom in understanding why we must forgive in this way has made it impossible for us to "turn the other cheek."[179]

How tragic it seems when one suffers accusation and hatred from those who would call themselves Christian, instead of the required compassion and love for one another that Christ is clearly calling upon us to demonstrate. Is it any wonder that 'Christians' are collectively slandered as a result of the anger, aggression, hatred, judgment and violence emanating from a handful of those predominating the news who would dare to claim they represent Christianity?

Our direction should be clear and the path well lit.

Be wise as serpents . . . and harmless as doves.[180]

*****

To come out of the world is not easy.

I praise God that He continues to remove me from its influence so gently that I hardly notice its happening. Of myself, I assure you, there was no strength in me for such a task. And yet, though the Lord makes it clear in His Word time and again that we are to become separated from the things of this world, there are relatively 'few' who have the capacity to understand such a life.

Phillip Keller[181] writes boldly of such a walk in his book *The High Cost of Holiness*. Much courage is required in order to face the seldom talked-about tough truths of the walk of a true Christian contained within those pages.

In my pilgrimage out of the world, though many entreated me to resist doing so, my heart echoes the fervent cry of Paul in Philippians 3:8 as I understand perfectly these precious words.

. . . I count all things but loss for the excellency of Christ Jesus my Lord: for whom I have suffered the loss of all

*things, and do count them but dung, that I may win
Christ.*

If you must attempt to discern who I am now and who I am becoming, it would do well to note the various stages of development over the years in both my faith and the understanding of the Scriptures. I do not claim to be there yet, but "I press toward the mark of the high calling"[182] and in that process, hope that some light will be shed upon others who may have considered joining this worthy race.

Beyond this, I would counsel you to have little or no interest in who I am, but to turn your attention toward Christ, for "if your eye be single, then your whole body will be full of light."[183]

*****

To write about the Lord is the greatest privilege for me, and for which privilege I am extremely grateful. There is an endless discourse … countless miracles … wonders of mercy … boundless grace … enduring love.

> *And there are also many other things which Jesus did, the
> which, if they should be written every one, I suppose that
> even the world itself could not contain the books that
> should be written.*
>
> ~*John 21:25*

*****

I have often been asked by pastors and mature Christians alike if I thought that Satan had somehow influenced any of my decisions along the way. My honest opinion is that it may not be impossible. However, the Word of God tells me that "all things work together for good to them that love God."[184]

This definitely qualifies me.

I think that, doctrinally, where many Christians have difficulty is that they refute the things associated with innocence; having become 'a little learned,' they often border quite handily upon Phariseeism.

When someone writes a book of this nature, their life and that of their family members may come under close scrutiny and the end result is often cross-examination and ridicule. Nonetheless, in spite of this tremendous uncertainty, the Lord continues to encourage me to press on.

I risk it all for "the one lost sheep"[185] that may be saved as a result of the testimonies which are offered here, in both humility and the deepest appreciation for the Lord's influence on my life. If just one person comes to better know what it is to call our Saviour 'friend,' I will be fully rewarded and all attacks upon my personal life will be happily endured.

*****

Over the years, through countless afflictions, persecutions, personal or financial downfalls, it has been often said to me, in spite of what I seemingly had not...

"I want what you have."

That which I have is a peace...

...*a peace that "passeth all understanding."*[186]

It is the peace of God.

*****

*****

Throughout these pages …
…what I have has been offered to you …
…in the person of Jesus Christ

As Jesus spoke in what is known as
His final Discourse to His Disciples
Let His words speak to you now …

*****

*****

Peace I leave with you, my peace I give unto you;
not as the world giveth, give I unto you.

Let not your heart be troubled,
neither let it be afraid.

~John 14:27

*****

Recommended Reading &

Dake, Finis Jennings. *Dake's Annotated Reference Bible*. Lawrenceville, GA: Dake Publishing, 1985.

Hybels, Bill and Rob Wilkins. *Descending into Greatness*. Grand Rapids: Zondervan, 1994.

Keller, Phillip. *A Shepherd Looks at Psalm 23*. Grand Rapids: Zondervan, 1970.

Keller, Phillip. *The High Cost of Holiness*. Eugene, OR: Harvest House Publishers, 1991.

Murray, Andrew. *The Power of the Blood of Jesus*. New Kensington, PA: Whitaker House, 1993.

Peck, M. Scott. *People of the Lie*. New York: Touchstone, 1983.

Ravenhill, Leonard. *Why Revival Tarries*. Minneapolis: Bethany House, 2004.

Rollin, Betty. *First You Cry*. 1976, Philadelphia: Lippencott.

Spurgeon, Charles. *What The Holy Spirit Does in a Believer's Life*. Compiled and edited by Robert D. Hall. Copyright © Lance C. Wubbels. Lynnwood, WA: Emerald Books, 1993.

Endnotes and Scriptures ❧

For ease of study, referenced Scriptures have also been printed within the notes where feasible, and the page location within this book is noted at the end in parentheses (p. #).

---

[1] **John 10:3** ~ "To him the porter openeth; and the sheep hear his voice: and he calleth his own sheep by name, and leadeth them out."
John 10:27 ~ "My sheep hear my voice, and I know them, and they follow me." (p. xix)

[2] Finis Jennings Dake, *Dake's Annotated Reference Bible* (Lawrenceville, GA: Dake Publishing, 1985), New Testament 157. (p. xx)

[3] **1 John 2:20** ~ "But ye have an unction from the Holy One, and ye know all things." (p. xxi)

[4] **1 John 2:27** ~ "But the anointing which ye have received of him abideth in you, and ye need not that any man teach you: but as the same anointing teacheth you of all things, and is truth, and is no lie, and even as it hath taught you, ye shall abide in him." (p. xxii)

[5] Betty Rollin, *First You Cry* (1976, Philadelphia: Lippencott). (p. xxiii)

[6] **Matthew 16:24** ~ "Then said Jesus unto his disciples, If any man will come after me, let him deny himself, and take up his cross, and follow me." (p. 13)

[7] **Matthew 10:8** ~ "Heal the sick, cleanse the lepers, raise the dead, cast out devils: freely ye have received, freely give." (p. 13)

[8] Steven Spielberg (Director), *Schindler's List*. (United States: Universal Studios and Amblin Entertainment, 1993). (p. 14)

[9] Bill Hybels and Rob Wilkins, *Descending into Greatness* (Grand Rapids: Zondervan, 1994). (p. 18)

[10] M. Scott Peck, *People of the Lie* (New York: Touchstone, 1983), 264. (p. 19)

[11] **Matthew 27:42** ~ "He saved others; himself he cannot save. If he be the King of Israel, let him now come down from the cross, and we will believe him." (p. 20)

[12] **Malachi 3:6** ~ "For I am the Lord, I change not; therefore ye sons of Jacob are not consumed." (p. 21)

[13] **Mark 8:35-37** ~ "For whosoever will save his life shall lose it; but whosoever shall lose his life for my sake and the gospel's, the same shall save it. For what shall it profit a man, if he shall gain the whole world, and lose his own soul? Or what shall a man give in exchange for his soul?" (p. 22)

[14] **Matthew 7:1** ~ "Judge not, that ye be not judged." (p. 23)

[15] **1 John 2:27** ~ "But the anointing which ye have received of him abideth in you, and ye need not that any man teach you: but as the same anointing teacheth you of all things, and is truth, and is no lie, and even as it hath taught you, ye shall abide in him." (p. 23)

[16] **2 Timothy 4:3–4** ~ "For the time will come when they will not endure sound doctrine; but after their own lusts shall they heap to themselves teachers, having itching ears; And they shall turn away their ears from the truth, and shall be turned unto fables." (p. 24)

[17] **James 4:8** ~ "Draw nigh to God, and he will draw nigh to you. Cleanse your hands, ye sinners; and purify your hearts, ye double minded." (p. 31)

[18] **Revelation 2:4** ~ "Nevertheless I have somewhat against thee, because thou hast left thy first love." (p. 31)

[19] **Matthew 18:3** ~ "And said, Verily I say unto you, Except ye be converted, and become as little children, ye shall not enter into the kingdom of heaven." (p. 34)

[20] **Luke 23:34** ~ "Then said Jesus, Father, forgive them; for they know not what they do. And they parted his raiment, and cast lots." (p. 37)

[21] Andrew Murray, *The Power of the Blood of Jesus* (New Kensington, PA: Whitaker House, 1993). (p. 41)

[22] Enid Blyton, *The Sea of Adventure* (Greenwich, CT: Macmillan & Co, 1952). (p. 43)

[23] Enid Blyton, *The Castle of Adventure* (Greenwich, CT: Macmillan & Co, 1950). (p. 43)

[24] Charles Spurgeon, *What The Holy Spirit Does in a Believer's Life*, Compiled and edited by Robert D. Hall, Copyright © Lance C. Wubbels (Lynnwood, WA: Emerald Books, 1993), 103. (p. 47)

[25] Charles Spurgeon, as in #24 above, p. 106. (p. 47)

[26] **1 Corinthians 13:12** ~ "For now we see through a glass, darkly; but then face to face: now I know in part; but then shall I know even as also I am known." (p. 52)

[27] **Romans 9:21** ~ "Hath not the potter power over the clay, of the same lump to make one vessel unto honour, and another unto dishonour?" (p. 53)

[28] Leonard Ravenhill, *Why Revival Tarries* (Minneapolis: Bethany House, 2004). (p. 54)

[29] **1 Corinthians 12:12–27** (p. 55)

[30] See "About the Author" in *What The Holy Spirit Does in a Believer's Life*, as in #24 above. (p. 56)

[31] Charles Spurgeon, as in #24 above, p. 44. (p. 57)

[32] **Exodus 24:10** ~ "And they saw the God of Israel: and there was under his feet as it were a paved work of a sapphire stone, and as it were the body of heaven in his clearness." (p. 63)

[33] Matthew 5:48 ~ "Be ye therefore perfect, even as your Father which is in heaven is perfect." (p. 65)

[34] Andrew Murray, as in #21 above. (p. 66)

[35] Gideon's story can be found in **Judges chapter 7.** (p. 74)

[36] **John 1:1, 12, 14** ~ "In the beginning was the Word, and the Word was with God, and the Word was God...But as many as received him, to them gave he power to become the sons of God, even to them that believe on his name...And the Word was made flesh, and dwelt among us, (and we beheld his glory, the glory as of the only begotten of the Father,) full of grace and truth." (p. 77)

[37] 'Scripture' and 'Word' refer to *The Holy Bible*. Recommended is the King James Version. Others may be used as a comparative. (p. 77)

[38] **1 John 2:20** ~ "But ye have an unction from the Holy One, and ye know all things." (p. 80)

[39] **Matthew 5:39–42** ~ "But I say unto you, That ye resist not evil: but whosoever shall smite thee on thy right cheek, turn to him the other also. And if any man will sue thee at the law, and take away thy coat, let him have thy cloak also. And whosoever shall compel thee to go a mile, go with him twain. Give to him that asketh thee, and from him that would borrow of thee turn not thou away." (p. 84)

[40] **Matthew 5:44–45** ~ "But I say unto you, Love your enemies, bless them that curse you, do good to them that hate you, and pray for them which despitefully use you, and persecute you; That ye may be the

children of your Father which is in heaven: for he maketh his sun to rise on the evil and on the good, and sendeth rain on the just and on the unjust." (p. 84)

[41] **Matthew 5:46–47** ~ "For if ye love them which love you, what reward have ye? do not even the publicans the same? And if ye salute your brethren only, what do ye more than others? do not even the publicans so?" (p. 84)

[42] **John 8:32** ~ "And ye shall know the truth, and the truth shall make you free." (p. 85)

[43] **Matthew 7:7** ~ "Ask, and it shall be given you; seek, and ye shall find; knock, and it shall be opened unto you." (p. 86)

[44] **Matthew 6:33** ~ "But seek ye first the kingdom of God, and his righteousness; and all these things shall be added unto you." (p. 86)

[45] **Matthew 10:39** ~ "He that findeth his life shall lose it: and he that loseth his life for my sake shall find it." (p. 87)

[46] **Matthew 16:25** ~ "For whosoever will save his life shall lose it: and whosoever will lose his life for my sake shall find it." (p. 87)

[47] **Philippians 4:6** ~ "Be careful for nothing; but in every thing by prayer and supplication with thanksgiving let your requests be made known unto God." (p. 88)

[48] **John 14:26** ~ "But the Comforter, which is the Holy Ghost, whom the Father will send in my name, he shall teach you all things, and bring all things to your remembrance, whatsoever I have said unto you." (p. 88)

[49] **2 Chronicles 7:14** ~ "If my people, which are called by my name, shall humble themselves, and pray, and seek my face, and turn from their wicked ways; then will I hear from heaven, and will forgive their sin, and will heal their land." (p. 89)

[50] Emphasis mine. (p. 92)

[51] **Matthew 11:25** ~ "At that time Jesus answered and said, I thank thee, O Father, Lord of heaven and earth, because thou hast hid these things from the wise and prudent, and hast revealed them unto babes." (p. 93)

[52] **Matthew 26:52** ~ "Then said Jesus unto him, Put up again thy sword into his place: for all they that take the sword shall perish with the sword." (p. 96)

[53] Phillip Keller, *A Shepherd Looks at Psalm 23* (Grand Rapids: Zondervan, 1970). (p. 98)

[54] Finis Jennings Dake, *Dake's Annotated Reference Bible* (Lawrenceville, GA: Dake Publishing, 1985), Old Testament p. 591. (p. 99)

[55] From the Lord's Prayer, **Matthew 6:9–13** ~ "After this manner therefore pray ye: Our Father which art in heaven, Hallowed be thy name. Thy kingdom come, Thy will be done in earth, as it is in heaven. Give us this day our daily bread. And forgive us our debts, as we forgive our debtors. And lead us not into temptation, but deliver us from evil: For thine is the kingdom, and the power, and the glory, for ever. Amen." (p. 102)

Also note **Matthew 6:14–15** re: forgiveness ~ "For if ye forgive men their trespasses, your heavenly Father will also forgive you: But if ye forgive not men their trespasses, neither will your Father forgive your trespasses." (p. 102)

[56] Specifically **Hebrews 11:6** (N.B. All of Hebrews 11) ~ "But without faith it is impossible to please him: for he that cometh to God must believe that he is, and that he is a rewarder of them that diligently seek him." (p. 102)

[57] **John 3:3–8** ~ "Jesus answered and said unto him, Verily, verily, I say unto thee, Except a man be born again, he cannot see the kingdom of God. Nicodemus saith unto him, How can a man be born when he is old? can he enter the second time into his mother's womb, and be born? Jesus answered, Verily, verily, I say unto thee, Except a man be born of water and of the Spirit, he cannot enter into the kingdom of God. That which is born of the flesh is flesh; and that which is born of the Spirit is spirit. Marvel not that I said unto thee, Ye must be born again. The wind bloweth where it listeth, and thou hearest the sound thereof, but canst not tell whence it cometh, and whither it goeth: so is every one that is born of the Spirit."

1 Peter 1:23 ~ "Being born again, not of corruptible seed, but of incorruptible, by the word of God, which liveth and abideth for ever."

1 John 3:9 ~ "Whosoever is born of God doth not commit sin; for his seed remaineth in him: and he cannot sin, because he is born of God."

1 John 4:7 ~ "Beloved, let us love one another: for love is of God; and every one that loveth is born of God, and knoweth God."

1 John 5:18 ~ "We know that whosoever is born of God sinneth not; but he that is begotten of God keepeth himself, and that wicked one toucheth him not." (p. 103)

[58] **Matthew 7:16** ~ "Ye shall know them by their fruits. Do men gather grapes of thorns, or figs of thistles?"

Galatians 5:22–23 ~ "But the fruit of the Spirit is love, joy, peace, longsuffering, gentleness, goodness, faith, meekness, temperance: against such there is no law." (p. 105)

[59] **Matthew 7:16; Galatians 5:22–23** (as in #58 above) (p. 105)

[60] Emphasis mine. (p. 105)

[61] **Galatians 1:6** ~ "I marvel that ye are so soon removed from him that called you into the grace of Christ unto another gospel." (p. 107)

[62] **John 1:1** ~ "In the beginning was the Word, and the Word was with God, and the Word was God."
Revelation 19:13 ~ "And he was clothed with a vesture dipped in blood: and his name is called The Word of God." (p. 108)

[63] Known as the Beatitudes, from the Sermon on the Mount.
Matthew 5:3–12 ~ "Blessed are the poor in spirit: for theirs is the kingdom of heaven. Blessed are they that mourn: for they shall be comforted. Blessed are the meek: for they shall inherit the earth. Blessed are they which do hunger and thirst after righteousness: for they shall be filled. Blessed are the merciful: for they shall obtain mercy. Blessed are the pure in heart: for they shall see God. Blessed are the peacemakers: for they shall be called the children of God. Blessed are they which are persecuted for righteousness' sake: for theirs is the kingdom of heaven. Blessed are ye, when men shall revile you, and persecute you, and shall say all manner of evil against you falsely, for my sake. Rejoice, and be exceeding glad: for great is your reward in heaven: for so persecuted they the prophets which were before you." (p. 109)

[64] **Isaiah 55:8–9** ~ "For my thoughts are not your thoughts, neither are your ways my ways, saith the Lord. For as the heavens are higher than the earth, so are my ways higher than your ways, and my thoughts than your thoughts." (p. 110)

[65] **Matthew 24:42** ~ "Watch therefore: for ye know not what hour your Lord doth come." (p. 111)

[66] **Psalm 12:8** ~ "The wicked walk on every side, when the vilest men are exalted." (p. 112)

[67] **Isaiah 8:19** ~ "And when they shall say unto you, Seek unto them that have familiar spirits, and unto wizards that peep, and that mutter: should not a people seek unto their God? for the living to the dead?"
Isaiah 19:3 ~ "And the spirit of Egypt shall fail in the midst thereof; and I will destroy the counsel thereof: and they shall seek to the idols, and to the charmers, and to them that have familiar spirits, and to the wizards."

Isaiah 29:4 ~ "And thou shalt be brought down, and shalt speak out of the ground, and thy speech shall be low out of the dust, and thy voice shall be, as of one that hath a familiar spirit, out of the ground, and thy speech shall whisper out of the dust." (p. 112)

[68] 1 John 2:16 ~ "For all that is in the world, the lust of the flesh, and the lust of the eyes, and the pride of life, is not of the Father, but is of the world." (p. 112)

[69] Luke 3:14 ~ "And the soldiers likewise demanded of him, saying, And what shall we do? And he said unto them, Do violence to no man, neither accuse any falsely; and be content with your wages." (p. 113)

[70] Matthew 5:39 ~ "But I say unto you, That ye resist not evil: but whosoever shall smite thee on thy right cheek, turn to him the other also." (p. 113)

[71] Matthew 5:40 ~ "And if any man will sue thee at the law, and take away thy coat, let him have thy cloak also." (p. 113)

[72] Matthew 6:34 ~ "Take therefore no thought for the morrow: for the morrow shall take thought for the things of itself. Sufficient unto the day is the evil thereof." (p. 113)

[73] Romans 12:19 ~ "Dearly beloved, avenge not yourselves, but rather give place unto wrath: for it is written, Vengeance is mine; I will repay, saith the Lord." (p. 113)

[74] Matthew 5:44 ~ "But I say unto you, Love your enemies, bless them that curse you, do good to them that hate you, and pray for them which despitefully use you, and persecute you." (p. 113)

[75] Matthew 18:22 ~ "Jesus saith unto him, I say not unto thee, Until seven times: but, Until seventy times seven." (p. 114)

[76] Matthew 5:42 ~ "Give to him that asketh thee, and from him that would borrow of thee turn not thou away." (p. 114)

[77] Matthew 5:41 ~ "And whosoever shall compel thee to go a mile, go with him twain." (p. 114)

[78] Matthew 6:7 ~ "But when ye pray, use not vain repetitions, as the heathen do: for they think that they shall be heard for their much speaking." (p. 114)

[79] John 3:3–8 (see #57 above) (p. 116)

[80] Matthew 8:3 ~ "And Jesus put forth his hand, and touched him, saying, I will; be thou clean. And immediately his leprosy was cleansed." (p. 116)

---

[81] **Psalm 91:1** ~ "He that dwelleth in the secret place of the most High shall abide under the shadow of the Almighty." (p. 117)

[82] **Matthew 7:7** ~ "Ask, and it shall be given you; seek, and ye shall find; knock, and it shall be opened unto you." (p. 117)

[83] **Mark 10:15** ~ "Verily I say unto you, Whosoever shall not receive the kingdom of God as a little child, he shall not enter therein." (p. 117)

[84] Phillip Keller, *The High Cost of Holiness* (Eugene, OR: Harvest House Publishers, 1991). Original title same publisher 1988. (p. 124)

[85] **John 14:6** ~ "Jesus saith unto him, I am the way, the truth, and the life: no man cometh unto the Father, but by me." (p. 131)

[86] **John 10:1** (For greater clarity read John 10: 1 through 18, The Parable of the Good Shepherd.) ~ "Verily, verily, I say unto you, He that entereth not by the door into the sheepfold, but climbeth up some other way, the same is a thief and a robber." (p. 131)

[87] **John 10:7–8** ~ "Then said Jesus unto them again, Verily, verily, I say unto you, I am the door of the sheep. All that ever came before me are thieves and robbers: but the sheep did not hear them." (p. 131)

[88] **John 8:32** ~ "And ye shall know the truth, and the truth shall make you free." (p. 135)

[89] **John 9:3** ~ "Jesus answered, Neither hath this man sinned, nor his parents: but that the works of God should be made manifest in him." (p. 141)

[90] The **Book of Job** is a remarkable study of divine ordinances. Also see **John 9:1–3** ~ "And as Jesus passed by, he saw a man which was blind from his birth. And his disciples asked him, saying, Master, who did sin, this man, or his parents, that he was born blind? Jesus answered, Neither hath this man sinned, nor his parents: but that the works of God should be made manifest in him." (p. 141)

[91] **Matthew 6:22** ~ "The light of the body is the eye: if therefore thine eye be single, thy whole body shall be full of light."
Luke 11:34 ~ "The light of the body is the eye: therefore when thine eye is single, thy whole body also is full of light; but when thine eye is evil, thy body also is full of darkness." (p. 142)

[92] **John 8:32** ~ "And ye shall know the truth, and the truth shall make you free." (p. 161)

[93] **Matthew 6:8** ~ "Be not ye therefore like unto them: for your Father knoweth what things ye have need of, before ye ask him." (p. 187)

[94] **Mark 13:11** ~ "But when they shall lead you, and deliver you up, take no thought beforehand what ye shall speak, neither do ye premeditate: but whatsoever shall be given you in that hour, that speak ye: for it is not ye that speak, but the Holy Ghost." (p. 188)

[95] **Luke 16:10–11** ~ "He that is faithful in that which is least is faithful also in much: and he that is unjust in the least is unjust also in much. If therefore ye have not been faithful in the unrighteous mammon, who will commit to your trust the true riches?" (p. 192)

[96] **Matthew 6:34** ~ "Take therefore no thought for the morrow: for the morrow shall take thought for the things of itself. Sufficient unto the day is the evil thereof." (p. 196)

[97] **Job 38:41** ~ "Who provideth for the raven his food? when his young ones cry unto God, they wander for lack of meat." (p.196

[98] John Bartlett, *Bartlett's Familiar Quotations*, Seventeenth Edition, ed. Justin Kaplan (New York: Little, Brown and Company, 2002), 319. (p. 196)

[99] **1 Corinthians 4:5** ~ "Therefore judge nothing before the time, until the Lord come, who both will bring to light the hidden things of darkness, and will make manifest the counsels of the hearts: and then shall every man have praise of God."
John 7:24 ~ "Judge not according to the appearance, but judge righteous judgment."
Matthew 7:1 ~ "Judge not, that ye be not judged."
Romans 14:13 ~ "Let us not therefore judge one another any more: but judge this rather, that no man put a stumblingblock or an occasion to fall in his brother's way." (p. 197)

[100] **Matthew 6:9** ~ "After this manner therefore pray ye: Our Father which art in heaven, Hallowed be thy name." (p. 200)

[101] **Matthew 10:8** ~ "Heal the sick, cleanse the lepers, raise the dead, cast out devils: freely ye have received, freely give." (p. 202)

[102] **Matthew 5:41–42** ~ "And whosoever shall compel thee to go a mile, go with him twain. Give to him that asketh thee, and from him that would borrow of thee turn not thou away." (p. 202)

[103] **Philippians 4:17** ~ "Not because I desire a gift: but I desire fruit that may abound to your account." (p. 203)

[104] **Matthew 6:2, 5, 16** ~ "Therefore when thou doest thine alms, do not sound a trumpet before thee, as the hypocrites do in the synagogues and in the streets, that they may have glory of men. Verily I say unto you, They have their reward…And when thou prayest, thou shalt not

be as the hypocrites are: for they love to pray standing in the synagogues and in the corners of the streets, that they may be seen of men. Verily I say unto you, They have their reward…Moreover when ye fast, be not, as the hypocrites, of a sad countenance: for they disfigure their faces, that they may appear unto men to fast. Verily I say unto you, They have their reward." (p. 203)

[105] **James 1:22** ~ "But be ye doers of the word, and not hearers only, deceiving your own selves." (p. 203)

[106] **1 Corinthians 12 (p. 204)**

[107] **John 8:28** ~ "Then said Jesus unto them, When ye have lifted up the Son of man, then shall ye know that I am he, and that I do nothing of myself; but as my Father hath taught me, I speak these things."
John 5:30 ~ "I can of mine own self do nothing: as I hear, I judge: and my judgment is just; because I seek not mine own will, but the will of the Father which hath sent me." (p. 204)

[108] **2 Timothy 3:5** ~ "Having a form of godliness, but denying the power thereof: from such turn away." (p. 204)

[109] **Psalm 127:1** ~ "Except the Lord build the house, they labour in vain that build it: except the Lord keep the city, the watchman waketh but in vain." (p. 204)

[110] **Psalm 33:12** ~ "Blessed is the nation whose God is the Lord; and the people whom he hath chosen for his own inheritance." (p. 204)

[111] **Matthew 25:40, 45** ~ "And the King shall answer and say unto them, Verily I say unto you, Inasmuch as ye have done it unto one of the least of these my brethren, ye have done it unto me…Then shall he answer them, saying, Verily I say unto you, Inasmuch as ye did it not to one of the least of these, ye did it not to me." (p. 205)

[112] **1 John 2:16** ~ "For all that is in the world, the lust of the flesh, and the lust of the eyes, and the pride of life, is not of the Father, but is of the world." (p. 205)

[113] **Matthew 25:31–46** (p. 205)

[114] **Matthew 26:11** ~ "For ye have the poor always with you; but me ye have not always." (p. 206)

[115] **Matthew 15:14** ~ "Let them alone: they be blind leaders of the blind. And if the blind lead the blind, both shall fall into the ditch." (p. 206)

[116] **2 Corinthians 5:17** ~ "Therefore if any man be in Christ, he is a new creature: old things are passed away; behold, all things are become new." (p. 207)

[117] **Philippians 4:6** ~ "Be careful for nothing; but in every thing by prayer and supplication with thanksgiving let your requests be made known unto God." (p. 207)

[118] **Luke 9:23** ~ "And he said to them all, If any man will come after me, let him deny himself, and take up his cross daily, and follow me." (p. 208)

[119] **Matthew 4:19–20** ~ "And he saith unto them, Follow me, and I will make you fishers of men. And they straightway left their nets, and followed him." (p. 208)

[120] **Matthew 19:27** ~ "Then answered Peter and said unto him, Behold, we have forsaken all, and followed thee; what shall we have therefore?" (p. 208)

[121] **Matthew 19:29** ~ "And every one that hath forsaken houses, or brethren, or sisters, or father, or mother, or wife, or children, or lands, for my name's sake, shall receive an hundredfold, and shall inherit everlasting life." (p. 208)

[122] **Philippians 3:14** ~ "I press toward the mark for the prize of the high calling of God in Christ Jesus." (p. 209)

[123] **1 Corinthians 4:9–13** ~ "For I think that God hath set forth us the apostles last, as it were appointed to death: for we are made a spectacle unto the world, and to angels, and to men. We are fools for Christ's sake, but ye are wise in Christ; we are weak, but ye are strong; ye are honourable, but we are despised. Even unto this present hour we both hunger, and thirst, and are naked, and are buffeted, and have no certain dwellingplace; And labour, working with our own hands: being reviled, we bless; being persecuted, we suffer it: Being defamed, we intreat: we are made as the filth of the world, and are the offscouring of all things unto this day." (p. 209)

[124] **Matthew 8:19** ~ "And a certain scribe came, and said unto him, Master, I will follow thee whithersoever thou goest." (p. 209)

[125] **Matthew 8:20** ~ "And Jesus saith unto him, The foxes have holes, and the birds of the air have nests; but the Son of man hath not where to lay his head." (p. 209)

[126] **1 Timothy 6:16** ~ "Who only hath immortality, dwelling in the light which no man can approach unto; whom no man hath seen, nor can see: to whom be honour and power everlasting. Amen." (p. 210)

[127] **John 1:10** ~ "He was in the world, and the world was made by him, and the world knew him not." (p. 210)

[128] **Matthew 10:22** ~ "And ye shall be hated of all men for my name's sake: but he that endureth to the end shall be saved. (p. 210)

[129] **Matthew 10:23** ~ "But when they persecute you in this city, flee ye into another: for verily I say unto you, Ye shall not have gone over the cities of Israel, till the Son of man be come." (p. 210)

[130] **John 15:22** ~ "If I had not come and spoken unto them, they had not had sin: but now they have no cloak for their sin." (p. 210)

[131] **John 15:20** ~ "Remember the word that I said unto you, The servant is not greater than his lord. If they have persecuted me, they will also persecute you; if they have kept my saying, they will keep yours also." (p. 210)

[132] **Galatians 5:22–23** ~ "But the fruit of the Spirit is love, joy, peace, longsuffering, gentleness, goodness, faith, meekness, temperance: against such there is no law." (p. 211)

[133] **James 4:2** ~ "Ye lust, and have not: ye kill, and desire to have, and cannot obtain: ye fight and war, yet ye have not, because ye ask not." (p. 212)

[134] **2 Corinthians 12:9** ~ "And he said unto me, My grace is sufficient for thee: for my strength is made perfect in weakness. Most gladly therefore will I rather glory in my infirmities, that the power of Christ may rest upon me." (p. 213)

[135] **Matthew 26:39** ~ "And he went a little farther, and fell on his face, and prayed, saying, O my Father, if it be possible, let this cup pass from me: nevertheless not as I will, but as thou wilt." (p. 213)

[136] **Luke 22:44** ~ "And being in an agony he prayed more earnestly: and his sweat was as it were great drops of blood falling down to the ground." (p. 214)

[137] **Matthew 16:25** ~ "For whosoever will save his life shall lose it: and whosoever will lose his life for my sake shall find it." (p. 215)

[138] **2 Corinthians 5:17** ~ "Therefore if any man be in Christ, he is a new creature: old things are passed away; behold, all things are become new." (p. 227)

[139] **John 8:28** ~ "Then said Jesus unto them, When ye have lifted up the Son of man, then shall ye know that I am he, and that I do nothing of myself; but as my Father hath taught me, I speak these things." (p. 227)

[140] **Isaiah 14:13–14** ~ "For thou hast said in thine heart, I will ascend into heaven, I will exalt my throne above the stars of God: I will sit also upon the mount of the congregation, in the sides of the north: I will

ascend above the heights of the clouds; I will be like the most High." (p. 228)

[141] **2 Timothy 3:5** ~ "Having a form of godliness, but denying the power thereof: from such turn away." (p. 228)

[142] **Mark 8:35** ~ "For whosoever will save his life shall lose it; but whosoever shall lose his life for my sake and the gospel's, the same shall save it." (p. 229)

[143] **Matthew 5:45** ~ "That ye may be the children of your Father which is in heaven: for he maketh his sun to rise on the evil and on the good, and sendeth rain on the just and on the unjust." (p. 233)

[144] **Acts 10:34** ~ "Then Peter opened his mouth, and said, Of a truth I perceive that God is no respecter of persons." (p. 233)

[145] **John 10:10** ~ "The thief cometh not, but for to steal, and to kill, and to destroy: I am come that they might have life, and that they might have it more abundantly." (p. 233)

[146] **Matthew 5:42** ~ "Give to him that asketh thee, and from him that would borrow of thee turn not thou away." (p. 235)

[147] Bill Hybels, as in #9 above. (p. 238)

[148] **John 3:30** ~ "He must increase, but I must decrease." (p. 238)

[149] **Matthew 23:5** ~ "But all their works they do for to be seen of men: they make broad their phylacteries, and enlarge the borders of their garments." (p. 238)

[150] **Matthew 6:8** ~ "Be not ye therefore like unto them: for your Father knoweth what things ye have need of, before ye ask him." (p. 241)

[151] **Matthew 6:25–34** (p. 242)

[152] **Matthew 6:33** ~ "But seek ye first the kingdom of God, and his righteousness; and all these things shall be added unto you." (p. 242)

[153] **Matthew 6:19** ~ "Lay not up for yourselves treasures upon earth, where moth and rust doth corrupt, and where thieves break through and steal." (p. 242)

[154] **Matthew 6:20–21** ~ "But lay up for yourselves treasures in heaven, where neither moth nor rust doth corrupt, and where thieves do not break through nor steal: For where your treasure is, there will your heart be also." (p. 243)

[155] **Matthew 6:24** ~ "No man can serve two masters: for either he will hate the one, and love the other; or else he will hold to the one, and despise the other. Ye cannot serve God and mammon." (p. 243)

[156] **Revelation 3:15–16** ~ "I know thy works, that thou art neither cold nor hot: I would thou wert cold or hot. So then because thou art lukewarm, and neither cold nor hot, I will spue thee out of my mouth." (p. 243)

[157] M. Scott Peck, as in #10 above. (p. 243)

[158] **Luke 23:35, 37** ~ "And the people stood beholding. And the rulers also with them derided him, saying, He saved others; let him save himself, if he be Christ, the chosen of God…And saying, If thou be the king of the Jews, save thyself." (p. 246)

[159] **Matthew 27:42–43** ~ "He saved others; himself he cannot save. If he be the King of Israel, let him now come down from the cross, and we will believe him. He trusted in God; let him deliver him now, if he will have him: for he said, I am the Son of God." (p. 246)

[160] **Matthew 16:17** ~ "And Jesus answered and said unto him, Blessed art thou, Simon Barjona: for flesh and blood hath not revealed it unto thee, but my Father which is in heaven." (p. 246)

[161] **1 Corinthians 4:5** ~ "Therefore judge nothing before the time, until the Lord come, who both will bring to light the hidden things of darkness, and will make manifest the counsels of the hearts: and then shall every man have praise of God." (p. 247)

[162] **2 Thessalonians 3:3** ~ "But the Lord is faithful, who shall stablish you, and keep you from evil." (p. 247)

[163] **1 Corinthians 9:11** ~ "If we have sown unto you spiritual things, is it a great thing if we shall reap your carnal things?" (p. 250)

[164] **Matthew 16:24** ~ "Then said Jesus unto his disciples, If any man will come after me, let him deny himself, and take up his cross, and follow me." (p. 252)

[165] **John 15:20** ~ "Remember the word that I said unto you, The servant is not greater than his lord. If they have persecuted me, they will also persecute you; if they have kept my saying, they will keep yours also." (p. 253)

[166] Andrew Murray, *The Best of Andrew Murray* (Grand Rapids: Baker Book House, 1991), 71. (p. 253)

[167] **Luke 12:32** ~ "Fear not, little flock; for it is your Father's good pleasure to give you the kingdom." (p. 254)

[168] Bob Farrell and Greg Nelson, "No Place to Lay My Head" © 1993 Gentle Ben Music (admin. by Dayspring Music)/Dayspring Music (a

div. of WORD INC.)/Summerdawn Music and Steadfast Music (admin. by Copyright Management Inc.) All rights reserved. (p. 254)

[169] Sandi Patti, *LeVoyage*, compact disc, Word Records, 1993. (p. 254)

[170] **1 Corinthians 6:11** ~ "And such were some of you: but ye are washed, but ye are sanctified, but ye are justified in the name of the Lord Jesus, and by the Spirit of our God." (p. 256)

[171] **Romans 3:23** ~ "For all have sinned, and come short of the glory of God." (p. 256)

[172] **Matthew 10:39** ~ "He that findeth his life shall lose it: and he that loseth his life for my sake shall find it." (p. 256)

[173] **Luke 6:37** ~ "Judge not, and ye shall not be judged: condemn not, and ye shall not be condemned: forgive, and ye shall be forgiven." (p. 256)

[174] **Matthew 7:16** ~ "Ye shall know them by their fruits. Do men gather grapes of thorns, or figs of thistles?" (p. 257)

[175] **Luke 9:23** ~ "And he said to them all, If any man will come after me, let him deny himself, and take up his cross daily, and follow me." (p. 258)

[176] **John 8:7** ~ "So when they continued asking him, he lifted up himself, and said unto them, He that is without sin among you, let him first cast a stone at her." (p. 258)

[177] From the Greek, *ekklesia*, describing the "church" translated as "called-out ones." (p. 258)

[178] **Luke 23:34** ~ "Then said Jesus, Father, forgive them; for they know not what they do. And they parted his raiment, and cast lots." (p. 258)

[179] **Matthew 5:39** ~ "But I say unto you, That ye resist not evil: but whosoever shall smite thee on thy right cheek, turn to him the other also." (p. 258)

[180] **Matthew 10:16** ~ "Behold, I send you forth as sheep in the midst of wolves: be ye therefore wise as serpents, and harmless as doves." (p. 259)

[181] Phillip Keller's most familiar work is *A Shepherd Looks at Psalm 23*, providing a unique understanding of both the shepherd and the sheep. Having been a shepherd in South Africa, he speaks from personal experience. (See #53 above) (p. 259)

[182] **Philippians 3:14** ~ "I press toward the mark for the prize of the high calling of God in Christ Jesus." (p. 260)

[183] **Matthew 6:22** ~ "The light of the body is the eye: if therefore thine eye be single, thy whole body shall be full of light." (p. 260)

184 **Romans 8:28** ~ "And we know that all things work together for good to them that love God, to them who are the called according to his purpose." (p. 260)

185 Parable of the lost sheep: **Luke 15:3–7** ~ "And he spake this parable unto them, saying, What man of you, having an hundred sheep, if he lose one of them, doth not leave the ninety and nine in the wilderness, and go after that which is lost, until he find it? And when he hath found it, he layeth it on his shoulders, rejoicing. And when he cometh home, he calleth together his friends and neighbours, saying unto them, Rejoice with me; for I have found my sheep which was lost. I say unto you, that likewise joy shall be in heaven over one sinner that repenteth, more than over ninety and nine just persons, which need no repentance." (p. 261)

186 **Philippians 4:7** ~ "And the peace of God, which passeth all understanding, shall keep your hearts and minds through Christ Jesus." (p. 261)